Praise for *Thea's Song*

"Sister Thea Bowman was a song sung by God. One of the most significant figures in modern Catholicism, Sister Thea was a radiant example of what happens when you let God's joy enter your life decisively. Read this marvelous new biography and meet a woman who will show you what it means, even in the midst of death, to *live*."

—James Martin, S.J., author, *My Life with the Saints*

"Just like Sr. Thea, this book is mesmerizing and drenched in inspiration. The writers engage the reader's heart and soul with *Thea's Song*. The story is told in such a moving manner that the reader is with Sr. Thea as she confronts racism, becomes the most powerful woman on the campus of Viterbo College, laments the death of Rev. Dr. Martin Luther King Jr., advocates for justice, dances and sings in Nairobi at the 43rd International Eucharistic Congress, is interviewed on *60 Minutes*, addresses the United States Conference of Catholic Bishops and holds on in hope and faith as she struggled with cancer. You will stand in awe of what God can do through a faithful and willing soul. This is an unforgettable story about an unshakable woman of faith."

—Therese Wilson Favors, Director,
African American Catholic Ministries

"Such a rich and loving life as Thea Bowman's certainly needs to be talked about! Here you will get all the beautiful stages of her extraordinary life. Read, and be transformed yourself!"

—Richard Rohr, O.F.M., Center for Action and Contemplation

"*Thea's Song* is the perfectly titled biography of one of the greatest voices in the contemporary American church. While she lived among us, Thea Bowman's ministry of music and joy set countless hearts free to live their lives to the fullest. Her song empowered others to walk in love instead of fear. This book is the perfect read for weary souls who need to keep on steppin', who want to keep the dream alive by singing her song."

—Brother Mickey McGrath, author/artist, *This Little Light:*
Lessons in Living from Sister Thea Bowman

"The authors have chosen a very appropriate title for Thea's biography, for in the words of the psalmist, God put a 'new song' in her mouth (Psalm 40), which she continues to sing today, challenging us to be instruments of God's peace and love."
— Sister Antona Ebo, F.S.M., founding member
and past president, National Black Sisters Conference

"This captivating biography of a woman beautiful in every way describes a life that is almost hard to believe it is so filled with the adventures of a humble, selfless, brilliant, and highly talented woman. Not only was she a distinguished intellectual, philosopher, and teacher; she was also one of the most outstanding patriots of our times. What is also very moving about her is the tender love she had even with all her busy-ness in the world, to go home and care for her ailing parents. This is a story that will rivet your attention from beginning to end."
— Fr. Joseph F. Girzone, the Joshua Foundation

"Sr. Thea was friend, teacher, and mentor for people of many races and faiths. This perceptive study illuminates why, and introduces Thea for a new generation. Her passionate intelligence and deep faith resonate throughout these pages. The authors make Thea come alive and sing anew." — Bryan N. Massingale, S.T.D., President,
Catholic Theological Society of America

"She sang . . . she taught . . . she told the old story,
She prophesied, . . . she inspired . . .
She made us listen . . .
She taught us to hear."
— Cyprian Davis, O.S.B.,
St. Meinrad Archabbey

Thea's Song

Thea's Song

The Life of
Thea Bowman

Charlene Smith and John Feister

ORBIS BOOKS
Maryknoll, New York 10545

Founded in 1970, Orbis Books endeavors to publish works that enlighten the mind, nourish the spirit, and challenge the conscience. The publishing arm of the Maryknoll Fathers and Brothers, Orbis seeks to explore the global dimensions of the Christian faith and mission, to invite dialogue with diverse cultures and religious traditions, and to serve the cause of reconciliation and peace. The books published reflect the views of their authors and do not represent the official position of the Maryknoll Society. To learn more about Maryknoll and Orbis Books, please visit our website at www.maryknollsociety.org.

Library of Congress Cataloging-in-Publication Data
Smith, Charlene.
    Thea's song : the life of Thea Bowman / Charlene Smith and John Feister.
       p.   cm.
    Includes index.
    ISBN 978-1-57075-868-3 (cloth)
    1. Bowman, Thea. 2. African American Catholics – Biography. 3. Franciscan Sisters of Perpetual Adoration (La Crosse, Wis.) – Biography. I. Feister, John. II. Title.
BX4705.B8113S65 2009
271′.97302 – dc22
       [B]   2009035420

For the myriad friends of Thea

Pray for me as I will for thee,
until we meet merrily in heaven.

— Sir Thomas More —

CONTENTS

Part Four
THEA AT VITERBO

Part Five
BACK TO CANTON

ACKNOWLEDGMENTS

Thanks to:

The Franciscan Sisters of Perpetual Adoration (FSPA) community for generous support during the research and writing of *Thea's Song*. I express with pleasure my deep gratitude to all my Franciscan sisters.

FSPA profession classes of 1957 and 1958, who journeyed with Thea from her Franciscan beginnings and recalled, reminisced, and answered questions about our unforgettable classmate.

FSPAs who ministered at Holy Child Jesus Mission in Canton, Mississippi, for invaluable contributions about their and Thea's work in the South.

FSPA Julian local community members Jean Kasparbauer, Nancy Lafferty, Katie Mitchell, Silvana Panza, Marlou Ricke, and Corrina Thomas for ongoing, enduring encouragement over the years of this biography project.

Sister Thea Bowman Black Catholic Education Foundation board members and executive director Mary Lou Jennings for professional acumen and optimism, all the while handing on the legacy of Thea by financially supporting Thea scholars since 1989.

Thea News editors 2002–8: Maria Friedman, FSPA, Beth Erickson and Mary Pat Hill, OSM, for gathering and reporting news about Thea since her 1990 homegoing.

Siblings Audrey, Jill, and Niles and their spouses Bill, Dick, and Ginny, nieces and nephews, for their love and unwavering belief.

Co-author John Feister, who persevered for two years and whose interviewing and writing helped make *Thea's Song* sing.

Secretaries Carolyn Grimm, Elizabeth Bungard, and Nancy Chapman, who generously assisted with printing, scanning, transcribing, et cetera.

"Friends for Now" book club members who listened, advised, and cheered.

Friends of Thea who are legion throughout the United States — black, white, yellow, red, and brown — women and men religious, priests, ministers, parishes, teachers, parents, children, singers, artists, musicians, doctors, nurses, elders and especially Dorothy Ann Kundinger, FSPA, housemate, helpmate, and traveling companion to Thea during her last years.

Orbis Books' award-winning editor-at-large Michael Leach and his New York team whose encouragement and wisdom and patience make the publishing process a joy.

Charlene Smith, FSPA

La Crosse, Wisconsin
June 30, 2009

❖ ❖ ❖

Thanks to Sharon Sumpter, assistant archivist, University of Notre Dame, to the archival staff at Catholic University of America and the editorial staff of Catholic News Service, both in Washington, D.C., and to many friends of Thea who were interviewed for this book.

Also, thanks to Dr. Cecilia Moore, Vanessa White, DMin, and Rev. Clarence Williams, CPPS, PhD, for critical reading of the manuscript, to Jack Wintz, OFM, for leading me to Thea in 1984, to Terri Biertzer for efficiently transcribing many hours of interviews, and to Jesse Feister for diligent draft corrections.

Finally, thanks to my beloved wife, Cathy, whose encouragement allowed my part of this book to happen.

John Feister

Cincinnati, Ohio
September 30, 2009

CHRONOLOGY

1937   Bertha Bowman is born in Yazoo City, Mississippi.

1947   Bertha, raised Protestant to that point, at age nine joins
            the Catholic Church and, in 1949, enrolls in the FSPA's
            Holy Child Jesus School.

1953   Bertha, age fifteen, joins the Franciscan sisters as an
            aspirant, moving to the FSPA motherhouse in La Crosse,
            Wisconsin.

1955   Bertha tests positive for tuberculosis and is moved to River
            Pines Sanitorium, in Stevens Point, Wisconsin, for ten
            months.

1956   At the beginning of novitiate, Bertha asks for and is given
            the name "Thea."

1958–1959   Thea professes first vows and, in 1959, is assigned to teach
            at an elementary school in La Crosse.

1961   Thea is assigned to teach elementary students at her alma
            mater, Holy Child Jesus School, in Canton, Mississippi.

1965   Thea receives her bachelor of arts degree from Viterbo
            College.

1966   Thea enrolls at Catholic University of America for graduate
            study in English. She is among the founders of the National
            Black Sisters Conference and emerges as a vocalist and
            public speaker.

1969   Thea is awarded a master of arts degree from Catholic
            University.

1972   Thea, focusing on Sir (Saint to Catholics) Thomas More,
            is awarded a PhD from Catholic University.

1972–78   Thea teaches, eventually becoming chair of the English Department at Viterbo College and also works in the La Crosse community.

1978   Thea returns to Canton to care for her aging parents. She is recruited by Mississippi's Bishop Joseph Brunini to develop outreach from the Catholic diocese to nonwhite communities and to help develop intercultural awareness among all races. She continues and expands her speaking and singing ministry nationally and, in a few cases, beyond.

1980   Thea is among the founders of the Institute for Black Catholic Studies at Xavier University in New Orleans, where she teaches until 1988. She is also an annual speaker at the University of Mississippi's Faulkner Conference.

1980–1990 Thea receives numerous national, regional, and local awards as her fame grows.

1984   Thea is first diagnosed with breast cancer. Her parents both die before year's end.

1985–1986 Thea travels to Nairobi, Kenya, for the International Eucharistic Congress. She edits *Families: Black and Catholic, Catholic and Black*. Isolated cancer treatments occur until 1988.

1987   CBS's *60 Minutes* airs a segment on Thea. She contributes to and helps to edit *Lead Me, Guide Me*, and discusses an autobiographical film with Harry Belafonte and Whoopi Goldberg.

1988   Widespread cancer returns. She conducts workshops for Maryknoll Sisters in Africa, records *Songs of My People*, and begins biographical interviews with Margaret Walker.

1989   Thea gives a historic speech to Catholic bishops; Clarence Williams produces *Sr. Thea: Her Own Story*, featuring Thea. Sister Thea Bowman Black Education Foundation is founded.

1990   Sister Thea Bowman dies on March 30, at age fifty-two. She is buried at Elmwood Cemetery in Memphis beside her parents.

THERE IS A BALM IN GILEAD

Her grandfather's family were freed slaves; she held a PhD in English language and literature. She was an expert on William Faulkner and a gifted vocalist and speaker. Echoing across a Mississippi church leading a schoolchildren's choir or in a northern cathedral filled with people of all races; across the United States in one parish or another; in New Orleans at the Institute for Black Catholic Studies; eventually, on national television, or, even later, stricken with cancer leading "We Shall Overcome" in the halls of the U.S. Catholic bishops; written about in newspaper after newspaper — all along the way her voice and her presence were unforgettable.

She was Sister Thea Bowman, a sister both in the African American, soulful sense of the term and also a sister in the more formal, vowed sense of the Roman Catholic community. She was a black sister and she was a Catholic, Franciscan sister, one who, as a teen, moved a thousand miles from home, outside of her culture, yet developed a deep sense of her cultural identity nonetheless. As she discovered her identity, the identity of a beautiful, black, Mississippi woman, she couldn't contain it. And people around her couldn't help but notice.

In the years after the peak of the civil rights movement, in the 1960s and especially in the 1980s, as the nation grappled with the questions of racial identity and equality, hers became a mesmerizing presence wherever she went. Singing the songs of her African American people with operatic skill, she worked with people of all races to help them to see their own lives in a new light. Through music and reflection, she helped people everywhere she went to explore their identity and to find their deepest humanity.

The balm in Gilead, that Old Testament image of comfort for a people in captivity, was the Spirit that drove her from her Mississippi roots to a Franciscan convent in La Crosse, Wisconsin. It was that Spirit that gave her the comforting, enlivening gift of music, a music that flowed from her to become both a balm and a challenge for others. It was that Spirit that brought her back to Mississippi as an accomplished adult, in 1978, where her career blossomed.

It is one of life's mysteries that a life so engaging, so promising, could fall to a terminal illness "midlife." Yet that is a key part of Thea's story, one of a black childhood in a majority-black region, among the former plantations of central Mississippi, of formative adulthood in an all-white setting far north of her home, then of a growing national reputation as a beacon of intercultural awareness. It is a story of a person who ultimately said, "Let me live until I die," and showed those around her how to drink deeply of life's promise to the very end, even as she spent her final years struggling against cancer.

Now, sit back awhile and imbibe the roots of the story of an unlikely black heroine. It is a story that starts in Mississippi.

Part One

Childhood

Chapter 1

IN THEA'S OWN WORDS:
LIFE IN CANTON

Who better could talk of Thea's Canton than Thea herself? In 1959, as a young college student far from home, she wrote at length about her home, a home trying to avoid what would become inescapable: the growing civil rights movement. At the start of Thea's story, before we begin the telling, here is that snapshot of Canton, Mississippi, in Thea's own words.[1]

◆ ◆ ◆

Of the eighteen states south of the Mason-Dixon line, I have visited only seven, and even in my home state I have neither traveled nor observed extensively. But one little Deep South city I have known intimately, and its people I have dearly loved. Of it and of them I shall tell you.

The place is Canton, a town of about eight thousand, half of whose population is Negro. Its climate is moderate with a nine month's season of growth and pasturage. Extensive heating and housing are not required. The average winter temperature is 53.6 degrees, but short spells of bitter cold are experienced, as are days of summer-like heat. Moisture is usually adequate, and magnolias, azaleas, camellias, oleander, crepe myrtle, and wisteria grace the city's streets.

Canton is an architectural conglomeration. Stately antebellum mansions of white Confederate descendants contrast sharply with ultra-modern residences, neat bungalows, and the small, dilapidated, almost uninhabitable dwellings of the very poor. Segregation is an invulnerable tradition. Whites have their streets and residential sections, as have the Negroes, and except for purposes of business, there is scant intercourse between the races. For this reason, the only people in Canton of whom I could hope to write are the Negroes. I lived across the road from white folks, shopped at their stores, passed them on the streets, but there was never a single southern white that I really knew.

But to get back to the matter at hand, segregation is, and ever has been, the vogue. In 1955, the railroad took down separation signs in Canton's railway depot. The white folks nailed them up again, and I, as a postulant on a home visit, saw them upside down or askew, but in place. Segregation reached even the house of the Lord. When, as a fervent new convert, I first visited the white Catholic church in Canton and took a place in an empty pew half way up the middle aisle, I was calmly relegated to the back seat by a dear firm little old lady who said she wouldn't mind my sitting farther front, but the others might not like it, and, after all, they had been nice enough to buy a whole back pew just for the colored folks who came to their church to greet the Lord. But, to the everlasting credit of those people and of the Catholic Church, Canton's white Catholics now welcome the little dark angels who on occasion invade their precincts en masse.

Mississippi was the second state to join the Confederacy, and "Old Miss" must ever hold on to her traditions, fly her confederate flags, and insist on the inalienable supremacy of the great white race. Mississippi state law requires separate education of the races. When in 1954 the Supreme Court declared such measures unconstitutional, Mississippi repealed her compulsory education laws (which never affected Canton's Negroes in the least), strengthened her precepts on segregation in other areas, and made serious plans to abolish the public school system.

The attitude of my people toward segregation is one of submission and acceptance. They have lived with it for longer than they remember, and few expect to see its decline. Six or seven years ago on a Chicago streetcar, the driver asked a Negro woman factory worker to stand so that a dainty little white maiden could take her seat. She stood her ground and said in none too gentle a voice, "I paid for my seat, and I'm going to keep it." The driver glared; Negro men aboard the car began to seethe; I looked for the nearest way out. The point I am trying to make is this. In Canton, no such scene would have occurred. My people through three centuries have accepted the last places, borne insults meekly, bowed and scraped to the white and "superior" race. They know that they will not be admitted to the *public* library, the *public* stadium, or the *public* swimming pool. They expect to be regarded as an inferior breed. And many of them are convinced that the whites are better than they — more intelligent, more beautiful, more gifted in every way.

What the white folks tell us is so much nonsense: "You can't have equal schools because you don't pay equal taxes. You don't pay equal taxes because you can't have equal jobs. You can't get paying jobs because you aren't educated, and if you are educated you're black, so what's the difference." That's the vicious circle aspect of many a Cantonian Negro's existence. People who have not paying jobs, no matter how strong their backs, how lofty their ambitions, how sterling their ideals, cannot, simply cannot, better their conditions.

Many of the younger generation, really qualified to hold good positions and lead their people, become disgusted and leave the South for distant parts where they can work hard, rear their families without constant stress, and live decent normal lives. Their desertion, which one can in no way censure, does nothing to better the Negro's position in Canton. My people need leaders, prudent, capable, and strong. They are not clamoring for integration, but they want equal rights — jobs, educational facilities, equitable public services. Those who are able join the NAACP [National Association for the Advancement of Colored People], giving financial support to their attempts to secure justice for our race. Some few complain, others pray, more simply wait.

Politically, we can do nothing. We cannot serve as senator, representative, jurist, policeman, constable, or county clerk. Mississippi has granted Negroes the right to vote, but their voting is discouraged. I lived through the days when Senator Bilbo paraded up and down Main Street — his resolve to keep "niggers" away from the polls. I was not old enough to vote, but I am old enough to remember the Bilbo cartoons that plagued our papers and my elders' conversations of deceit, trickery, and violence used against Negroes at Mississippi polls.

Bilbo's adherents still do their work in Canton, but quietly and underhandedly. Prominent Negro men are insulted at the polls; birth certificates and genealogies are required; ludicrous and irrelevant questions are asked. Mississippi's constitutions have clauses purposely intended to eliminate Negro voters. Residence restrictions are very stringent; those who have not paid poll tax are automatically disenfranchised; only persons able to read or interpret any article of the constitution are eligible to vote. Young Negro army veterans, trained in their political privileges by Uncle Sam himself, go through the formalities and appear at the polls with their wives and families. A few other citizens insist on their right to vote. But most, technically disqualified or simply discouraged, forsake the fight and leave it up to our good white friends to vote for the better man.

One thing that will ever strike me as an anomaly is this: though most of Canton's white inhabitants professedly look upon their dark-skinned brothers as an inferior breed, they pride themselves on the number and efficiency of the Negro servants they hire to clean their homes, cook their food, and rear their children. Some wealthy families hire a Negro maid, laundress, gardener, housekeeper, one or more "nurses" for the children, one or more cooks. Uniformed servants in starched white, black, or blue, with dainty aprons and frilly collars are a familiar early morning sight.

Negro servants are always made to feel like servants. They are hired help. They use the servant's entrance, eat their meals alone, refrain from conversation with visitors, respond to requests with a little bow and a polite "Yes, Ma'am," do their work silently and well. Southern etiquette demands that this be so, and neither servants nor masters would wish things differently. In some cases, Negro servants work in a family for generations and are passed on like treasured heirlooms. But in other instances, people, forced by necessity to take the first jobs available, are unmercifully exploited. Wages are low — sometimes less than fifteen cents an hour, and work is all too strenuous.

As in almost any U.S. town, in Canton there are Negroes who are indigent from sloth or because they have squandered their earnings in Harlem ramblings or Saturday night "Pearl Harbor" sprees, but most of our poor people are relentless workers and frugal livers — like Ada who as a high school student clerked in a grocery store from four until midnight with no time off on weekends, and that while keeping up a full high school schedule; or Jamie, an old-timer, who until the year she died picked five hundred pounds of cotton every weekday in the season.

Canton is an agricultural center, and cotton is the staple crop, but within the city surrounding the dwellings of the poor, one sees small gardens, poultry, pigs, even an occasional cow. Sweet potatoes, sugar cane, peanuts, pecans, figs, persimmons, pomegranates, watermelon, or kale and collards are Canton truck farm products typically southern. Small farmers sometimes produce a few bales of cotton on private enterprise, but most of the cotton is grown on large estates or plantations.

Sharecropping and plantation farming as I have seen them are two of the most flagrant evils of southern life. In cotton-picking time, no *free* man, however, need go hungry. Cotton pickers are paid from $2 to $5 dollars for a hundred pounds, and some skilled pickers can pick five hundred pounds a day. Even four-year-olds are able to drag a sack, and pick as well, though not as rapidly or steadily, as their elders. Mississippi has had child labor laws since 1912, but luckily they are not enforced. Many of our children help to support their families with summer cotton-picking money. Unfortunately, the cotton-picking season usually closes in late October, and other means of livelihood must be sought.

A fertilizer factory, a casket factory, saw mill, oil mill, and creosote plant provide jobs for some men and women. Others are teachers, preachers, mechanics, owners of small businesses. Canton has two Negro doctors and one Negro dentist. Some Negroes go to white doctors, most of whom will, under no circumstances, make night calls to Negro homes. Since most of our babies are born at home (hospitals are expensive places) and babies show a preference for being born at night, this makes for confusion and usually ends up with Dr. Black shouldering night calls and deliveries for Dr. White.

My people have more than their share of unwed mothers, and what most amazes outsiders is that these girls and women are not social outcasts. They rear their own children and many eventually marry. Why are unwed mothers so common? One can only conjecture. Maybe it is a foggy conception of the moral law, maybe a hangover from slave days when men and women were mated like cattle or the later age of common law love, maybe a demonstration of the fact that when human beings are denied normal and licit pleasures they descend to those which are natural but illegitimate.

Through the centuries my people have been a starry-eyed happy people of hope — hope for the future and for better days.

ANCESTRAL HISTORY
OF HOPE

Thea Bowman's ancestors were indeed people of hope. During the century before the Civil War, itself a century before the civil rights movement, the "old folks," ancestors so loved by Thea, came into Mississippi, slaves to their white plantation owners.

This is the land of King Cotton. It is the land of magnolia trees and mockingbirds, of a mild climate north of Jackson, subtropics to the south. Although cotton's ascendency had once rocketed the state to one of the nation's wealthiest, the wealth was not shared widely. In the decades after the War between the States, Mississippi became known as a poor state and is now ranked consistently among the poorest in the nation.

Into this land of plantations and slaves, Thea's ancestors came as slaves. In her cadence, Thea wrote:

> Most of my ancestors came to the Americas in chains, from thousands of towns and villages, from many racial stocks and many tribes — from the spirited Hansas, the gentle Mandingos, the creative Youlas, the Ibos, Efiks, Krus, the proud Fantirs, the warlike Ashantis, the Dahomeans, the Binis, and Senegalese. Some were captured in native wars and sold to Europeans. Some were kidnapped. Some were sold into slavery for infractions of native laws.
>
> They came to this hemisphere and met with the other side of my family — island dwellers from Cuba, Jamaica, Haiti, and the Caribbean, French traders, and Native Americans with whom they mixed and married; Spanish conquistadors and Portuguese traders and owners and overlords who claimed their bodies as well as their labor.

In America, no matter what their percentage of Negroid blood, they were called sambos, niggers, nigras, colored, negroes, blacks, and this is what I am.

We came to North America as chattel labor — chained, stripped naked and examined, sold and branded. Having no property, owned, not owning, we were found everywhere, but chiefly in Mississippi, Georgia, Tennessee, South Carolina, North Carolina, Maryland, and Virginia, those states where cotton was king.

We were valued because we were strong. We could work in unshaded fields where noonday temperatures reached 140 degrees.[1] We planted and harvested your cotton, cooked your food, washed your clothes, reared your children, built the antebellum mansions in which you take so much pride. Even after we were freed from slavery by law and fought your wars and helped to build your nation less than fifteen years ago, many of us were, by law, denied equal opportunity, the right to equal education, even the right to vote.[2]

This was the heritage of Thea's people. Before President Abraham Lincoln freed the slaves in 1863, the Benton, Mississippi, Bowman family "owned" Nathaniel and Katherine Bowman, who were the parents of Edward Bowman, Thea's paternal grandfather, born in 1874. Nathaniel and Katherine belonged to a southern "white" family comprised of both white and black progeny.

Edward and his wife, Sallie Elizabeth Washington Bowman, (daughter of Benjamin and Harriet Washington), a housewife who died in 1934, lived in Yazoo City, Mississippi (about forty-five miles northwest of Jackson). Both were Methodists. On September 13, 1894, Theon Edward Bowman, Thea's father, was born. He had two younger siblings: a sister, Bertha Catherine Bowman, who remained single and lived in Memphis throughout her life, and a brother, J. Charles Bowman, a Memphis drugstore owner and pharmacist. J. Charles and his wife were the parents of Thea's only first cousins, Sallie June and Carl Edward Bowman (both of Memphis). Before Thea's father, Theon, was a teenager, his parents, Edward and Sallie Bowman, moved the family to Memphis, where Edward got a job as a mail porter at Memphis Light, Gas, and Water Company. Edward, Thea's grandfather, died in January 1954, at age seventy-nine.

Thea's father, Theon, attended elementary and high school in Memphis and graduated from college in Nashville. In 1918, he received his medical degree from the first medical program for African Americans in the United States, Nashville's Meharry Medical School. He was a medical resident in New York City, and an intern at Jane Terrell Hospital in Memphis. In 1921, Dr. Theon Bowman, age twenty-seven, decided to practice medicine in Canton, Mississippi, because there were no African American doctors in that area. Canton, located about forty-five miles from his birthplace, would be home for him, his wife, and his daughter for many years to come.

He set up his office on West Peace Street, the main east-west artery through Canton. Later, Dr. Bowman moved his office several blocks south to Short Hickory Street, which was within easy walking distance from 136 Hill Street, the Bowman home. Dr. Bowman practiced medicine for over fifty years in Canton and throughout the Madison County area, mostly for black families.

Thea's maternal lineage was through the Coleman family. Her maternal grandfather, Jerry Coleman, son of Gabriel and Mary Coleman, was a respected businessman in Greenville, Mississippi, a town on the Mississippi River, about a hundred miles northwest of Jackson, just north of the state's midpoint. He operated a lumberyard and fuel business, was a fine orchidist, and had once been a cotton-farm operator. His birth date is unrecorded; he died December 28, 1910.

Greenville's renowned educator Lizzie Williams Coleman was Thea's maternal grandmother. She was born in Yazoo City, on a date unrecorded. Lizzie Coleman taught public school for forty-seven years (1890s to 1930s) and served as principal of the largest "colored school" in Greenville. Thea came by her teaching and leadership talents honestly!

A *Delta Democrat Times* newspaper clipping in 1976 recounting historical events to celebrate the U.S. Bicentennial notes, "Church Women United Name Woman of Influence, Greenville's Lizzie W. Coleman." She is described as "woman of vision, far ahead of her times."

In 1923, the local school board renamed a small brick high school on Redbud Street as the Lizzie Coleman Public School, in her honor because of her years of service to Negro education and her contribution to individual pride and citizenship. She was described as a "born teacher." Even though she was not a college graduate, Mrs. Coleman was always a student, a lifelong learner. "Burn the midnight oil!" and "Be prepared!" were her watchwords. She died on May 28, 1931.

Thea's mother, Mary Esther Coleman, was born on November 25, 1902, in Greenville. After graduating from Tougaloo College, in Jackson, Mississippi, in 1919, she attended summer school classes at Chicago Normal College. During the academic year, she taught public school in her hometown of Greenville. Mary and Theon seemed destined to be together.

THE PARENTS:
MARY AND THEON IN LOVE

"If you want smart kids, get smart parents!" goes an old saying. In a similar sense, it could be said that loving parents beget loving children. To appreciate the depths of love their daughter would share with the world, it would be good to study her parents. Luckily, there is ample record.

On Sunday, June 1, 1924, the youthful Mary Esther Coleman and Dr. Theon Edward Bowman met in the home of her aunt, Mrs. E. A. Chue, in Yazoo City. An immediate mutual attraction blossomed into a love that lasted a lifetime.

Many years later a story in *Mississippi Today,* a Catholic weekly in Jackson, recalled their courtship in a Valentine's Day feature about local couples. The paper recalled the story of Theon's father's advice about Mary Esther Coleman, of Greenville, a teacher and family friend: "Marry her as soon as you can! That's the wife for you!" Another friend concurred, said the article, and the two got together.[1]

After courting for several months, they became engaged on Christmas Eve, 1924. The ring Mary Esther received from Theon was white gold set with a diamond. The couple set their wedding date for the following August.

Some hint of the strength of the Coleman and Bowman families that contributed to the happy marriage can be found in a prayer that Mary kept in her scrapbook:

Prayer

Lord,

Bless and preserve the dear person whom Thou hast chosen to be my husband.

Let his life be long and blessed, comfortable, holy, and let me also become a great blessing and comfort unto him, a sharer in all his sorrows, a meet helper in all his accidents and changes in the world; make me amiable forever in his eyes, and forever dear to him.

Unite his heart to me in tenderest love and holiness, and mine to him in all sweetness, charity, and compliance.

Keep me from all ungentleness and unreasonableness of passion and humor.

And make me humble and obedient, useful and observant, that we may delight in each other according to Thy blessed Word; and that we may both rejoice in Thee, having our portion in the love and service of God forever. Amen.[2]

At the time of their courtship and marriage in 1925, both Dr. Theon Bowman, thirty, and teacher Mary Esther Coleman, twenty-two, were members of the respected professional black middle class in the prosperous portion of the Mississippi Delta. According to newspaper accounts from these years, the citizens of Greenville had a genuine sense of noblesse oblige. The Coleman-Bowman wedding was celebrated with matching elan.

Several well-attended bridal showers, plenty of gifts, and a highly social aura surrounded the whole event. Relatives and friends from Clarksdale, Greenville, Yazoo City, and Memphis who could attend, descended on the Coleman home for the wedding. The bride recorded names of over fifty persons who presented wedding gifts. Probably over thirty or more people attended, in addition to the wedding party members. Adding to the excitement of the festivities, two telegrams arrived for the happy couple at the Coleman home on the wedding day. One was from Uncle C. A. Bowman from Richmond Hill, New York, and the other from the Washingtons in Chicago.

In "The Bride's Memory Book," Mary Esther described her wedding day:

The ceremony was performed on the lawn. On the south end of the green, an altar was made and draped with ivy, vines, and tiny white blossoms. The powerhouse had burned the day before so we had to depend on lamps, candles, and the lights from the cars for illumination. The altar was lighted by white candles in tall silver candlesticks. The candlesticks were loaned by Mrs. Eustis and originally belonged to Mrs. Theobald, for whom our street was named.[3]

Reverend S. A. Morgan of the Episcopal Church officiated at the ceremony, assisted by Methodist pastor Rev. J. R. Rowe. (Theon was Methodist; Mary Esther was Episcopalian.) Members of the wedding party processed and took their places at the altar to the strains of the "Wedding March" from Mendelssohn's "Midsummer Night's Dream," played by Mrs. McGhee, at the piano, and Ruby C. Harris on the violin. Little Geraldine Overton, fairy-like in pink organdie with tiny roses, tossed flowers in the path of the bride. She was followed by bridesmaid Miss Daisy Miller and best man, Theon's brother, J. Charles Bowman. The guests were seated in chairs on the lawn and in cars parked along the road.

Mrs. Bowman's scrapbooks contain details of dress style, songs, and the rest. By all accounts, including one Mary had submitted to her college paper, it was a gala affair.

A planned trip to New York was toned down into a drive to Memphis for a honeymoon of several days, August 24–29. The newlyweds were eager to begin married life in their Hill Street house on Canton's south side. Arriving in Canton, Mary Esther was keen to explore her new home, but they went to Theon's office first so he could check his messages and make sure there was nothing urgent pending among his patients. Then the doctor swept up his bride and carried her over the threshold into her new home.

Mary Esther investigated the entire house and then acquainted herself with the garden, the chickens, the spaciousness of her new surroundings. Equipped with a subtle sense of humor, Mary Esther and Theon arranged to mystify and surprise their friends by having their wedding thank-you notes mailed with a New York postmark. (They accomplished the little subterfuge by sending the completed notes to Theon's uncle in New York, who in turn mailed them to their final destinations.) Both Theon and Mary often smiled with amusement at this memory.

Throughout the many years of their life together, Dr. Bowman continued his practice of medicine for the black community in Canton and all of surrounding Madison County. During the late 1920s and into the next decade, people from the nearby areas considered Canton, with a population of eight to ten thousand, a major draw. Canton was the place to come for church, school, health care needs, business transactions, and shopping. Besides being the seat of the county government, the town had churches of assorted denominations — African Methodist Episcopal (A.M.E.), A.M.E. Zion, Baptist, Episcopal, Holiness, Methodist, Catholic — several banks, public schools (segregated, of course), local businesses, doctors' offices, department stores, movie theaters, restaurants, and cafes.

Madison County was predominately black in the early 1900s. Blacks however, owned little, and most of the jobs held by blacks were menial. For the men, there was field work and day labor. For women, there was cooking, laundry, and housekeeping. The division between white and black neighborhoods was deep. That deep division continued until after the civil rights movement of the 1950s and 1960s and beyond. Central Mississippi was one of the nation's most oppressive regions with regard to its racial discrimination. That situation affected blacks and whites with brutal consequences.

It was in this environment that the Bowmans lived. They were middle class, well-to-do in Canton's black community. It was very prestigious for Dr. Bowman to own his office and medical practice. The new Mrs. Bowman was privileged to resume her education, returning to Jackson's Tougaloo College, a private, liberal arts African American college, which was religious and ecumenical. The Bowmans were aware of their many blessings and lived modestly. They, in fact, dedicated their lives to helping those less fortunate than they were.

Chapter 4

YOUNG BERTHA

Advent, the time before Christmas, is a time of hope, a time of waiting for the coming of a promise, for Christians, the birth of Jesus. For the Bowmans, Advent meant the same and more. Their engagement had been at Christmas time. Now, after thirteen years of trial and hope, during Advent of 1937, they finally were pregnant. What could be more filled with promise than awaiting a child during the season of light and giving! The impending birth of a baby now was a wondrous, generous gift.

Later in life, their daughter, named Bertha in childhood, would remember that she had been a much-loved and much-desired child. She heard stories of her birth and childhood so often and so lovingly that she was able to regale her many friends with tales of her birth and escapade-filled growing-up years. These stories always began or ended with the line, "I am an old folks' child." In the story of her birth, the woman who became Sister Thea declaimed to her rapt audiences, "My parents were o-o-o-ld when I was born." She started this way, emphasizing the "old," particularly when her parents were around. She loved to tease them, and they grinned from ear to ear when they heard her carry on.

But, at the time Bertha was born, Mary Esther, at age thirty-five, was indeed considered "o-o-old," at an advanced age for birthing a first child. That's why, during mid-December of 1937 in balmy Mississippi, Theon drove her from Canton to 301 Calhoun Street in Yazoo City, where she would remain during the last days of her pregnancy at the home of her good friend and registered nurse Miss Alice Luse. There, she would be close to that city's hospital for blacks, the Old African Hospital. Canton did not have a hospital for blacks. Also close by was Dr. L. T. Miller, who had once practiced medicine with Dr. Bowman. Dr. Miller was a good friend of the soon-to-be new father and had attended the Bowman wedding. It seemed everyone involved was at the ready for the eagerly anticipated, blessed event. But babies sometimes come by surprise! Bertha snuck up on her parents.

18

Years later, Sister Thea recounted the story she had heard so many times from her parents:

My mother, they tell me, went downtown Wednesday morning, December 29, the fifth day of Christmas, to make some last-minute purchases for the new baby. But she went into labor, and had to return home as quickly as she could. Miss Alice Luse called my father at his doctor's office in Canton. He got into his car and immediately drove the forty-five miles to Yazoo City. Then Miss Alice called Dr. L. T. Miller.

Dr. Miller said it was too soon. He took his time driving to the Luse home. By the time Dr. Miller arrived, my own father had delivered me! When Dr. Miller finally arrived, Miss Alice, having swaddled the brand new, perfect and beautiful, six-pound baby girl, answered the door with the child in her arms, just to prove that Dr. Miller wasn't always right.[1]

"I saved him $25!" Thea would crow when telling the story. Afterward, she would gaily maintain, "And I was not too soon!" The newborn was a mighty crier, according to her parents and those attending to her. Mary Esther, who remained with the as-yet-unnamed baby in Yazoo City a little over a month before she returned home to Canton, often recalled that Charlie Luse, Alice's husband, during the first days of the infant's life frequently sang "Sweet Rose Marie." As a result, Mary Esther considered naming her new daughter Rose Marie. However, Theon's sister in Memphis, Bertha Catherine Bowman, prevailed upon everyone to name the child Bertha, after her. She threatened never again to speak to the new parents if they did not! Aunt Bertha's great desire won out.

A January 1938 church bulletin from St. Mark's Episcopal Church in Jackson says: "The first news of interest is the announcement of the arrival of a most precious gift to Dr. and Mrs. T. E. Bowman. The newcomer — Bertha Elizabeth — already wields the scepter of a queen ruling with the power of innocent sweetness in the hearts of parents and all who come within her domain. St. Mark's greets lady Bertha Elizabeth and welcomes her into our midst, with best wishes for many years of health, happiness, and honors."[2]

On February 13, 1938, the new baby was christened Bertha Elizabeth Bowman at St. Mark's. Reverend Arthur Buxton Keeling, who was also Bertha's godfather, officiated.

As Baby Bertha grew, her proud new parents faithfully recorded her growth and development in a padded, silk-taffeta-covered book that they, using a label, renamed *Baby Days*. The actual title of the memory book is *Tot to Teens;* it was a gift to Bertha from a family friend. Inches grown, pounds gained, all of the standard milestones of early childhood were lovingly recorded here with delight and approval, even if amid images of white babies. Glistening locks of hair with pink ribbons still attached were included for posterity.

On October 10, 1938, Mary Esther wrote of a visit to the circus, "Baby applauded the circus acts by clapping her hands, waved at the performers, and dances [*sic*] to the music...liked the trapeze acts and the elephants."[3] When Bertha later would leaf though these pages, she marveled at how much her parents loved her and how much they apparently cherished every aspect of being new parents.

In 1938 Bertha spent her first Easter in Memphis, visiting her grandfather, aunt, and uncle. She adored her grandfather, Edward Bowman, known as "Grandpa Ed." It was mutual. She loved recalling the story about a cherished rocking chair she kept through her adulthood. As it happened, when she was only three or four years old, she went to a concert by a famous visiting singer with her parents and grandfather. Outside the concert hall, vendors hawked products for sale. Native Americans from the nearby reservation displayed handmade crafts. At one booth Bertha sat in a little rocking chair sporting a woven swamp-grass seat. Just as Grandpa was ready to make the purchase, Bertha's parents noticed it was time to proceed into the concert hall. They suggested Grandpa wait to buy the chair until after the concert.

As fate would have it, when the concert was over, the vendors and their wares were gone. Bertha teared up, she later recalled. Grandpa Ed told her not to cry. "I'll find the Indians; I'll buy the rocking chair for you," he promised. A man of his word, Grandpa Ed went to the reservation, purchased the chair, and presented it to young Bertha. She found comfort and joy rocking in her favorite chair. Even decades later when, after losing weight during treatment for cancer, Sister Thea could again ease her weary body into that chair, she rocked away, perhaps enveloped in memories of her beloved grandfather.

Recorded also in Bertha's baby book were vaccinations, inoculations, "measles from April 20 to 29, 1941," and other health notations. We discover, "baby's first tooth appeared during her seventh month." We read that Bertha later "lost her first tooth on February 18, 1943." Mrs. Bowman indicated that her darling daughter's first toy was a "rattle with Mickey Mouse on it, given by Uncle Tony." At four months, "baby's" favorite toy was a rubber rabbit. At eleven months, her favorite was a rubber baby doll that she called, "Berta Elizabeth's Baby." Having studied music, Mary Esther paid particular attention to her baby girl's vocal chords, her lung capacity. She was thrilled when, at eleven months, Bertha showed a "sense of rhythm and love of music." She added, "We hope she is really musical." Mary Esther and Theon encouraged Bertha's musicality. For Christmas 1941, a then almost four-year-old Bertha received a Victrola (phonograph, or record player) "from which she received a great deal of pleasure." Listening and singing along to records contributed to Bertha's rapidly developing musical talent.

The Bowmans encouraged Bertha's literacy and education. "Baby, at two, knows several nursery rhymes, counts to ten, and can pick out several letters. Bertha Elizabeth, at three, still dances, sings, knows numerous rhymes and stories, and can spell B-E-R-T-H-A." When Bertha was only two years old, her favorite story was "Ding Dong Bell." At age two and a half, her favorite book was *A Child's Garden of Verses*.[4]

Remembering her love of reading and of learning, the newly renamed Sister Thea, at age nineteen, recalled her childhood days in a written assignment during her education with the Franciscan sisters:

"Mama, read me a story!" And Mama read — bedtime story hours; daytime interruptions. "Please, Mama, my *Child's Garden of Verses* or *Peter Rabbit* and some nursery rhymes! Mama, just one more!"

Then Ma grew tired of reading, so one day she came home with a bright, red reader, and soon I was introduced to Father and Mother and Bob and Sally. "See Mother. See Father. See Bob and Sally. Bob and Sally run."

Mama was patient. Eventually, *Little Bo Peep* and *The Three Billy-Goats Gruff* came within my grasp. *Little Red Riding Hood* was my favorite, despite its Big Bad Wolf, and I was charmed by the fair Snow White, "a face as white as snow, lips like a drop of blood, and hair like ebony." *The Little Engine That Could* taught me a first, needed lesson in perseverance, and from Peter, the Naughty Rabbit, I learned that obedience pays dividends. Toby, Dumly, a simple Bambi, *A Child's Picture Dictionary*, Bible stories, animal books, nursery rhymes, and fairy tales completed my own personal library.

I learned to read, and while Bertha read aloud, Mama, listening for the "real hard" words that I spelled through the kitchen window, was able to do her housework undisturbed. Domestic bliss reigned.

With all of Mama's tutelage, I was able to bypass the first-year crowd and mingle with my "grown-up" friends in second grade. Moreover, my love of nursery rhymes and children's tales and fairy lore has never died.[5]

Bertha's baby book was also filled with information about her pets. On Easter 1939, she was given "a chicken named Peep." Peep was a color-tinted baby chicken who, when grown up, "won first prize at the October Fair as a white leghorn cockerel." Later, Bertha had a rabbit named Honey Bunny. On her third birthday, she received a puppy she christened "Bozo."[6] "Baby," or "Birdie," as Bertha was called by her doting parents, captured the center of everyone's attention in the happy Bowman home at 136 Hill Street in Canton.

By all accounts, her childhood was a joy. In her teenage years, she often talked to her friends about her childhood. She told them her earliest memory was from age three. She remembered being carried about on the shoulders by Grandpa Ed. Smiling, she remembered an Aunt Thelma who vied with her mother over who would change Thea's diapers. She delighted in telling friends she was a naughty child on occasion.

As an adult, in unpublished interviews with Margaret Walker Alexander (the pioneering black poet and author who wrote as Margaret Walker), the grown Sister Thea impishly recalled a few of her stories. On one occasion, her mother had given young "Birdie" a child-size broom and mop with which to clean up after herself when she had an accident in the house. Spying her mother's new shoes in the entrance, she decided to go to the bathroom there. After her mother's discipline, Birdie didn't try such a smart-aleck trick again!

On another occasion when her parents took her to a Marian Anderson concert in Jackson, Birdie concealed a cooked chicken leg in her purse. While the renowned coloratura Miss Anderson was singing, Bertha pulled out her chicken leg, to her father's amusement and her mother's embarrassment and irritation.

Young Bertha loved to tease her dad. When she saw him returning home after work, she would latch onto his leg making him swing her back and forth along the driveway into the house. She knew she was a nuisance and at the same time understood that her dad did not know how to unfasten her grip gently.

The last time Mrs. Bowman put a hand to Bertha was when she was in the fourth or fifth grade. Mrs. Bowman laughed then and both laughed later retelling the story to relatives and friends. While the petite Mrs. Bowman attempted to discipline, by spanking, the now five-foot-tall Bertha, the impetuous daughter said to her mother, "I hope you realize the only reason why you are doing this is because I am standing here letting you." Her mother knew that was true and resorted to non-corporal discipline thenceforth. On the other hand, Bertha said her dad never struck her because he probably would have killed her. He told her he did not want to start something he did not intend to finish.[7]

That "naughty child," though, was turning into an educated child all along that early way. Beginning the summer of 1941, three-year-old Bertha attended nursery school at Asbury United Methodist Church, where Mrs. Burton was the teacher. In the fall of 1942, Mrs. Bowman taught Bertha kindergarten at home and at the Calvert Street School.

Bertha was a voracious learner at school and at the knees of her mother-teacher and father-doctor. From her father, she recalls learning a lesson in compassion, affection, and, most of all, irony. She recounts this in an essay she wrote, as Thea, in 1953 for a high school English assignment:

Sometimes dads can be awfully funny people, and oh well, there's something that I could never quite figure out. My dad was a doctor, not a fancy surgeon or a specialist of any kind, just a plain family doctor, and a good one, if I do say so myself. One bright summer's morning when I was at his office a man came in. His chest was deeply gashed and his clothing was one big mass of dirt and blood.

Dad washed his hands, donned a sterile gown, and calmly went to work. The man's heart had grown too weak to stand an anesthetic, so he lay there and groaned, but Dad didn't mind, because he knew that he was doing the right thing. He must have taken thirty stitches in that poor man's chest, and he did a fine job of it. I handed him cotton, thread, gauze, then finally, adhesive bandages, and in less than an hour, his patient was all fixed up and ready to go home for a few days' rest.

Dad was tired and hungry, so we went home and pleaded with Mom for a little lunch. We sat down and started to talk; Mom was cutting meat and "Oh!" her knife slipped. Her hand was cut, and it was bleeding profusely. "Dad, Dad, do something quickly!" Dear Dad didn't move. He was scared stiff, and he sat there and looked "as though the sky was falling." I fixed up Mom's hand; the cut wasn't deep, and I had had two years of first aid.

After it was all over, Dad managed to say, "Does...does...does it hurt?" Mom and I held our sides to keep from laughing aloud, but as for Dad, he didn't eat his lunch. He just wasn't hungry.[8]

Perhaps that love of learning that Mary Esther wanted for her daughter, Bertha, is the reason she clipped the poem "Motherhood," by Frances White, and attached it to *Baby Days*. A mother's message for her child, the poem is an appropriate entry from the daughter of a renowned, beloved teacher to a baby who was destined to follow in the footsteps of her maternal grandmother, becoming herself a renowned, beloved, master teacher.

Motherhood

I know now/I have learned;
Why birds guard eggs so patiently.
Know a miracle is there;
Why death is faced so valiantly
If danger comes to whelping lair;
Why wind and sun and rain in spring
Tiptoe so softly as they go
Preparing things/and whispering
Encouragement to earth in throe;
And I have learned that life is sweet
It has crooned a lullaby,
And smoothed a path for stumbling feet
And watched a laugh leave young eyes dry.
I know now. I have learned.[9]

As a child Bertha was spiritually sensitive. For her and her friends, going to church was fun. It was there in those "old black churches," the adult Sister Thea would later say, "I learned what they called the 'old-time religion.' I wanted to grow up so I could be a preacher."[10]

Bertha was fascinated when women in the congregation stood and shouted and swayed up the middle aisle of the church. She and her childhood friends sat at the edge of their seats mesmerized each Sunday awaiting a weekly blessed event that they dubbed the "angel thing." Exciting, too, was preaching that got, in the girls' parlance, "real good": real good preaching that enticed the congregation to shout and say "Amen" and moan and sway. Sister Thea would later quip that she could never understand why folks would shout "Amen" but not "A-women!" As children, Bertha and the others did not really understand what was happening, but they knew it was important. Bertha held a deep fascination for her elders, who were so expressive of a faith born in slavery. Theirs was a treasure of her heritage, a treasure Bertha absorbed.

When Bertha started public school at age three, she also started Sunday school. Sunday school introduced her to Mother Ricker, a Canton neighbor and Sunday school teacher, who often gathered children in her home to teach them Gospel songs. From Mother Ricker, Bertha learned the powerful combination of faith and music.

Then there was Mrs. Ward, Bertha's next-door neighbor. Every week, Bertha and the other children saw Mrs. Ward leaving early in a maid's uniform, off to take care of some white folks' laundry and other domestic chores, and returning late. On Sunday, though, Mrs. Ward dressed in her best for church and carried herself with a different dignity. Throughout the week, the children heard her after hours, singing church songs in her yard, on her porch, doing her housework. Then in church on Sunday, Mrs. Ward said "Amen" and sang with a "Good News" kind of dignity. Her face and her body announced the joy she had deep in her heart. It was from her elders, people like Mrs. Ward, that Bertha learned religion.

In *Sister Thea: Songs of My People,* Thea recalled, in the late 1980s:

I grew up in a community where the teaching of religion was a treasured role of the elders — grandparents, old uncles and aunts, but also parents, big brothers and sisters, family friends, and church members. Many of the best teachers were not formally educated. But they knew Scripture, and they believed the Living Word must be celebrated and shared. They did not struggle to ask, "Did this biblical event occur? When or how did it happen?" Somehow they intuited that the stories were concerned with truth more than with

factuality. They asked only, "What does this story mean? What did
it mean in biblical times? What does it mean in our lives today?
What does it call me to do?"

Their teachings were simple. Their teachings were sound. Their
methodologies were such that, without effort, I remember their
teachings today: songs of Adam, Eve, Noah, Abraham, Moses,
Joshua, Miriam, David, Dives, Ezekiel, Daniel, Jonah, John, Mary,
Jesus: his birth, his life, his teachings, his miracles, his disciples, his
Passion, his glory, his promise to us all of eternal life.[11]

Given her rich exposure as a child, a spiritual quest would be natural
for Bertha. Her quest would eventually lead her to meet and mingle with
the priests, brothers, and sisters of the Catholic Order of the Missionary
Servants of the Most Holy Trinity, who came to Canton in the 1940s.
Attracted by the good she saw the Catholics trying to do, young Bertha
took instructions to become a Catholic. Later in life, when people would
wonder how something apparently so unlikely could happen, she would
insist that that was her primary motivation for becoming Catholic and
for becoming a sister. This daughter of charitable parents wanted to love
in the way that she saw the sisters love.

In a 1958 spiritual autobiography she composed as a Franciscan
novice, she wrote: "Before I met Catholicism in 1947, I had tried the
Methodist, Baptist, Episcopalian, Adventist, A.M.E., and A.M.E. Zion
churches, but once I went to the Catholic Church, my wanderings ceased.
I knew I had found that for which I had been seeking. As Momma always
says, 'God takes care of babies and fools.' "[12]

At age nine, on the first Sunday in June 1947, she was baptized
a Catholic at Holy Child Jesus Mission in Canton by the Rev. Justin
Furman of the Missionary Servants of the Most Holy Trinity, then pastor at Holy Child Jesus Church. The following day, she made her First
Communion.

In an article for a religious educators association,[13] she later wrote
that her attraction to Catholicism was a result of personal witness. It
wasn't that she recognized anything formal; rather, she recognized and
resonated with the lifestyle of prayer, community, service, and faith that
had been nurtured in her already. Thea's conversion was so powerful
that it inspired her parents. Dr. and Mrs. Bowman followed in their
daughter's footsteps and joined the Catholic faith several years later,
first Mrs. Bowman and then Dr. Bowman.

Chapter 5

SCHOOL DAYS IN CANTON

The day I was born, my father went out and started a separate bank account for my education. As far back as I can remember, education was a top priority in my family on both sides. My mother's mother was a teacher and a school principal. Even today, the school she founded in Greenville is still named after her. And, my father's father was a slave,[1] but he managed to go to school through the second grade. So the expectation was that education was important, not just for yourself, but for your family and your community. And it brought [the] responsibility to try to help somebody else. That's a different kind of teaching from what many families believe today.
— Sister Thea Bowman[2]

It was challenging for the Bowmans to get a first-class education for their daughter. In segregated Canton, black public schools were in sad condition. Centuries of legalized slavery allowed white citizens in the United States to exercise a pseudo-superiority. After the Civil War and Reconstruction, segregation was enforced and hardened by the unjust Jim Crow laws for the better part of a century. In the Deep South, and most especially in Mississippi, everything in the dominant political system and culture was geared to oppress African Americans.

Bertha, who attended public school for first to fifth grades, learned early that she lived in a racist society. She was pained when she and her friends had to drink from segregated drinking fountains. "Colored Only" signs sharply offended the exquisitely sensitive, intelligent child. One day when she wanted some water, she helped herself from the "Whites Only" fountain. Mrs. Bowman, Bertha recalled, "had a fit." Under no circumstances did she want her child in trouble with local authorities.

But as a young girl, Bertha knew her natural sensibilities were similar to those of white people's. She knew she could feel hurt or happy, just

27

as white people could. She knew discrimination was unfair and unjust. Her young consciousness swirled with moral confusion and cynicism. She had been taught that the United States Constitution proclaimed "all men are created equal," yet her people were not treated as equals to whites.

Being the daughter of a physician and a teacher, being the talented, precocious child of "old folks," gave Bertha rich, diverse, wondrous, and, simultaneously, searing experiences. When asked, she recalled bitter encounters with segregation, racism, religion, education, poverty, cruelties blacks had to endure, shootings, discrimination, indignity, men being called "boy," clerks and some professionals addressing married women by their first names instead of, for example, the polite "Mrs. Bowman."

Perhaps the earliest incident pricking Bertha's realization she lived in a racist society took place in her father's office. She told friends:

> One day, three white men burst in. One of the men had been severely injured; he was covered in blood. The white man wanted Dr. Bowman to treat his wounds. Bertha heard her father ask, "Who is your regular doctor? I suggest you go to your regular doctor." There I was thinking my dad was not honoring his Hippocratic oath. He should have attended to that injured man. Then, in a flash, I realized those three white men were in some kind of complication, or they would not even have been in a black Canton neighborhood. And I had the insight that if my dad had treated them, he might have been punished and put in jail.
>
> This was not a pretty learning for me as a very young child.[3]

Examples abounded. One time white kids picked on one of Mary Bowman's godsons, and he fought back. Tensions developed. Blacks had to hide the young man, terrified of what would happen if the white kids found him. Relatives and friends of the family lived in fear until they could spirit him out of Canton.

On another occasion, grimly similar to the infamous Emmett Till case (which helped spark the civil rights movement), a Cantonian youth Bertha knew as a child had moved from the neighborhood to Milwaukee. Upon his return south in his late teens, whites judged he had become "uppity." One evening from her bedroom Bertha heard police questioning him. He had an attitude. He refused to be courteous, to say, "Yes, sir. No, sir." The police shot him. The youth ran though the Bowman's yard and dropped to the ground in an adjacent yard. Bertha remembered the old woman who lived there saying, "We got to soak up the blood so the children won't be scared." Adults put sand on the ground to clean away the blood stains.[4]

Another horror Bertha experienced — the kind of story that is scarcely believable unless you appreciate the blatant oppression of many parts of pre–civil rights Mississippi — was with a family who lived nearby. The father had charged furniture from a white storekeeper, an event that did not sit well with some of the local troublemakers. Soon these three white men, accompanied by the storekeeper, who had no doubt been pressured by them, came to the man's house carrying weapons. The whites pulled Bertha's neighbor out of the duplex, and under threat of violence, forced him to sit in humiliation, downtown in front of the Seale-Lily Ice Cream store, until the family came up with dollars. At the time, his wife was heavily pregnant. She had to plod house to house, begging. This went on for several days, during which the whole town, including Bertha and her friends, witnessed the poor man haplessly sitting in front of Seale-Lily Ice Cream. Soon his wife went into labor. A neighbor lady delivered the baby. Finally enough money was collected and the family brought the humiliated husband home.[5]

When her beloved grandfather, Grandpa Ed, in the workplace at Memphis Power and Light talked about being taunted, "Boy! Come here, Boy! Pick that up, Boy! Do this, Boy," her sensitive spirit recoiled. She realized her grandfather was slick in his reply, "Yes, sir, boss, whatever you say, boss."[6] She understood that her people were treated unfairly, inhumanly, and that they coped for survival.

Still a young girl, Bertha drove with her dad to Yazoo City's Old African Hospital to remove a child's tonsils. Because his family could not afford to hospitalize the boy, he returned with the Bowmans. "I got to hold the can so the kid can spit," Bertha recounted.[7]

Discrimination in Mississippi was not limited to blacks. There were Chinese immigrants, brought from Cuba to Mississippi in the early twentieth century as indentured servants to supplement black labor. Eventually they moved into society, especially as agricultural laborers and merchants. Neither black nor white, they received a mixed welcome, one that vacillated during this first half of the century, a topic beyond this book. When Chinese families arrived in Canton, the children were not welcome in the town's white school, but enrolling them in the black school proved a disaster too. During the World War II years,

Mrs. Rogers, the principal of Bertha's school, lined the children in marching formation outside the building and then went inside to play patriotic songs on the piano. On one occasion, as the children marched in, Canton police officers suddenly swooped in, forcefully dragging the Chinese children away. Not able to attend the white or black public schools, the families had to move out of town.[8] Some had intermarried with African Americans; hence they were dubbed "black Chinese." Segregation laws did not permit them to mingle with or marry whites.

Bertha's soul cringed as she observed these indignities. Indignity and discrimination were a constant, destructive teacher for this daughter of the South, who later would become a teacher and healer in her own right. As an adult she winced recounting the episodes. As a child she witnessed the whites' hurtful oppression. In college later, she studied and excelled in Shakespeare, often quoting Shylock's speech from "The Merchant of Venice" when her instruction was about discrimination:

> Hath not a Jew eyes? Hath not a Jew hands, organs, dimensions, senses, affections, passions; fed with the same food, hurt with the same weapons, subject to the same diseases, heal'd by the same means, warm'd and cool'd by the same winter and summer as a Christian is? If you prick us, do we not bleed? If you tickle us, do we not laugh? If you poison us, do we not die? And if you wrong us, shall we not revenge? If we are like you in the rest, we will resemble you in that. If a Jew wrong a Christian, what is his humility? Revenge. If a Christian wrong a Jew, what should his sufferance be by Christian example? Why, revenge. The villainy you teach me, I will execute, and it shall go hard but I will better the instruction. — Act 3, scene 1

It was precisely indignity spewed by segregation and racism that the Bowmans refused to accept. Nor would they allow their daughter, ultimately, to accept indignity. When the Bowmans realized that their gifted and talented only child, after five years in segregated, "tremendously disadvantaged and understaffed"[9] black public schools, could not read on a fifth-grade level, they took action.

Bertha had begun school in 1941. At that time some Catholic missionaries were turning their attention toward Canton's black community. The priests, brothers, and sisters from the Missionary Servants of the Most Holy Trinity, based in Alabama, were serving white Catholics at Sacred

Heart Catholic Mission in Canton. They had turned to the black community and established Holy Child Jesus Mission for African Americans. Not long afterward, they held a meeting with Canton's impoverished blacks, a few of whom were Catholic. The group determined their top priority for the new mission would be education for poor children.

Achieving their goal would not be easy, but it held the support of the Roman Catholic Church, a tiny minority in most of Mississippi, but a large, multinational institution nonetheless. Racism's prominence in the civic and church culture in Mississippi conflicted with Catholic Church teachings on social justice. Based in Natchez, bishop after bishop had valiantly fostered outreach to the black majority in Mississippi (we'll discuss this further in chapter 16). Because of scarce finances and little support from the white Catholic population, the results were meager. The task ahead for Holy Child Jesus Mission was daunting. Still, with the blessings of the bishop, whose diocese at the time encompassed all of Mississippi, they set about enlisting a community of teaching sisters to come to Canton.

With some recruiting, the Wisconsin-based Franciscan Sisters of Perpetual Adoration, known as Franciscans or by their familiar abbreviation, the FSPAs, agreed to come.* It started with:

> ... a few retired sisters who toiled quietly to support the missions at St. Rose Convent motherhouse in La Crosse, Wisconsin. Gathering monetary and other donations, making dollars by selling cancelled stamps, the Franciscans donated to missionaries throughout the country. One donation was sent to Gilbert Hay, ST (Missionary Servants of the Most Holy Trinity) at Holy Child Jesus Mission in Canton, Mississippi. Father Hay immediately thanked the nuns and informed his community about the FSPA generosity.
>
> Another member of Father Hay's community, Father Andrew Lawrence, was preaching in the Midwest at the time (in 1942). He got himself invited to talk with the sisters at St. Rose Convent, pleading Father Hay's need for sisters to teach at the school. Both priests were persuasive. Father Lawrence began correspondence

---

* The early focus of the Franciscan Sisters of Perpetual Adoration was to educate children of German Catholic immigrants. The community has continually adapted to meet the ever-changing needs of humankind. The sisters' recurring desire to share God's love is strengthened by the FSPA's defining practice of Perpetual Adoration. Since August 1, 1878, at least two adorers have prayed day and night before the blessed sacrament. See *www.fspa.org/Prayer/perpetualadoration.html*.

with the sisters. He frequently expressed hope that they would accept the challenge of starting a school in one of the southern communities he served. In 1946, Mother Rose Kreibich, FSPA, major superior (head of the community), visited Canton and, realizing the need, promised Father Lawrence that the sisters would help with one of the "most urgent needs of the mid-twentieth century."[10]

Father Lawrence was delighted. In an August 25, 1947, letter to Mother Rose, he wrote, "Daily in the Mass when I give memento to you and your esteemed Congregation, I think, 'Dear Lord, how long?' And then the day passes and another dawns — and again, 'Dear Lord, how long? . . .' " The letter continues in that vein.[11]

Father Gilbert Hay became pastor of the mission in September 1947 and began organizing the school. Four months after his arrival at Canton, Father Hay wrote a new appeal to Mother Kreibich, telling her of the establishment of the school and of its important mission: "Mother, despite the opposition to the Church and her teaching in this part of the country, I think your sisters will enjoy building up the Church in this neglected corner of Christ's vineyard, and will like working with our children here. They are eager and affectionate, and religious at heart. With the sisters to lead them, in God's good time, the harvest of souls should be great."[12]

His efforts paid off. Finally, four sisters arrived in Canton in the summer of 1948. By then, Bertha, also called "Birdie," was ten. Little did she know how her whole world would expand. Sisters Vita Burger, Vincenza Naumann, and Judith Quinn were assigned as teachers for the first six grades. Sister Genedine Melder, a registered nurse, handled medical services and housekeeping. The nurse was a necessary addition, considering the shortage of medical services in the black community.

Sister Mileta Ludwig, FSPA, in her history of the Franciscan sisters, *A Chapter of Franciscan History,* describes the situation the new FSPA missionaries would face:

> Once the FSPA had come to Canton and established the new school, they knew how important their role was, and they dedicated themselves to it without one look back. In every sense, the term "mission" is applicable to Holy Child Jesus School. In Mississippi, where the colored make up one half of a total population of 2,200,000, Catholics number about forty-four thousand; of those forty-four thousand, fewer than five thousand are colored.

In the Canton area, Negroes constitute about seventy-eight per cent of the population. Very few of them are Catholics. More than two-thirds belong to no church whatever. Holy Child Jesus Mission is one of the nine diocesan centers by means of which the Church is trying to bring the message of Christ to these masses.

Since Canton is located in a typical share-cropping region, the Negroes are, for the most part, extremely poor. Their homes are often mere sheds almost unfit for human habitation.

The work is further handicapped by prejudice and other unfortunate social conditions. Many colored have had no opportunities for formal education. Most of the approximately 90 pupils enrolled in the mission school for the 1948–49 term actually had to be classified as ungraded. Not even one-fifth of the children were Catholic, but all were docile and receptive to the Faith. In view of the rapid increase of the Negro population in the country, the Church and the nations must look to the youth of the race as an important factor in the future happiness and security of both; for, as the founder (Thomas Augustine Judge, Boston) of the Missionary Servants of the Most Holy Trinity often said, "Save the child, and you save all."[13]

Flonzie Brown-Wright, then known as Flonzie Brown, along with Bertha, was a member of the charter class. Looking back in 2008, from her Ohio home, she remembers, "Thea and I were little girls together — she was three years older than me."[14] Flonzie's house was just across the street from the sisters' convent, about an eighth of a mile from Bertha's. She remembers the old barracks that had been moved there, "a ripe opportunity for developing."

After the Franciscan sisters first opened the convent, back in the mid-1940s, it was a while before the school actually opened, because they spent much of their days recruiting black students to attend the school.[15]

As soon as the opening of Holy Child Jesus School was announced, the Bowmans enrolled Bertha in grade six. It was there that Bertha accelerated her reading and learning. Years later, she would reflect on her transfer from public school to the new mission:

Because my mother wanted me to have a chance in life, she sent me to a Catholic school. The black public schools were tremendously disadvantaged and understaffed. At the black Catholic school, I remember using books given to us by St. Angela's Academy in Carroll, Iowa, and Aquinas High School in La Crosse, Wis. We shared gym clothes with students in Breda, Iowa. The sisters begged a lot, and because they did, our school was much better supplied. Men and women all over the country gave a dollar or two to help us get an adequate education.

The priest, brothers, and sisters brought an extraordinary kind of dedication to the education process. They involved us in fundraising and helped us to educate ourselves. That was the key. They also worked with our parents and never left us feeling indebted. They made us feel that we contributed to the process.[16]

Flonzie remembers well the school situation before the sisters arrived. "The books that we had were books that had been used year after year," she says. "Some of the backs may have been torn or torn off, just very very poor quality. The convent provided an opportunity for families to send their children to school with low tuition, and certainly better opportunity. This was, for us, a culture shock . . . to see all of these white women and white men coming, and having Mass, burning incense — this was an entirely new culture for our people."[17]

As Thea recalled to interviewer Judy Ball many years later, "The everyday niceties were few. The school itself was a reclaimed army barracks. Old orange crates served as bookcases. But the Franciscan sisters who came into our world spent quality time with us."[18]

Additionally, amazingly to the blacks, Holy Child Jesus School did not discriminate on race, class, or even religion. Sister Thea wrote later in life:

The vast majority of the students were Baptist, Methodist, Holiness. There were at most two dozen Catholics in a student population of 180. Holy Child was a good place to be.

We loved our teachers because they first loved us. For a handful of Catholics, for devout Protestants, for the children of a surprising number of ministers, deacons, elders, and evangelizers, and for children who rarely went to any church, the Catholic school was a graced and grace-filled environment. We all went to Mass each week, sang in the choir, learned, if we wished, to serve Mass (boys only) or to care for vestments and altar (girls only).

We all prayed before every class. We all studied catechism. With Father Gilbert [Hay] and Father Justin [Furman], religion class was a time to be anticipated and treasured — stories of Jesus and the saints, songs, and prayers, and Catholic doctrine. Our pastors loved us. They entertained us as they taught us. Some of my friends and schoolmates developed insights and skills (reading, thought, judgment, song) which enabled them to become young leaders in the Protestant churches of Canton.[19]

In another reflection, this time for a school fundraising letter, Sister Thea remembered cleaning up the old army barracks by washing windows, polishing desks, the works. She recalled the first day of school, when about seventy children, herself among them, showed up:

What an amalgam of children we were — some hungry; some afraid; some eager and inquisitive; some shy; some far too behind ever to catch up academically; some far too old, even for sixth grade; most already discouraged with school and learning; some too poor to pay even the $2 per month tuition that was asked but not required.

She reflected on the transition from an overcrowded, underfinanced public school to a "very different school environment," one that was not overcrowded and where children were expected to learn. If a child didn't come to school, Sister or Father would visit the home to inquire why. "Homework had a purpose, and you'd better do it at home or you would find yourself the next day doing it in the classroom after school and getting the help you needed to do your best."

There were clean books for everyone, which was definitely not the case in the segregated public school, where children were considered lucky to get a hand-down book that had been used for five years by white children. Everyone pitched in to make the school work. Students made flash cards and bulletin-board learning devices. They helped prepare the school lunch. They wrote thank-you notes to benefactors from all over the country who contributed to the school.

We cleaned the school, sanded the desks, cut the grass, painted beaverboard walls. We worked in groups. Ada helped me with math. I helped Walter and Willie with reading. We all learned to flash flash-cards and to hear spelling drills. We older children supervised the younger children on the playground. We taught them songs and games and dances. We wiped their noses and soothed their tears.

Under the priests' and sisters' supervision, Holy Child Jesus School operated as a "big school-family, sharing stories and songs, jokes and signifying, faith, and hope, hard work, and love."

> The results were tangible and incredible: Children who had wasted time in the segregated public schools now became learners. We walked and talked and thought and felt different. We knew we were learning every day. We knew we were growing. We wore those Holy Child Jesus uniforms, even the most faded ones, with pride. HCJ was our school. We thought we were special.[20]

Tellingly, she wrote, "Academically, I made it because Holy Child Jesus School had given me a chance."[21] The impact Holy Child Jesus School had on Bertha and her fellow students was indeed life-changing. In a climate of racism, segregation, and injustice suffered at the hands of whites, Holy Child Jesus School brought tremendous hope and a sense of dignity and pride to the black and poor of Canton.

Flonzie Brown-Wright remembers the sisters: "They made quite a significant impact in the community, economically and socially. This is one of the things that Thea talked about: one of the things that won her to the Catholic faith was not the liturgy or the doctrine, it was that these nuns would walk the streets and find these children, and clean their nose, and give them a cookie, or invite them over to play...."[22]

Not only was there an expectation of academic achievement at Holy Child Jesus School; Holy Child Jesus Catholic mission also worked on social relations. The Franciscan sisters who came to Canton became one with the black community, which is no small achievement in 1940s Mississippi. They worked to educate the white community about the humanity of the blacks, and in turn they helped the black community to see the humanity in their white neighbors. The sisters organized "after-school and weekend activities.... They taught first aid and nutrition classes to impoverished young pregnant women."[23]

The mission also sponsored a used clothing store, known as the "sale house" or "HCJ Emporium," where clothing and other goods donated from around the country were sold at bargain prices. Wrote Sister Thea, "I have seen what a dainty little green dress bought for two nickels and a dime did for the morale of an eight-year-old who had worn only dingy, none too dainty hand-me-downs for eight years. I have seen also what nice, attractive used clothing has done for the self-respect of a little mission parish over a period of nine or ten years. It has put stars in their eyes, armed them with self-confidence, made ideals attainable, given men and women courage to look the world in the face and smile at it." To an "already happy people," wrote Thea, the mission brought joys, and the promise of good things to come.[24]

Bertha Bowman wasn't the only child whose life was radically affected by the Holy Child Jesus Mission. She later recalled how many of her classmates moved on to successful lives outside of Canton: "We are educators, health professionals, lawyers, journalists, print and TV journalists, social workers, politicians, church workers, etc., etc. We are parents and grandparents, capable, competent, loving, caring people, doing well, making life better for ourselves, our families, our communities, our people."[25]

It was that opportunity to serve in some bigger way that drew Bertha closer to the Franciscan sisters. Her friend and classmate, Flonzie, who later became a prominent Mississippi civil rights activist, remembers, "We were going to become nuns together. We were on the same track, and so much so, that in the evenings (I lived right across the street from the convent, and her Daddy would bring her back to my house, or we would visit together every Sunday) we would go over to the sisters, and they just loved us!" She recalls them imitating the sisters, the sixth-grader Bertha with the third-grader Flonzie: "We would take headscarves, and we would fold them in a little triangle, and we would put those little headscarves on our hair, and we would pin them down by our ears, so that when we walked over to the grounds of the convent," there were bandanas "waving in the wind."[26] The sisters indulged them: "The sisters would walk with us around the grounds, they would do their rosary and we would do our rosary."[27]

At age fifteen, Bertha announced her intentions to move to St. Rose High School, the La Crosse, Wisconsin, motherhouse of the Franciscan sisters who had come to Holy Child Jesus school. Flonzie recalls: "Her mother and father did not approve of her going into the convent — there was a lot of discussion about that, but Bertha was determined."[28]

Her parents, naturally hoping for grandchildren — and naturally wondering what having a Catholic sister in the family might mean for the future of all three of them — forbade Bertha to leave home. They pleaded with her to change her mind, but she was adamant. When the Bowmans did not relent, Birdie refused to eat until she finagled her parents' permission to go to La Crosse.

Alarmed by their daughter's persistence and rapid weight loss, Dr. and Mrs. Bowman reluctantly acquiesced. Next, Dr. Bowman tried to talk Bertha into joining a community nearer home, for example, a community of mostly black Catholic sisters in New Orleans. Holy Child Jesus Mission pastor Fr. Justin Furman echoed Dr. Bowman's counsel.

Buoyed by her love of God, her love of her Wisconsin teachers and mentors, she doggedly resisted considering any congregation other than the La Crosse Franciscans. Thea later told interviewer Judy Ball that her father had warned her, "They're not going to like you up there, the only black in the middle of all the whites." Bertha's response was, "I'm going to *make* them like me."[29]

In addition to the unfamiliar Catholic-convent world, there were other questions: Would a black girl be safe going into the Far North, so far from home? Bertha prevailed. In an act not uncommon for Catholic teenage girls of the day, she made the trip to Wisconsin with a sister from the community and took on the community as her guardian.

A prayer card she took with her, saved in the family scrapbook, expresses well her parting sentiment:

> Leave all things and ye shall find all.
> Who shall declare the sweet delights
> which the Lord showers on those
> who have given up all things to follow him?[30]

Part Two

Thea in La Crosse

Chapter 6

FOLLOWING ST. FRANCIS—
TO WISCONSIN

Bertha Elizabeth did indeed leave all things behind as she took the trip north to become a Franciscan sister. Inspired by the compassionate, effective modeling of the Franciscan sisters who staffed Holy Child Jesus Mission School, teenager Bertha responded to an urgent, inner call to be a woman religious, a sister, and follow the example of her Franciscan teachers.

One was Sister Lina Putz. In the 1950s, she taught science at St. Rose High School in La Crosse. Her heart led her also to be an advocate for the poor. After she traveled to Mississippi in 1953 for summer work at Holy Child Jesus Mission, congregation leaders then asked Sister Lina to accompany Bertha "Birdie" Elizabeth Bowman on the thousand-mile Milwaukee Railroad train trip to La Crosse.

In Canton, Sister Lina and teenaged Bertha boarded the fabled City of New Orleans train traveling north to Chicago. In those pre-civil-rights days, blacks were required to ride in the baggage cars. The sisters negotiated with train officials to allow Bertha to ride with Sister Lina in a passenger car.[1] One can only imagine the delicacy of that trip. The second leg of the trip from Chicago to La Crosse was on the regionally famed Hiawatha.

Bertha penned a two-cent postcard to her parents in Canton while en route on the Hiawatha via R.P.O. (Railroad Post Office). The card began Bertha's written chronicles about her new status.[2]

On Wednesday, August 19, the traveling duo de-trained in Chicago. A stopover at a Notre Dame sisters' convent provided a refreshing respite during the longest train adventure of Bertha's young life. While in the "City with the Big Shoulders" the travelers dutifully and eagerly shopped for specific items requested by the Canton FSPAs for their mission store. From the stopover Bertha saved a white table napkin with rose and lace border, imprinted with "Welcome to our house" received as a gift from their Notre Dame hostesses. She remembered the sentiment, treating it as a sign she would be welcomed in Wisconsin, too. Verifying the experience for her parents, she wrote on the napkin "Notre Dame Convent, Chicago, Ill."[3] The passengers arrived in La Crosse on Friday, August 21, 1953.

Looking back, a senior sister remembered Bertha's arrival: here was an attractive, mocha-skinned, sparkling-eyed woman walking on Winnebago Street to the entrance of Maria Angelorum Chapel: Bertha, dressed in a white eyelet dress with an embroidered border on its skirt, sauntered into the chapel with Sister Lina. The inspiring beauty that Bertha saw in Maria Angelorum remained with soon-to-be Thea throughout her life. Her heart was happy there in the chapel; she intuited genuine her call to become a sister. She had aligned herself with God's will and, though tempted, never wavered from her newfound calling.

What were the temptations? From time to time in the tumultuous decades ahead for most people in the United States — and especially for blacks — Thea surely must have been tempted to leave the convent, to renounce her vows. It's a question we'll return to, but for now, suffice it to say that she genuinely perceived a call from God. Friend and fellow FSPA sister Dorothy Ann Kundinger, who lived with Thea for years at the peak of Thea's career, says, "You know, I think it's because she made a commitment at age fifteen when she entered. She just knew it was right for her. . . . I just think she was so true to herself and saw herself doing right." Or, in other words, says Sister Dorothy Ann, "I guess that the calling was just so prevailing that nothing else made a difference."[4]

Shortly after the required first act for new entrants coming to La Crosse — visiting the chapel — Bertha changed to aspirant attire, a simple black dress. Later, in a formal ritual, all the new aspirants were given sheer black veils for chapel wear.

From the time she arrived at La Crosse, at age fifteen, until her death thirty-seven years later, Bertha often made news. Being black and in the public at the cusp of the civil rights movement (and, later, a public speaker during the women's movement) often thrust her into "first" or "only" status. The civil rights movement kept African American demands for justice on the front pages in local, regional, and national publications.

An August 1953 issue of the La Crosse Catholic diocesan paper, the *Catholic Register,* greeted readers with a story about Bertha Bowman entering St. Rose Convent. Her blackness was news in western Wisconsin. In the accompanying photo, Bertha is pictured with her parents and several Franciscan sisters in Canton in front of Holy Child Jesus Mission. The headline: "Negro Aspirant":

> Bertha E. Bowman, aspirant for St. Rose's Convent, La Crosse, bids farewell to her parents, Dr. and Mrs. T. E. Bowman, Canton, Miss. Bertha, a junior in high school and a convert, is the first girl to enter the St. Rose aspirancy from the Holy Child Jesus Mission conducted for the Colored in Canton by the La Crosse Franciscans. At the completion of her junior year Bertha hopes to enter the senior aspirancy and to become a postulant in February of that year. A two-year novitiate will follow the six-month postulancy. Miss Bowman anticipates returning to the South as a professed Sister to work among her people.[5]

Though in a state of high excitement, sensitive Birdie knew her mother's and father's hearts were hurting when they bade farewell to their only and beloved daughter back in Canton. Bertha was sad, too, and yet simultaneously eager to walk the first steps in her journey to becoming a Franciscan sister.

She did all she could to console her "Mama" and "Daddy," to whom she was deeply devoted. They had provided for her a sheltered, loving, and happy family life, which extended to the wider family circle. As her mother had given her a prayer card to remember her by, so, too, Bertha had presented her mother with a prayer/poem, "Lily of the Cloister," from the Franciscan sisters, signed, "Birdie." It says in part:

> Yet now you part with your darling,
> You will miss her girlish smile,
> But think she is safe forever,
> From the storms of life and guile.
> So weep not, but be joyful, Oh Mother,
> At the choice that your daughter has made,
> For she is one of the lilies,
> Safe in the cloister's shade.
> There before the altar adoring,
> So silently and sweet,
> Till angels shall bear her to Heaven
> To rest at the Savior's feet.[6]

This sister would be a lily of a different color!

Impressionable Bertha from her earliest days was captivated by all things holy. Going to various churches, "church-hopping," had been a weekly adventure in Canton. Sunday school was fun. Bible stories were thrilling. She remembered nursery rhymes, fairy tales, and children's stories learned at her mother's knee; she also remembered beloved sacred stories, songs and poems. She had collected, saved, and recycled articles, poems, quotations, songs, that drew her spirit closer to God. She committed to memory many of the best of these. Later, during her professional ministries, she sprinkled her talks, lectures, and singing performances with zesty favorites.

Now that Bertha was away from home, she became a prolific letter writer. Mrs. Bowman gathered Bertha's correspondence, clippings, award certificates, programs, and other printed materials which she read, savored, reread, and sometimes held close to her heart. Occasionally clipping personal parts away, Mrs. Bowman pasted "historical parts" of Birdie's letters in Bowman family scrapbooks. She must have known that her beloved daughter indeed was about something unusual.

From the summer Birdie stepped into the convent until she stepped back to Canton twenty-five years later to care for her aging parents, she wrote letters home dutifully.

On the one hand, they read as authentic, vital, first-hand accounts of her life story, depicted through correspondence with her parents, community, colleagues, and friends. But some of her letters were the kind that any young person might write to reassure her parents that everything was fine, carefully skipping the more difficult moments.

On September 3, 1953, less than two weeks after Bertha Elizabeth arrived in La Crosse, her traveling companion, Sister Lina, wrote a chatty letter to Dr. and Mrs. Bowman that gives a good picture of the moment from Sister Lina's perspective:

A few days ago I received your lovely letter. Thanks so much.

Yes, we certainly did enjoy our trip North, Bertha and I. We had no difficulty whatever, and, I think, we walked and rode over half of Chicago before we had completed all the "odd jobs" we had planned.

Bertha was a very lovely companion. I imagine she wrote you of the time we had in that "clothes bureau." It really can't be written, it will have to be told, because so many funny incidents were connected with it. The sisters can tell you we captured quite a few "handy articles of clothing" that they could use in the sale houses.

We shipped the cartons from Chicago to La Crosse on our tickets and then sent them out, via parcel post, to Sister Vita, Canton.

Bertha is now pretty well settled in her new home, and likes all her class work. I imagine she has written you all about it, but I'll just state briefly that she has both Sister Olive Lepine and me as two of her teachers. I have her in the botany section of biology, and we're having a great time. We've covered the first unit, so are sending on a copy of the work to Sister Vita Burger as she is also teaching that subject this semester and may appreciate the outline. I know library facilities are so meager down there.

Bertha would like to make her biology notebook using "Plants from the South" so she asked me to have you do a little "job" for her. She'd appreciate getting a sprig of the various weeds (pressed). . . . Then we'd like a leaf from the different trees (size makes no difference.) In fact, any flower or leaf that grows down in Mississippi will be welcome. The other members of her class have used or are using flowers, leaves, plants from their sections of the country. Most of them, of course, are using "Flowers of the North." Would it still be possible to find a pink bloom, also, a white one of the cotton plant? A pod, closed or open, would also be nice. I wish Bertha and I could have foreseen this; we certainly would have gathered specimens, galore, for our class.

There's one thing Bertha doesn't like about the North, and that's the mosquitoes. It's been so very hot up here since we're back that, I don't think she has noticed much difference in the temperature. . . . The humidity is intense back here.

I'm told Bertha eats and sleeps well, and, everyone likes her much. God be praised![7]

High school graduates or college students, immediately upon entering the convent, were "aspirants"; in a period called "aspirancy." It was a somewhat mysterious world to the newcomer.

Following aspirancy came postulancy, a six-month period beginning on February 2, the Feast of the Presentation of Jesus in the Temple, extending to reception into the novitiate the following August 12, then the feast day of thirteenth-century Francisan St. Clare of Assisi. Novitiate lasted two years, followed by six years of temporary profession of vows, and finally profession of perpetual vows. Bertha negotiated all these steps with her classmates during formation.

Immediately after walking over the threshold into the formation wing, new aspirants were excused to change out of lay clothes. Quickly they donned one of the two black, simple dresses they had been instructed to bring with them to La Crosse. Later, they were fitted with dress uniforms. Opaque black cotton stockings and "sensible" black shoes completed their ensemble. For chapel wear, a see-through black mantilla-like veil covered their hair, until that time, their crowning glory.

The plain black uniform was a major contrast to the fashionable, handmade attire Bertha knew as the daughter of an accomplished seamstress. Replaced permanently were the colorful clothes that Bertha and the other young women entering the Franciscan community had worn previously. It was not unlike the dramatic change of wardrobe that St. Francis, son of a fabric merchant, and St. Clare, daughter of nobility, had made so many centuries ago.

Adjusting to the daily schedule, the *horarium* in convent jargon, was a new aspirant's first task. Rising early for prayer, attending 6:30 a.m. Mass on weekdays, eating all meals in common, eating breakfast and supper in silence while one of them read aloud from a spiritual book, doing household tasks, attending high school and/or college classes, choir practice, study time, recreation in common, then attending evening prayers filled the aspirants' waking hours. In the beginning adjusting to convent style, coupled with getting to know the other young women seeking the same vocation, may well have delayed the severe culture shock the southern teenager and Catholic convert eventually experienced.

Exchanging a large, sunny room of her own for a metal-rail-framed, curtain-enclosed bed-unit in a large dormitory made Bertha's eyes blink in amazement. Many of her classmates had a similar reaction to their "cells" — the traditional name for their modest personal space. The draped area housed a bed, a chair, and a dresser with storage space for a wash basin, soap dish, wash cloth, towel, and undergarments.

During the day the curtains were drawn open. At night they were pulled closed along the railings, affording a modicum of privacy. The dormitory decor was mostly white: white bed curtains, white bed spreads, white nightgowns, white towels. There were, however, khaki army blankets, brown furniture, and black house robes.

When Bertha entered the La Crosse Franciscan community, close to two hundred new sisters lived in the five-story convent. As did Bertha, many of the young women hailed from small towns. Their eyes bugged as they were invited into the spacious, high-ceilinged, architecturally renowned chapels and motherhouse departments. Parlors, offices, and music rooms were well appointed. General areas, including the kitchen, food service area, bakery, laundry, sewing room, and community rooms, were sizeable, well equipped, and designed for efficiency.

Three times a day all residents sat down to meals in the same building, at the same time. The professed sisters used the large main dining room, while the Viterbo College sister faculty had a smaller dining room, as did the sisters who taught at nearby La Crosse parochial schools. The young formation groups — aspirants, postulants, and novices — ate in separate dining rooms. All dining tables were rectangular; each seated six and included table drawers containing individual place settings. After meals, dishes were cleared at each table of sisters. Aspirants, postulants, and novices performed assigned kitchen or serving room duties before meals with clean-up responsibilities afterward. Efficient organization was the order of the day. Meals were nutritious, often delicious and home-style.

In Bertha's case, adjusting from southern cuisine to that of a German-Irish community was a challenge borne with goodwill, but not without effort. Resolute to do all things the way they were supposed to be done in this new community environment, Bertha partook even though the food was foreign to her palate. What she secretly salivated for, of course, were sweet potatoes, black molasses, southern fried chicken, catfish, pecan pies, collard greens, hoe cakes, chitlins, okra, sweet tea — none of which were even remotely on the menu. Nonetheless, like most persons away from home in a residential academic environment, Bertha, and many of her classmates gained the traditional first-year-at-school-away-from-home pounds.

But there was more than unfamiliar food to deal with. In the 1950s, in western Wisconsin, which had little exposure to black Americans, there was overt racism — even (to a degree perhaps unsurprising in those times) inside the convent. This is by no means to say that the environment was universally intolerant, but there were definitely sisters who were ignorant about black people, and there were those who weren't shy about keeping this young aspirant in her place. We'll take that up in the next chapter.

To mark feast days and holy days, the aspirants sometimes created programs and skits for their own and others' edification and amusement. In late fall of her first year in the convent, Bertha wrote a prayer called "Consecration to Mary," which sounded much like others in that pious genre. The Feast of the Immaculate Conception of Mary, patroness of the United States, on December 8, was marked with a festive convocation. Bertha's prayer was read at the end of the program. The prayer, though, was not in the style of the prayers she had prayed back home. By then, it was clear that Bertha delighted in her choice to enter the convent. Earlier, only a few weeks after her arrival, she had written home:

> This letter comes to thank you for the delicious cookies that you sent us. My but they were good. It seems that the aspirants are always hungry. I have not gained but twelve pounds. Sister Rosita (Weiler, aspirant mistress) told us that we didn't have to weigh three hundred by Christmas.
>
> Today Sister Lina and I opened the box that you sent us for biology. You must have put some real work into collecting all those plants. How many did you pull, Daddy?
>
> I have so little time. I asked Sister Rosita if I could please write tonight during recreation. She said yes, but just this once. Sister's so nice to us. I think that she is just about ideal. When we laugh she laughs with us, and most of the time she tells the jokes.
>
> I am taking harmony. Tell that to Sister Vincenza [Naumann]. I think that she knows how awful it is. Aside from that I like all the subjects that I am having. I love chorus. We have music appreciation. Every day. Delightful. We have so much fun. I always say that musicians are all alike . . . [a line points to the treble and bass staff notation at the bottom of the page, with the comment, "Pretty, not! Compliments of Sister Rose Cecile Korst. She gave it to me because it was southern."][8]

While a student at St. Rose High School, Bertha excelled in things academic. She was a serious, disciplined, curious student. This educator's daughter had exposure to the history and literature of her native South and incorporated her knowledge and love of it to the hilt in class discussions, assignments, and research papers. Spiritual exercises, high school classes, recreation, conversations, singing, and sharing with classmates filled her days and kept the young aspirants busily occupied.

Bertha, a true daughter of her record-keeping mother, who compiled scrapbooks from Bertha's birth onward, in the first months away from home, soon instructed her parents to keep a scrapbook of her convent life. Early on, the Franciscan aspirants were encouraged to use the pronoun "our" instead of "my" to denote a communal life of nonownership. Bertha did so dutifully.

On October 4, 1953, in a letter permitted in honor of the Feast of St. Francis, she directed: "I'm sending you 'our' place markers. Start a scrapbook. I'll send home all my place markers." Accompanying that directive, she enclosed in a thick envelope individual place cards, a miniature pair of brown-colored-paper Franciscan sandals, a cut-out Franciscan friar complete with a tiny, folded cowl (neckpiece) and a real white-rope cincture (the rope worn about Franciscans' waists), and the beloved Prayer of St. Francis of Assisi, "Lord, make me an instrument of your peace," along with a gray feather (symbolic of her nickname, "Birdie").[9]

Less than four months after she left the South, Bertha experienced and endured her first winter in the North — a cold winter indeed, starting in November. Then she discovered Wisconsin winters were white. In the beginning, snowfalls were fun for frolic. Snowfalls were often even beautiful. Then, to her amazement, for five months straight, the grounds were freezing cold and white with snow.

Shoveling sidewalks was a responsibility assigned to the strong young aspirants. Sniffles and colds sometimes followed. Dressing for outdoors took Bertha longer than ever before in her life. Sweaters, scarves, coats, boots, ear muffs, knit caps, gloves, mittens had to be donned. Fortunately, on the coldest days heated tunnels (not unusual in the region) connecting the convent with the college and hospital provided an alternative way to get to Viterbo College (now University) or St. Francis Hospital when aspirants, postulants, and any of the sisters needed to go there. Bertha and others who shivered in the cold were grateful to the tunnel builders, even if some of these young women did complain of feeling like moles!

School brought academic awards. In November 1953, Bertha enjoyed her first published works: an essay and a poem recognized by the National Essay Association and the National High School Poetry Association. In addition, a telegram composed for an English assignment was awarded a Certificate of Merit by Scholastic Magazines in cooperation with Western Union. Such awards, though fairly common for the bright students, were encouraging.

A seven-day group retreat came that first December, the first of many for any Sister. Bertha wrote, "We had a wonderful retreat. Father Roemer was our retreat master, and I am certain that he is a saint himself. He was more quiet than Father Howard or Father John W. Bowman (our black priests), and he spoke so simply that I could understand everything that he said. It was inspiring."[10]

Next on this teen's busy agenda were plans for Christmas vacation. The high school junior would head to Canton on December 21, 1953, traveling under the care and supervision of Sister Dolorita Heiting, for a brief stay at home.

On stationery headed with gold "Notes from Bertha" and music notes on a staff, Birdie somewhat diffidently wrote, wondering if her parents would enjoy having her home for the Christmas holidays. A humble side of Bertha was being cultivated. "All the other junior aspirants will be going home for Christmas this year. If you would like me to, I'd love to spend this Christmas in Canton, because next year we won't be allowed home at this time of year. If I come home, I can stay for about a week and a half. Wouldn't that be grand?"[11] The Bowmans, one can safely assume, enthusiastically gave their daughter a positive response.

Christmas vacation in the South was wonderful. Bertha enjoyed the warmer temperatures, basked in the attention of her doting parents, ate home-cooked, southern-style food, celebrated the holy day liturgies at Holy Child Jesus Church, visited friends, the Franciscan sisters at Holy Child Convent, and relatives.

After her week-and-a-half respite, she headed back to La Crosse, evidently happy to return. In a letter to "Mama, Daddy, Grandpa," she wrote:

Thank you for a lovely Christmas visit. . . . We aspirants are so happy to be all together again after two whole weeks of separation. Everyone had a Merry Christmas, but still it's good to be back. . . .

Everyone brought back food. Aunt Bertha sent me a cake which said, "Happy Birthday, Bertha." We also had a box of candies from Father Gilbert, handkerchiefs from Lea Oden, but Pauline's package didn't come as yet.

I have about eight "thank you" letters to write. Sister Rosita [Weiler] said that considering the way I write letters that wouldn't take very long.

I forgot our little Yogo Bird. Last night we dressed the little boy doll, which we now call Teddy, in a novice's veil and habit. He makes a darling little sister.

Love to all.

God bless you,

Bertha E. and Teddy

"I like the convent too." — Teddy[12]

Sad news came within a few weeks. Her parents called to tell her that her beloved Grandpa Ed had died, at age seveny-nine. His obituary provides details about his "widely known" life:

> ...He worked for forty-five years as an employee of the Memphis Power and Light Co. He retired several years ago. During his retirement he spent most of his time between his two sons' professional and business establishments, the drugstore of Dr. J. C. Bowman, of Memphis, and the office of Dr. Theon E. Bowman, of Canton. He was equally devoted to his daughter, Miss Bertha C. Bowman of Memphis.
>
> Mr. Bowman was best known for his conscientiousness on his job, where he was a dependable and trusted employee for almost half a century. He was a Mason and a member of the Mt. Olive AME church.[13]

Bertha affectionately responded, by return mail: "When I first came to the convent, I gave everything to Jesus through Mary. I am sure that she will care for him. During retreat I prayed for Grandpa and for both of you, for Grandpa, that he might hurry to heaven, for you, that some day we might be one in the faith."[14]

A few weeks later, she signed off for Lent, when writing letters was not permitted. *Receiving* letters was allowed. She encouraged her parents to write.

STEPPING UP

After the rush of newness wore off, the realization of the major step Bertha had taken — entering religious life in a community far from her southern home — set in.

It was culture shock. Bertha, who had rarely seen white people in her part of Canton, now saw *only* white people. In Canton, buildings were small; at St. Rose Convent there were large buildings, expansive spaces, institutional community living. Close-knit Canton was replaced by a La Crosse convent where intimacy, closeness, dancing, singing were not evident. A decidedly German-American, northern culture pervaded — a far cry from southern, African American Mississippi.

The Franciscan sisters in La Crosse, with the exception of a few sisters from China, were Caucasians. Priests were white, as many priests had been in Mississippi. High school teachers and college instructors in La Crosse were white. Not until the 1960s did a philosophy professor who was Chinese teach at Viterbo. Classmates from Iowa, Washington, and Wisconsin were white. New friends were white. Students at St. Rose High School and Viterbo College were white. The choir director was white. The organists were white. The kitchen staff was white. The bishop of La Crosse was white. Doctors and dentists were white. Delivery persons were white. The postman was white.

For a young black girl from the Deep South, it was a jolt. Bertha kept it mostly repressed, but to her trusted classmates, she frequently, softly remarked, "You all are so pale around here!" The doctor's daughter asked sometimes, "Is everybody up here anemic?" For chocolate-skinned Thea, the "uncommon" paleness of many northerners was a bemusement.

In the 1950s almost everyone who entered the Franciscan Sisters of Perpetual Adoration was from an all-Catholic family. A few persons moving into religious life were the offspring from "mixed" marriages, but that was rare. Vanished were the Baptists, Methodists, Holiness,

Episcopalians, and other denominations she had interacted with from childhood in her hometown.

But Mrs. Bowman's Episcopalian background was a help (Dr. Bowman, at the time, was Methodist). Especially before the Roman Catholic changes of the 1960s, Episcopalianism looked and felt a lot like Roman Catholicism, even in its black communities, so far as the ritual actions themselves. "If you didn't know the subtleties you wouldn't even recognize the difference between Catholic liturgy and Episcopalian liturgy, on a theological level," says Adrian Dominican Sister Jamie Phelps, professor of theology. But there was an obvious practical difference: the language. In those days, Phelps observes, the Roman Catholic liturgy was in Latin; the Episcopalian liturgy was in English. And the Episcopalians, especially in the black community, would have plenty of exposure to people and services of various faiths — there simply weren't rigid barriers among the various black faith communities.[1] Roman Catholics in Wisconsin, and everywhere else at that time, kept to themselves when it came to worship.

Nevertheless, Bertha fell into step. From the moment she entered St. Rose Convent, she was convinced she was called to become a Franciscan, called to religious life, called most seriously to share the Good News she learned in the Gospels. Accordingly, she sought to emulate in every detail the sisters ministering in Canton, whom she had grown to admire, trust, and love. She wholeheartedly embraced the program of religious formation.

It was more of a challenge to refrain from whole-body, whole-spirit, whole-voice living. Often she discovered there was, for this culture, a "proper" way to pray, a "proper" way to walk, to laugh, to sing, in the convent. She learned it was not "proper" to sashay, to sway, to prance, to dance, to break into song at the least provocation any time of the day or night. She strove to please, and mostly she hid her cultural identity.

If ever she veered from her newly chosen course, she was gently guided by her mentor, Sister Charlotte Bonneville, back to the proper path. Some tried to persuade her that the postulants did not have to be perfect all the time. But Bertha firmly disagreed. As she progressed through the formative years in religious life, sincerely wishing to conform to every practice the convent required, indeed many considered her a model aspirant, a model student, a model postulant, a model novice, and, eventually, a model teacher.

It is also a fact that to others, some of whom, aforementioned, harbored prejudice and ignorant intolerance, she was not a model religious at all. Some experienced her as loud, ungainly, and too demanding, expecting others to meet her consistent high standards. She tried hard to diminish her gifted black self, incomprehensible as it may have seemed to her. Her extraordinary talents could hardly be contained, but it would take years for her to own that.

Church in this new, almost all-white world was hugely different from the Bible Belt South. In the 1950s the sisters at St. Rose Convent prayed some of their common prayers in Latin. The time was pre–Vatican Council II, which, from 1962 forward, brought changes for Catholics that those outside of Catholic culture can scarcely appreciate. Before the Council, during Bertha's formation, in this country music, frequently lovely, was European. Processions were sedate. People sat decorously in their pews, sometimes quietly attentive, sometimes in private prayer, with little movement, and by no means with humming, moaning, or shouting "Amen," as was common in the black community.

When Bertha came to the convent, La Crosse exhibited a general unawareness of cultures different from its own — Caucasian, German, Irish, Catholic, Lutheran, Swedish, Nordic. La Crosse assumed the racist prejudices about African Americans of 1950s mainstream American popular culture. It may seem hard to believe today, but black people were seen as slow, lazy, stupid, inferior to whites, evil, never on time, not dependable.

La Crosse evidenced a decided lack of interest in the black customs and culture that were integral to young Bertha. Many of the sisters at La Crosse were not concerned about or aware of black music, black art, black traditions, southern cuisine, or black style of prayer. In the 1950s "Negro" was the polite word most often used in reference to African Americans; everyone knows other derogatory words that were used in varying degrees around the country. Caucasians took for granted that their white ways were superior, for talk, laugh, church services, funerals, music, art, even for manner of walking.

In La Crosse, at St. Rose Convent, as Bertha was ushered into the white world of the Franciscan Sisters of Perpetual Adoration, she enrolled in her junior year at St. Rose High School. Here she met, mingled, and lived with classmates, friends, teachers, mentors. They were white; they were from Catholic families. Bertha navigated carefully in her new white world.

Decades later, Sister Thea told confidant Maryknoll Sister Norma Angel, who, though twenty years younger, had endured her own share of racial bias in her own community, some of what had happened during Thea's first years at Viterbo. Norma remembers Thea telling her that there were older sisters who said to then-sixteen-year-old Bertha, "Black people go to nigger heaven together with the dogs and other animals."[2]

Then there was just plain curiosity, not malicious, but trying nonetheless, about a girl from a novel culture. Says lifelong friend Sister Dorothy Ann ("Dort") Kundinger, of Thea, "She liked being FSPA, yet I still hear stories of how hard it was for her like when people asked her, about her hair, 'Why do you have to do it that way'?"[3]

Sister Jamie Phelps, Thea's contemporary, says that's no surprise: "Back in those days, [black sisters were] a novelty. Congregations were not really prepared to receive black women. And if they received us, we had to pass all the tests." Those "tests," says Phelps, were higher standards of expectation than those of the white girls.

"In my own situation," she recalls, "my classmates and I laughed later as we started talking about our experiences" of that higher standard. "It was not a conscious thing, but nevertheless we got a thorough inspection."

Why was it so hard for a black woman to join a white community? Explains Phelps, the encounter with a black sister likely would have been the first time the white sisters had ever met a black person. "If you were one of the first blacks in your religious congregation," she says, "you had to dispel people's negative expectations of you.... They were startled that we were in habits, but they just didn't have a model of expectation for black women as sisters." Negative expectations were dispelled, she adds, "simply by being who you were."[4]

But Sister Francesca Thompson, an African American from the Oldenburg, Indiana, Franciscans, says, "I do think that Thea felt that she had been called.... She felt that nobody white, black, green, or yellow would have a right to tell her that Jesus didn't want her just because of the color of her skin."

Francesca heard many reports of blatant racism over the years. The FSPAs were typical of their time: black women often encountered similar environments in predominantly white women's communities in those early years. Francesca recalls a woman from an unnamed community: "I had a black sister friend that told me a horror story that made my hair stand on end.... I said 'Why, why did you stay?' She said, 'I knew that God wanted me. I knew that Jesus called me. I wasn't going to let a group of stupid white women tell me that I could not go the way God wanted me to go!' "

She recounts another report of a sister who wouldn't invite her parents to her own investiture (acceptance into the community), profession, or final vows, "because she did not want them to know that she was not allowed to make her vows with the other sisters. As her Reverend Mother told her, 'We wouldn't want to offend our white parents.' " And there were numerous communities who simply would not accept black members.

In short, religious communities were not immune from the problems of racism that were present throughout society, and they were by no means uniform. In decades past, some of their members were just as insensitive, inexperienced, and, in some cases, even prejudiced, as the dominant culture. But, as one sister charitably said to Thompson, "Oh, Francesca, they can't help it; they are white!"[5]

Sister Norma Angel recalls Thea telling her, many years later, that Thea's parents were, indeed, apprehensive about sending their young Bertha "up north with all these white people," Norma says. She adds, "There was no way that they would have allowed her to stay if they found out some of the horrendous earlier experiences that she had." Some of Bertha's letters home, says Norma, surely were meant to gloss over the hardships, so that her parents wouldn't be concerned.[6]

But Bertha's difficult, negative experiences must be understood in a broader context. On the whole, hers must have been a marvelous and rich experience; her letters, rosy as they are, bear an authenticity and youthful fervor as well.

Getting to know all these new people was fun but also a challenge. She willed to make it work, and friendships flourished. Many of the white girls found that they were more similar to their classmate from the South than they were different. For Bertha, the first year of school in La Crosse from August 1953 through May 1954 passed quickly and happily. She excelled in her eleventh-grade high school classes despite the culture shock.

The upcoming summer was packed with activities for the aspirants. For Bertha, it included a June visit home in Canton, then a six-week change of scenery at St. Mary's School for the Indians at Odanah, in northern Wisconsin. Sister Rosita Weiler, aspirant mistress, informed Bertha in a letter about her 1954 summer assignment at Odanah.

" ... You will take biology and sewing this summer. You may sew for anybody you wish, and even bring material and pattern if you like."[7]

The Franciscan Sisters of Perpetual Adoration had begun their missionary work at St. Mary's School for the Chippewa Indians in 1883, where they staffed a boarding school. Odanah, in northern Wisconsin, was exhilarating for any aspirant who went there in the 1950s. It was six weeks of classes, getting to know the vivacious Native American children, and fun in a region that was a vacation destination for many Midwesterners.

After summer school in the North and after-school activities with the Chippewa children at Odanah, the aspirants spent two weeks at Villa St. Joseph, the home for retired Franciscan sisters in the scenic Coulee Region, fifteen miles east of La Crosse.

In one of the few letters to her parents that summer, written just after she arrived at Villa St. Joseph, Bertha expressed that the six weeks had flown by: "While I miss the children," she admitted, "there is no school to contend with."[8] The paucity of correspondence during Bertha's first summer in the convent attests to the changing, full, and varied schedules; to classes and tasks; to interacting with the Chippewa children at Odanah, to visiting the retired sisters at the Villa; to prayers, gardening and travels — all activities the aspirants engaged in. Busy from sunrise to sunset, the aspirants had time only to show up: there was no time allotted for homesickness.

Back at St. Rose Convent, Bertha wrote to her parents in a letter dated August 29, 1954: "I guess that we have changed our address for the last time for a while, and by now we are all settled down with Sister Charlotte Bonneville, senior aspirant and postulant mistress. This seems to be the beginning of a wonderful school year (grade twelve), although there's lots of work and little time."[9] In August 1954 when Bertha was about to advance to the senior aspirancy, she and the other postulants were put under the care of Sister Charlotte Bonneville. Sister Charlotte was former head of the English Department at Viterbo College.

An immediate rapport developed and flourished between Bertha and Sister Charlotte. This bond continued during subsequent years, when Bertha, having been groomed to teach English at Viterbo College, stepped into the shoes of Sister Charlotte, replacing her as head of the English Department in the 1970s. The southern "old folks' child" detected warmth through Sister Charlotte's somewhat stern exterior. The fire in Sister Charlotte's eyes reflected the equally bright fire in Bertha's sparkling brown eyes. Unlikely as some thought it was, the two of them became soul sisters.

Charlotte, a profoundly spiritual, literate, intelligent, empathetic woman, understood the culture shock the teenager from Mississippi suffered in a totally white world. Reveling in their friendship, Bertha proudly revealed to a classmate, "Sister Charlotte reads black writers like Langston Hughes and Richard Wright."[10] At that time they were authors of Bertha's interest but unknown to her classmate.

Sister Charlotte wielded considerable influence in the community. Besides her leadership role at Viterbo, she served on many committees for the Franciscan Sisters of Perpetual Adoration and was an elected delegate to successive chapters (assemblies for governance). Bertha was blessed that Sister Charlotte took the time to nurture a personal interest in her. Charlotte encouraged Bertha and challenged her. Bertha responded enthusiastically.

In the fall of 1954 a large group of new Franciscan seekers entered St. Rose Convent in August and September, joining Bertha's class. This peaceful, prosperous time for Catholics in the United States was accompanied by a surge in entrants to religious communities everywhere.

That winter, for Bertha's seventeenth birthday, Bertha's mother came to Wisconsin to see the convent for herself. She encountered a rich environment: decorations were colorful, liturgies were inspiring, meals were festive. Bertha wrote later to her father, "I was so happy for her to see the place and I think she enjoyed it almost as much as I."[11] Bertha's resolve to become a model sister intensified. In her later years she reflected on methods she learned in the convent that honed her skills as a disciplined person: doing what she was told, when she was told to do it, at the same time others were doing the same thing, walking, standing, sitting, kneeling with the proper posture; practicing etiquette flawlessly in speaking, eating, communicating. Convent life was not charm school, but sisters were expected to practice good manners, to be models of womanhood. In the Franciscan spirit, they were to radiate joy.

Bertha had learned to pray from her beloved "old folks," the elders back in Canton. But prayer in the convent was decidedly different, less holistic. She went through the drill nevertheless.

Academically, Bertha continued her excellent way. In January 1955, she completed her twelfth-grade courses at St. Rose High School and graduated formally in May. Meanwhile college would start and formation would continue. Bertha the college student delighted in following in the footsteps of her educated parents. During her first month at Viterbo, she wrote to them: "College isn't so bad, but we do have tremendous assignments. I love speech. Did you ever think that I'd have to learn to talk? Well, 'I'm a college woman now!' For better or worse. 'In lettering I have learned to make one thing. An 'l.' As an assignment we had to make a whole page full. I also learned that India ink is indelible. I am living proof of that fact."[12]

Bertha's first semester at college was a mixture of courses taught mostly by sisters: Intermediate Latin (Sister Annella Bopp); Freshman English, Principles of Physical Science (Sister Ruthmary Waterstreet); Speech (Sister Julia Anne Maus); Fundamentals of Theology (Father Joseph Rohling); Ascetical Theology (Father Othmar Missler); Lettering (Sister Patrice Halligan); Physical Education (Sister Ruthmary Waterstreet). She seemed to admire and love them all.

Postulant Day was the first formal step to becoming a Franciscan. During the subsequent six-month postulancy period Bertha and the other young women took instructions in the Rule and Constitutions of the Franciscan Sisters of Perpetual Adoration.

Forty-two young women aspirants in Bertha's class (from high school and college) persevered. A small, detachable white collar was provided to wear with black street-length postulant dresses, given in a ceremony on February 2. Postulant attire included a short, opaque black veil, worn at all times. As aspirants they had donned sheer black veils only for chapel services and some formal occasions. Now they were to wear the more striking veil in public always. The photo of Bertha in her postulant uniform held a place of honor in the Bowman home for decades to come.

Postulant Day was a happy occasion for all. Laughter, tears of joy, good cheer, good food, thanksgiving, and celebration abounded. St. Rose Convent chaplain, Rev. Joseph Rohling, CPPS, a priest from Carthagena, Ohio, presided at the festive liturgy at 8:00 a.m. and delivered the homily. Friends of the postulants showered them with prayers, good wishes, and cards. Then the postulants returned to their routines.

Students at Viterbo College, with its strong fine arts program, attended many musical and dramatic programs. Bertha was impressed by them and shared her good fortune with her parents. Bertha sent along programs for her mother to save, along with a steady stream of newsy letters, a tradition she maintained over the years.

But once she was in the postulant class, the number of letters home was limited to one a month. Postulants could receive mail once a week.

Mrs. Bowman wrote faithfully each week, as did most of the postulants' mothers. To Bertha's surprise, Dr. Bowman also wrote to his only daughter faithfully each week. His letters were a badge of honor because, in the 1950s, not surprisingly, it was not common for dads to write letters to their daughters in the convent.

But that loving support is key to who Thea was, and to how she fared so well in the convent, especially this all-white convent. Sister Jamie Phelps observes, "Those of us who grew up black and were nurtured in positive black experiences, someplace along the way understood that we had to be ourselves, that ours would be a different brand of sisterhood." Our parents wanted us, she says, to develop fully as humans. "I'm sure Thea heard something in that language that was, 'You are equal and you can be and do anything that you want to.'"

Jamie recalls her own experience as an example: "My parents had to help me negotiate the white society. Now I'm the youngest of six and so there were certain things that my parents taught me like, 'You're equal to everybody and be responsible.' They would not let me use race as an excuse."

"Like any other [Catholic] sister," she says, "we committed ourselves to God, and we committed ourselves to the particular charisms of our congregations." But, she adds, "we would do that using particular cultural gifts and memories."[13]

Other African American religious echo the importance of their families in keeping things in perspective as they interacted with a dominant, and occasionally hostile, white culture. Oldenburg Franciscan Sister Francesca Thompson, another contemporary of Thea's, reflects on her own strong self-image, nurtured by her family. "I was very very young the first time I ever heard the word "nigger" and I can remember my grandmother saying to my father, 'You explain this one,' because I knew it was something bad and I knew that I had been insulted or whatever but I couldn't quite understand. The thing that I remember just as if it was yesterday was him pointing his finger at me saying 'Honey, there are many stupid people in the world, and they think that because they look differently than you do and because their skin is a different color they are better than you are. There are many, many dumb people who think that, because they look different than you do, they are smarter. I want you to remember this and never forget it: That is their problem. Don't ever make it yours.'"[14]

Franciscan Father Fernand Cheri, also an African American, would put it this way: "You take the child out of the community, and the child learns how valuable it is," ultimately giving that child a picture of how her culture fits into a broader, catholic family of cultures.[15] Bertha would discover this as she grew.

Bertha's college career was soon to be sidetracked by a health crisis. Because of that, and continuing formation and teaching responsibilities, completing college took longer than the usual four years. As the daughter of a doctor and a teacher, she would be a bit dismayed to wait ten years before receiving a bachelor of arts degree, although other studies were to follow. When she did finally graduate, she received honors, *magna cum laude,* in 1965. But in 1955 her way was temporarily blocked.

Chapter 8

LAID UP

As the eventful months in the postulancy flew by, Bertha, having gained weight when she moved to Wisconsin, now found herself shedding pounds precipitously. During her first year away from home she had sometimes been spirit sick, soul sick, heart sick, and a few times body sick. She caught colds the first year she was in Wisconsin. A few hung on for weeks at a time. Stoically, she deemed it best not to complain.

Yet Bertha may have intuited something. In the spring of 1955 she wrote to her parents, "Sometimes I'm tempted to miss you, but then I think you're just in another room of God's big house."[1]

Then came news. To everyone's puzzlement, doctors at St. Francis Hospital ordered Bertha to a lengthy hospital stay. Sister Charlotte Bonneville described Bertha's status in a letter dated April 18 (Easter Monday, 1955) written to the Bowmans. She told of the routine physicals, and how Bertha had tested positive for tuberculosis and had been put into confinement: "Since she is just across the street at St. Francis [Hospital], I may go to see her every day. She is amused at having to be in bed when she feels so well. She is very cheerful, too. We are praying that the x-ray is showing an old lesion and not a 'new' spot. . . . Bertha also wishes you to keep this a secret, although you may tell the sisters if you wish."[2]

Bertha wrote a long letter to her parents a few weeks later, describing her isolation and drawing a picture of a masked face: "Everyone who comes to see me almost looks like this."[3]

Because of her serious health condition, Bertha feared she would have been sent home had it not been for Sister Charlotte's intervention. Sister Charlotte walked across Tenth Street from St. Rose Convent to the hospital every day of Bertha's hospital stay, which expanded from weeks to almost three months. Sister Charlotte insisted that the congregation's major superiors permit Bertha continue her quest to be a Franciscan sister. Bertha relaxed, counting on Sister Charlotte's promise, "God will fix it."[4] Further tests and complete rest were prescribed for Bertha. While in Mississippi for a routine visit, Reverend Mother Joan Cramer and Mother Assistant Josina Roth, the community leaders, consulted with the Bowmans.

Sister Charlotte in her letter to Bertha's parents dated April 24, 1955, described new medical developments:

> Today, Dr. Robert E. McMahon told her that her temperature had been normal for two days. That was good news. In three weeks, he wants another x-ray. We are praying for the improvement that will shorten her days in the hospital. The doctor also told her that the smears taken from the stomach contents showed "bugs." Although the cultures have brought forth nothing so far, he is convinced that Bertha has TB. He is very optimistic, however, and reposes trust in the "shots" he had ordered for her. Stereocomyacin, I believe. (Perhaps the spelling is incorrect, but you'll know what is meant.)[5]

During her hospitalization, Bertha occasionally wrote to her parents. In one letter, she told of the many daily visits she received from various nurses, doctors, priests, and sisters of the community. "You can see that I am never lonely. Besides that, I get a letter from one or the other of the postulants almost every day and the four bawling babies on this floor could wake up the dead.... Don't let yourself get any new gray hairs over me, even though I do think that white hair is awfully pretty, because this thing is going to turn out for the best."[6]

In May came good news about Bertha's condition. Wrote Sister Charlotte to the Bowmans: "Bertha's x-ray of May 5 shows 'great improvement.' In fact, so much so, that Dr. McMahon thinks it may not be necessary for her to leave St. Francis. Monday, he is having a specialist check her and from his verdict, the decision will be made. The postulants and I are finishing, on Monday, a novena to St. Thérèse for Bertha's recovery.... I marvel at her consistent cheerfulness."[7]

Meanwhile, high school graduation at Maria Angelorum Chapel, in the motherhouse, happened without her, although, having completed her coursework back in December, she did receive her diploma outside of the ceremony. Sister Esther Burger, principal of St. Rose High School, penned a handwritten congratulatory and compassionate letter to her:

> "My dear Bertha, Though you cannot be with us for graduation you are in our thoughts! We shall do our best to have you share in

our joys . . . Sister Charlotte will give you or keep for you your high school diploma and the Latin Certificate. (Also essay, poetry, and journalism certificates.) My hearty Congratulations to you, Bertha! God wants you to spend a few more weeks alone with him. See how he loves you. Accept all as his will and you will be very happy no matter where you are."[8]

As the weeks progressed, medical consultants and Dr. McMahon determined that Bertha indeed had tuberculosis. Her treatment initially included streptomycin, but, because that medication was causing hearing loss, she was switched to perimenosalicylic acid (PAS). This toxic medication ate the stomach lining and caused nausea and vomiting. She was undergoing side effects of chemotherapy.

Sister Charlotte tried always to keep Bertha's parents informed about their daughter's condition, treatment, and disposition. She wrote on June 7, 1955: "I have a little news about Bertha that I do not think she will relay to you adequately when she writes this week. [Dr. McMahon, this week] said that Bertha was in good condition. Her lung had healed with a good scar. She has had no temperature for a long time. Her sedimentation rate, however, remains high. That might not prevent her from being up, but he is afraid to take risks."[9]

The doctor asked that Bertha be moved to a sanatorium for a few months to ensure the rest that would improve her chances for a full recovery. He noted how cheerful Bertha was, and how all the staff had become fond of her.

Sister Charlotte recounted another glimpse of Bertha's hospitalization: "The other day, I met one of the hospital chaplains. He said to me, 'Either she is consistently cheerful, or she is good at pretense.' And I, who am proud of Bertha's attitude, answered him, 'Father, what you see is the result of resignation to God's Will.' "

She wrote to the Bowmans about a home movie shown in Bertha's room (of the other postulants) and about plenty of reading material, including a steady stream of cards and letters from the other postulants. "She and I have a good laugh every once in a while over the liberal education she is now receiving," wrote Charlotte.[10]

With her parents' permission, the doctors and the Franciscan religious superiors admitted Bertha to River Pines Sanatorium, 115 miles northeast of La Crosse, in Stevens Point, Wisconsin. For any seventeen-year-old to have tuberculosis was scary, let alone a black teenager in the segregated United States in 1955, a thousand miles from her Deep South home. Bertha, daughter of a doctor, understood her health had been compromised. She was determined to take whatever steps necessary to recover. She wrote a letter home and invited her mother to come visit.[11]

Mrs. Bowman traveled by train from Canton as she had for Christmas six months earlier. She accompanied Bertha in the ambulance from La Crosse to River Pines Sanatorium for Tuberculosis in Stevens Point, administered by the Sisters of St. Joseph. She was the first African American patient and first postulant from a religious community admitted in the history of River Pines Sanatorium.

Bertha sent home a welcome message she had received from the sanatorium, advising a "cooperative and appreciative attitude," along with a letter to her parents, printed here in its entirety:

Dear Mama and Daddy,

Greetings from "the land of the sky blue waters!" Yes, this is that land, and to prove it, the Wisconsin River flows just outside our window. The San consists of building after building, each drawn against a background of blue sky and majestic oak and pine, and there is plenty of fresh, pine-scented air to shoo the buggies. What a beautiful place it is, but I won't go into details of description, because Mama has already seen the place, and Daddy, she's probably told you all about it already. Oh, Daddy, let me know if she enjoyed the nap that she took in the ambulance. I couldn't tease her properly then, because there was an audience. Thank you so much for sending her. I know that you would have come too if you were feeling well.

Mama, Mrs. Stanke sends greetings. She said that I should tell you that she didn't spank me yet. Today she brought up her family pictures to show me. She said that she has a boy in the University [University of Wisconsin–Stevens Point], another who is a junior in high school, and a "little gal, that's thirteen years old, and a real cute kid."

Hurrah! The birdies found me on Saturday morning, and I've had almost constant company ever since. They are the nosiest birds that you ever saw, regular pecking-Toms, and since they are too fat and lazy to work for their bread, they come to me most willingly, and are not one bit afraid. This morning a mother bird fed and chastised her young ones right in front of our window. She flew back and forth from our feeding station to her tree about four dozen times, hardly taking time to feed herself. The young ones are little gourmets. Jays, robins, sparrows, and orioles have visited me so far, and I have seen woodpeckers, cardinals, and four other birds which I don't know. Almost all of them have little ones.

There are also many bushy squirrels.

This is visiting day, and just a minute ago a sister announced over the call system, "Attention, visitors. We kindly ask you to leave now." She repeated the speech for extra emphasis and I almost rolled. At St. Francis they would have said, "It is now four o'clock. Visiting hours are over." Which sounds best?

I imagine that you would like to know something about my daily schedule. It reads about like this for the time being:

06:20	Communion
07:15	Breakfast
08:20	Absolute Rest Hours
10:00	Occupational Therapy
11:50	Dinner
01:20	Absolute Rest Hours
04:00	Occupational Therapy
05:30	Supper
06:30	Rest Hour
07:30	Recreation
09:00	Lights Out

My daily exercise consists in sitting in the chair while our bed is being made, and going to the bathroom once a day. Otherwise I have complete bed rest.

Sister Alvera Wiederin (an FSPA patient at River Pines) is very kind to me. She is out of bed for several hours each day, and she often comes to visit me. There are four sisters on this floor; nine in the whole San. There is also a priest patient. Mama, do you remember the altar outside our door? He says Mass there when he is able. I can hardly wait.

St. Stanislaus Band is giving a concert in the courtyard. Now they are playing a medley of Southern songs, "Sewanee River," "Lil Liza Jane," etc. The patients who are allowed out of doors have gone to see them, but the rest of us can hear from our windows.

Everyone is so nice here. It is such a happy place. The patients who are up are most solicitous for those who are in bed, and the whole atmosphere is one of friendliness. The person who said that TB victims are morbid should just drop in for a visit.

This is sufficient for today.

Two morning doves are preening themselves on the tree.

God love you,

Birdie[12]

At the sanatorium, Bertha was able to continue her studies via a correspondence course. Her topics reveal Bertha emerging as a strong, observant writer.

She wrote about what she knew best: her family, her southern roots, and her Stevens Point healing place. Of two surviving essays, one is a detailed observation of a breed of local woodpeckers; another drew on her experiences in her kitchen back home. The latter is stated to be "in the style of a TV chef," one of the emerging popular formats for the new medium. Her description of what she describes as "Dixie delicacies" (hoe cakes, corn pone and crackling), and modern ways of preparing food is as good an example of scriptwriting — if not better — as any similar show of the day.

In both essays, young Bertha reveals that, for all of her formation in the North and now her isolation, her southern roots remained close to her heart. Here's a brief excerpt from a much longer essay:

Our next Dixie delicacy is corn pone, a coarse, thick, heavy cake or patty valued for its rich, nutty flavor, its golden-corn color, and its economy; prepared by old, Southern cooks as a dinner-time vegetable accompaniment; and particularly relished when served with mustard or turnip greens, rum-covered ham, sugared yams, and buttermilk. Corn pone, some times called "ash-cake," was formerly baked on a shovel or pan covered with another pan and buried in a bed of hot ashes which formed a very satisfactory substitute for an oven.[13]

While Bertha had been at St. Francis Hospital, her high school classmates created and published a newspaper, "exclusively for Bertha E. Bowman." Entitled *St. Joseph's Journal*, the hand-printed, hand-written, usually four-page paper, was composed and sent eight times from April though June 1955. The journal grew out of a St. Rose High School senior

English class assignment. It ran articles and columns by and about any of Bertha's postulant class. There were informative reports about events, personalities, celebrations, classes, music recitals, kitchen occurrences, programs. The paper also carried poetry and weather reports.[14]

Each column was hand-written by a different writer, with copies of holy cards of Joseph and Jesus affixed to the front. The first "volume" describes a clean-up race among the postulants, followed by a tongue-in-cheek report of a strange "disesase" among postulants stricken by the absence of Bertha Bowman. There are reports of rat births in the science classroom, an upcoming field trip, a sentinmental poem penned by a postulant. The four marginless pages are chocked with newsy essays — essentially a collection of letters interspersed with sophomoric humor. The final piece:

> Wanted for desertion by the Postulants of St. Rose Convent — Bertha E. Bowman, no. 6, fairly tall, last seen wearing a black postulant uniform. If located please capture — be careful — and return promptly and safely to St. Rose. Reward: thirty-nine votes of deep gratitude plus innumerable prayers of thanksgiving. — F.B.I. Agent M.L.R.

Future issues, through the end of the school year, were equally chatty and sometimes silly. Clearly, the postulants missed their friend. The final issue closes with a note: "Our sincerest thanks to Postmaster General Mrs. Theon Bowman, for delivering this edition of the *Journal*. NOTICE — In case of change of address, please notify the editor IMMEDIATELY!"[15]

Up at River Pines, Bertha would also be written about in the sanatorium bulletin, notably, in the most glowing of terms: "Just walk into room 303. There you will find a bright girl who can do almost anything. If it's fancywork you want to learn, she's there to help you. If it's an ache or pain you're advertising, she has a prescription; a peppermint stick of chewing gum sometimes does the trick. And if you've got strep blues, her remedy comes forth."[16]

The sisters received good reports about Bertha's convalescence, and sent them along to her parents. Mrs. Bowman visited Bertha twice when she was in River Pines; her father made the trip once, by air travel.

At River Pines, Bertha made dozens of friends. She talked and wrote about them. She was especially drawn to patients with diverse ethnic backgrounds. She was delighted with a patient from Korea named Syng

Ai Lee. She wrote about Syng to the Bowmans in the fall of 1955, apparently at Mrs. Bowman's urging:

> So you want to know about Syng. First of all, Syng is a very uncommon name in Korea. Since it means Susie, most people here call Syng Susie but I am not numbered among the "most." Syng comes to see me on Mondays or Fridays, and she is the only one of the girls I really enjoy. She is from Seoul. During the war she pushed her little brother into a ditch and lay on top of him while the soldiers bombed. She is a ballet dancer, and she plans to study pharmacy.[17]

Bertha also shared poems from fellow residents, expressing a sentiment that must have been common for those resigned to life at the sanitarium:

> In lying still
> In letting His hand mold me
> Just as He will.
> In working or in waiting,
> May I fulfill
> Not ours at all, but only
> Our Master's Will.[18]

In November Sister Charlotte came to visit, and, afterward, helped arrange a surprise visit from Mrs. Bowman for Bertha's eighteenth birthday. The visit was part of a festive Christmas celebration that the St. Joseph sisters and staff arranged for everyone. One patient wrote, "You cannot help get the feeling deep down in the marrow of your bones: the quickened step, the broader smile, the merry twinkle in every Sister's eye, the bright 'comin'' of Doc Anderson, all give you the feeling that Christmas must be just around corner."[19]

Then on the fifth day of Christmas, 1955, to Bertha's glee, Mrs. Bowman arrived, on Bertha's eighteenth birthday. Birthday cake, songs, opening gifts, meeting Bertha's friends at River Pines, catching up on all the news from Canton filled their time together. No wonder Bertha remembered her eighteenth birthday among her favorites. The director wrote a letter to the sisters in La Crosse reporting what a splendid guest Mrs. Bowman had been, with her "kindness...charming personality, and loving thoughtfulness."[20]

A few months later, in March, Bertha finally was released from convalescence. The loving support of her community in La Crosse, the sisters and staff at Stevens Point, and her own family and friends back in Canton had helped her through it.

In her letter of release, Doctor Harry Anderson wrote: "Her lesion in the right lung has cleared almost without leaving any residual.... We have asked her superiors at the convent to have her continue her rest periods for some months to come, and she is to continue on Isoniazin [sic] (INH) and PAS for at least another year, which will make a total of two years of chemotherapy.... I would like to tell you what a pleasure it has been to care for Bertha. She is a fine girl and I am sure you and Mrs. Bowman are justly proud of her."[21]

Bertha returned, triumphant in spirit, healthy in body, to La Crosse on March 29, 1956. Sister Charlotte conveyed the good news on March 30. Bertha had been in ill health from spring 1955 through March 1956. She was now a year behind her classmates, and thus set her sites on entering the novitiate a year later, with the class of 1958.

Thea's father, Dr. Theon E. Bowman, was a graduate of Meharry Medical College in Nashville. A native of Yazoo City, he went to Canton, Miss. as the sole doctor to serve the black community.

Daughter of a well-known Greenville, Miss., educator, Thea's mother, Mary Esther Coleman, herself a teacher and vocalist, came to Canton as a newlywed with Theon.

Baby Bertha embellished her dad's pocket watch in a triumphant pose she often struck throughout life.

On the back steps of the Bowman Hill Street home, alert child "Birdie" poses near a favorite wooden bird. (1939)

Holy Child Mission Church, in Canton, Miss., was founded in the black district by the Missionary Servants of the Most Holy Trinity and eventually spawned Thea's alma mater, Holy Child Jesus elementary school, served by the Franciscan Sisters of Perpetual Adoration (FSPA). (Photo: 1947)

With bright red bows in her braids, young Bertha is set for school. (1949)

Bertha says goodbye to her parents and the Canton FSPAs after a home visit. She was an aspirant at the time. (1954)

Young teacher Thea, during a seven-year stint in Canton, gives individualized instruction to an HCJS student. (1964)

Thea lived with other FSPA sisters while attending graduate summer school at Catholic University in Washington, D.C. Visiting the Capitol, left to right, are: Sisters Mary Ann Gschwind, Nancy Lafferty, Thea, Rep. Vernon Thompson (Wis.), Sisters Christa Schmitt, Rochelle Potaracke. (1966)

Thea founded the popular, intercultural Hallelujah Singers at Viterbo College. Here they perform "He's Got the Whole World in His Hands." (1970s)

Thea always had a playful spirit. In Stratford, Ontario, Thea is locked in the stocks during a Shakespeare study tour she led. (1970s)

Thea celebrates her 25th Jubilee at Holy Child Jesus Church in Canton. (1983)

Thea's pioneering ministry attracted national attention. Mike Wallace interviews her in Canton for CBS 60 Minutes, *first broadcast in May 1987.*

Two civil-rights pioneers, Muhammad Ali and Thea Bowman, embrace at a Holy Ghost parish event in Jackson, Miss. (1980s)

Thea pauses to center her spirit before breaking into song in the early 1980s.

Chapter 9

BECOMING SISTER THEA

Novitiate is the time for which postulants yearned. During this two-year period of prayer and formal religious training, the novices' interest in religious life would be tested. If the calling proved authentic, at the end of novitiate they would profess vows to the community, beginning with "simple vows" for three successive years, then once for three years, culminating at final profession with a lifelong commitment.

At the start of novitiate year, in the days before Vatican Council II and its changes in the 1960s, the novices, now known as "sisters," were assigned new names. Typically sisters could choose from among names that had some meaning within the religious communities; more often than not they were names combined with Mary, in honor of Mary, the mother of Jesus. Ultimately the names were assigned, and those new names would signify the sister's new life as a woman religious.

On August 12, 1956, Bertha was given the name Sister Mary Thea. Thea, which literally means "of God," is a feminine version of Theon, Bertha's father's name. (All names had to be chosen from among the saints: St. Thea was a fourth-century martyr.) Thea relished her new name. Her baptismal name, from her aunt Bertha, to her conjured hugeness. "Big Bertha" was a particularly effective mortar gun used by the Germans in World War I. "Birdie" had been Bertha's nickname of choice. Sister Thea now had a name of which she could be proud. She found herself gravitating to other sisters who had similar names: Sister Theone Beres, Sister Theophilia Pehler, Sister Theodine Sebold. They formed a "Thea-Theo circle." She was especially close to Sister Theone Beres, a registered nurse who had ministered in Canton when Bertha was growing up. Bertha had been impressed that Sister Theone cared for "her people" by going into their homes to give them health care. Sister Theone was, like Dr. Theon, a healer.

Along with a new name and the new title "Sister," each novice was garbed in new attire: a black-pleated floor-length habit, a white *guimpe*

71

(a collar, of French origin), a white *coif* to cover the hair, a bright white veil and a white *cincture* (rope-like cord) used as a belt, knotted three times symbolizing the vows of poverty, chastity, and obedience.

Thea was enchanted, yet sometimes troubled by white novice veils. The veil symbolized the purity of a single-minded desire to follow her call to be as "perfect" as possible. At times though, Sister Thea seemed discomfited in the habit. Her veil was sometimes askew, her cincture not the proper length, her guimpe awry. These sentiments of not-quite fitting in would surface as time went on. The white veil added another layer to the overwhelming whiteness Sister Thea experienced in the North.

During the first year of novitiate the new novices devoted full time and energy to studying religious life, to learning about the vows of poverty, chastity, and obedience, about deepening meditation practice, about the life, spirit, and legacy of St. Francis of Assisi, about the Constitutions (Rule of Life) for the Franciscan Sisters of Perpetual Adoration, and about living in community as women religious.

In spite of being a fish out of water in many ways, a Mississippian among Midwesterners, she pressed on, sometimes with a heavy heart. She kept on "keepin' on," as she would later say. To comfort herself she sang her beloved spirituals to herself and, whenever she could, out loud. Having left an isolated world in Canton, she now immersed herself in a new Franciscan world, a closed world, the novitiate. Carefully, she listened to everything the novice mistress, Sister M. Josile Lynch, offered for consideration. Sister Josile was a veteran, serving as FSPA novice mistress (director) from 1946 until the late 1960s. Novice Thea followed Sister Josile's directions assiduously.

Brand new Sister M. (Mary) Thea focused on shapeshifting into the "perfect" nun. Her conduct was exemplary, her adolescent piety deep. One friend, a fellow novice (this very biographer Charlene), tested Thea's resolve to follow the strict rules, but try as she might, she could not coax Thea from the proper novice protocol. Her sense of commitment would not permit a detour of any kind.

That novice, who was in the class one year ahead of Thea's, thus a "senior novice," recalls the tough standards that the seniors set. Thea's class was smaller and a modicum more modest, or unassuming. To some people's surprise, they grew into splendid Franciscan sisters and accomplished professional women, however overshadowed they may have seemed at the time of their novitiate.

For the "white-veiled ones," the first year in the novitiate was filled with spiritual practices and development. The year was a peaceful, contemplative time. Spiritual practices and spiritual development continued through the second year, along with full-time college classes at Viterbo College for those training for professions in education or health care. Novices who planned to go into convent food service or housekeeping did clinical practice in St. Rose's kitchen and motherhouse. Chapel and motherhouse tasks were included in the daily life of a novice.

Mostly under twenty years old, the new sisters were cloistered, isolated from the world during the first year of the novitiate. Radios and the secular press were off-limits. In the United States, the years 1956 through 1958 were roiling with the incipient civil rights movement. In 1954, the U.S. Supreme Court ruled in *Brown vs. the Board of Education* that school segregation was unconstitutional. In 1955, Rosa Parks refused to give up her seat at the front of a bus in Montgomery, Alabama (250 miles east of Canton, Mississippi), launching the Montgomery Bus Boycott and its leader, Dr. Martin Luther King Jr. Through his marvelous juxtapositions of constitutional and biblical dicta, he inspirationally led blacks and their allies to nonviolent resistance against legalized segregation in the South. A few years later, in the 1960s, would come President Lyndon Johnson's Great Society programs.

The civil rights movement awakened people of color, women, and others into realizing that long-denied human rights were theirs to claim. Sister Thea was intensely interested in the movement toward justice and peace for black Americans.

Geography and commitment to the FSPA's formation program, designed to happen *outside* of the everyday world, kept her from actual involvement in the movement during her early years in La Crosse. In the novitiate in the North, however, she prayed, in the words of Old Testament prophet Amos, that "justice roll down like a river."

During their preparation years, the young Franciscans often wrote original skits and programs for in-house entertainment. An exception occurred with the profession class of 1958, Thea's class. With their considerable musical and dramatic talent they rehearsed and performed for St. Rose Convent and the city sisters, *The Complaining Angel*, then a popular musical for Catholic audiences.

When the senior novices professed vows on August 12, 1957, Thea presented her senior novice friends with a prayer card. On the back of the card she wrote a version of the opening lines from Isaiah 43, "Fear not, for I have redeemed you — the flames shall not consume you, because you are precious in my eyes. . . . " She believed those lines and loved to share them.

In her own style, she added after the verse, "I wish you blessings and all good. Pray for me as I will for thee." Already during novitiate she was quoting St. Thomas More, King Henry VIII's nemesis, known a few years later as the "man for all seasons," in Robert Bolt's 1960 play and film. Years later, she would choose an infrequently studied work of More's for her doctoral dissertation subject.

Having recovered completely from tuberculosis, Sister Thea remained healthy and strong. She relished her college courses, especially those in literature. She easily excelled academically. Her marvelous singing voice guaranteed her a place in the prestigious St. Rose Choir. She also sang in the more distinctive St. Rose Schola comprised of select singers. In Latin, and in Gregorian Chant, the schola sang the parts of the liturgies assigned for song.

Her formation phase passed quickly until the momentous day of first profession of vows. At age twenty, Sister Thea gleefully relinquished the white novice veil for the distinctive black veil of a professed sister.

At Profession Day Mass, the choir sang, "I will go into the house of the Lord" (Psalm 122) while the novices processed into the chapel. In Maria Angelorum Chapel on August 12, 1958, with nineteen classmates, Sister Thea Bowman professed first vows of poverty, chastity, and obedience for one year. Her proud parents were in the congregation. Each newly professed sister received the gold ring of the congregation during the ceremony. The ring symbolized their chosen life of dedication. High liturgy, festive meals, and visiting were the order of the day. No one was surprised that the Bowmans had traveled the thousand miles from Mississippi to share the profound experience and celebration with their joyous daughter.

Twenty sisters, including Sister Thea Bowman, made up the August 12, 1958, profession of first vows class. They had bonded with each other especially during the two years as novices and remained close companions and friends throughout the coming years.

Once again, the *La Crosse Tribune* ran an article about Sister Thea with a photo of her in the black veil. Under the headline, "First Negro," the story read, in part, "On August 12, the Franciscan Sisters of Perpetual Adoration of La Crosse will have their first professed colored member in this Community. . . . Following her religious profession, Sister Thea will continue her studies at Viterbo College as a preparation for the teaching profession."[1]

To catch up with courses missed while at River Pines Sanatorium, Sister Thea enrolled full-time at Viterbo College during the 1958–59 academic year. The Franciscan community recognized her obvious intellectual talent and, as with many sisters, they groomed her for the teaching profession.

Thea loved learning. She loved college. She exuded enthusiasm for intellectual stimulation. Next to the English courses, her favorite subject was Latin. She read and translated Cicero, Ovid, Virgil, and Horace. She also studied music, took voice lessons, and continued in the St. Rose Convent Choir and Schola.

Her free academic year quickly drew to a close. Summer school at Viterbo College followed for Sister Thea and most of the young temporary professed sisters. During the 1959 summer session she enrolled in a six-credit course called Drama Production, taught by Sister Margaret Mary Conway, with assistance from other Theatre Arts Department faculty. The course involved techniques of directing, set design, acting, costuming, make-up, lighting, sound, and business management.

One memorable episode during the make-up class occurred when Thea and another sister decided to make each other up. Thea put black make-up on the other sister's face and hands, and the other sister made up Thea as white. The illusion, enhanced by their black veils, was so convincing that the two young nuns kept the make-up on all day to the consternation, but then amusement and enchantment, of everyone they encountered.[2]

At this time in the United States, Catholic elementary school enrollment was swelling with children born after World War II. Because of the demand for teachers in the Catholic schools in the late 1950s and early 1960s, sisters from religious communities everywhere were compelled to begin classroom teaching before completing all their bachelor of arts degree requirements. The La Crosse Franciscans were no exception: an assignment was forthcoming for Thea.

Her college studies were delayed, but she would continue courses in the summers, between teaching commitments, until 1965. She ultimately graduated *magna cum laude,* having majored in English with a minor in speech and drama.

In the summer of 1959, she would receive her first assignment at a longstanding annual custom among the Franciscan sisters of La Crosse:

Appointment Day. On that July 26, the Feast of St. Anne (mother of the Virgin Mary) the reverend mother and her council distributed "mission slips," official appointments stipulating where each sister would be commissioned to live and work for the year and what her specific assignment would be. That could be teaching, nursing, study, or some other ministry, new or continued. It was a time of high drama. Accepted either way in holy obedience, sometimes tears of joy were shed; sometimes tears of sadness. Generally excitement abounded with happy talk of who was going where, who would be living with whom.

During her first years in the convent, Sister Thea had observed these exhilarating "mission slip" days. She was thrilled to discover her first assignment: teaching grades five and six at Blessed Sacrament Elementary School in La Crosse. At age twenty one, she was ready for her first foray into the world of professional teaching.

Teaching skills aside, she could only hope to be ready for her first assignment into teaching young Wisconsin white children. This was 1959, after all, and black people were generally unknown in La Crosse outside of newspaper and magazine stories. Blessed Sacrament, in northeast La Crosse, was upper middle class. Many parish members were La Crosse's professionals: educators, doctors, nurses, lawyers, business people. When a few parents realized their children would be in a classroom under the tutelage of an African American teacher, a conflict ensued.

Immediately, the parents requested a meeting in the principal's office. The principal, Sister Clarice Kleinheinz, FSPA, introduced Sister Thea Bowman to the assembled parents. As was her wont, Thea, with her professional manner and winning personality, instantly charmed them. Fears allayed, a crisis was quelled.

Thea determined, as one of her first goals, to connect the children at Blessed Sacrament School in Wisconsin with Holy Child Jesus Mission School in Mississippi. In her mind there was a deep chasm between where she was to teach in La Crosse and her native Holy Child Jesus Mission School and parish. She sought to build a partnership between Holy Child Jesus Mission School with its black students, many of whom were not Catholic, and her white Catholic Blessed Sacrament students. Through letters about each other's worlds with pictures, stories, and songs, a happy relationship developed.

Long before the end of her two brief years teaching at Blessed Sacrament, children claimed it a badge of honor to be a student in Sister

Thea's classroom. Students and their parents grew to admire, respect, and love the black teacher. Thea's grandmother Lizzie Coleman would have been proud.

A story shows Thea's extraordinary power with children. Celestine Cepress, FSPA, in *Sister Thea Bowman: Shooting Star,* wrote, "One little boy, who had gotten into trouble in another local Catholic school, was transferred to Blessed Sacrament. At the end of the first day in Thea's class, he eased into the social worker's car and said, 'Gosh, she's beautiful.' Magically, 'getting into trouble' days ended for that child."[3]

Today most of Thea's former Blessed Sacrament fifth- and sixth-graders are successful business and professional persons, and parents themselves. Many recall Sister Thea as their beloved, favorite, and most-remembered grade-school teacher.

On the feast of St. Anne the next summer, Sister Thea was again commissioned to teach grades five and six at Blessed Sacrament. Forty-nine children were enrolled to be in her care. They were delightful, just as her students had been the year before. Being a new teacher, being a professional woman, took energy, preparation, and time. Thea continued to share experiences with her parents through correspondence. On February 1, 1961, she wrote:

Dear Ma and Pa,

It is with deep apology that I write two weeks later to say that I received the beautiful, black, well-fitting, and conventual house-coat, fruit of a father's labors and work of a mother's hand.... Our school pictures have arrived, and I am sending you one as a peace offering, gift of gratitude, Valentine's day gift, and reward for patient endurance....

This week in music class I taught my children, "Couldn't Hear Nobody Pray." Now they are clamoring for more Negro spirituals. There are only two more in our book, so that will have to suffice. I never saw them work so diligently in music class before.

By the way, I have collected a picture story of Leontyne Price [pioneering African American opera singer] for the bulletin board by the Infant Jesus at HCJM. The next thing will be to inveigle one of the HCJM sisters to put it up for me. I've got the most scrumptious idea for what I can do when I am missioned in Canton. Can hardly wait to see if it will work.

In the interim, tell Sister Enrico Pudenz that one of our Girl
Scout troops has promised to make and collect diapers for the
salehouse....
    Enough.
    Abruptly yours,
    Sister M. Thea, FSPA
    P.S. After I get Reverend Mother's permission to go to Catho-
lic U., I'll write you a masterpiece of an epistle. SMT[4]

Thea, along with some of the other young sisters, surmised she would
get to teach in her hometown the next school year. In May 1961, four
weeks before the end of the school year, Sister Thea wrote to her mother:

Dear Ma,
    ...Today I had a very exciting afternoon. Sister invited me down
for a music appreciation class. I went and took my forty-nine along
and gave a demonstrated talk about Negro folk music. The eighth-
graders were as nice as my angels, but I wouldn't trade mine for all
the rest of the school put together....When we got back upstairs
they gave one of their "outdoor" cheers. Hip Hip Hurrah! — so
loud that the teachers all over the building heard it, and Sister
Superior heard it at the convent. No kids can scream and holler
like my kids.
    Four more weeks of school and then pretty soon I'll be south-
ward bound. I hope my homecoming won't resemble what happened today. Sister Sharonne's little niece Sharon, here on a visit,
saw me in the corridor, put up both hands and took off like a streak
of lightning. Sister Sharonne (and friends) spent a large portion of
the afternoon trying to convince Sharon that (1) I was nice; (2) I
wouldn't hurt her; (3) I was their sister; (4) I looked just like them.
She didn't believe a word of it, and I can't say I blame her, but such
is life.[5]

Sister Thea included a separate, chatty epistle to her dear dad. A longer
letter came on Mother's Day, 1961:

Dear Ma,
    Thank you very much for your lovely bouquet of roses. They
were beauties — all red and long-stemmed and still in bud stage.
The Sisters teased me because you sent me flowers for Mother's
Day. They thought it should have been the other way around. I

could have stopped their remarks by telling them that the roses were not for me but for Mary, but why spoil their little joke.

... On Ascension Thursday we were invited out to the seminary for a pontifical High Mass. It was so exciting. Before anything happened we were taken on a tour of the seminary. Then almost as soon as we were settled in the chapel the organist started to play like fury, the trumpets — six of them started blowing, the choir began the "Ecce Sacerdos," and the cross bearer started up the aisle followed by four acolytes. The music was magnificent. Wished you were there....

Do you remember the nice housecoat you sent me for Christmas? Sister Sharonne hemmed it up for me and I am wearing it nightly and morningly....

Love, S.M.T.[6]

Teaching two years at Blessed Sacrament ended successfully. To her complete delight, she was assigned to teach that fall at Holy Child Jesus, her alma mater, in Canton. Six weeks of summer school courses at Viterbo passed rapidly. With a happy heart, eight years after she had first left, Sister Thea boarded the train to her beloved South.

Chapter 10

CIVIL RIGHTS FROM AFAR

Thea, though far from her Mississippi home, was paying close attention to the growing civil rights movement. Her beloved Magnolia State was considered to be the most racist of states in the heart of the Old South. Between 1955 and 1965, civil rights activists, empowered with the liberating message of the Gospel nurtured in the black Christian community, supported by the new medium of television and helped by students from across the country (along with a minority of white sympathizers and religious leaders in the South), were staging actions that led to federal protections for the rights of African American citizens.

There was the Council on Racial Equality (CORE), the National Association for the Advancement of Colored People (NAACP), and Dr. Martin Luther King Jr.'s Southern Christian Leadership Conference (SLC). There were the lunch-counter sit-ins that spread from Greensboro, North Carolina, across the South and beyond. The violence and arrests associated with these actions garnered national attention. CORE and the Student Nonviolent Coordinating Committee (SNCC) sponsored Freedom Rides, following the 1960 Supreme Court decision *Boynton v. Virginia,* during which interracial groups of riders boarded interstate buses. They were met by violent mobs, yet they persisted, inspiring people across the South, including those most oppressed in many ways, rural blacks, to take a stand. Jackson, Mississippi, became a focal point for the riders, who sought to fill the local jails. There were a number of lesser known civil rights organizations as well, all of which played a part in a myriad of actions.

During this decade, the nation saw images of southern violent reaction on the nightly news that it could scarcely believe. There were lynchings, sheriffs' posses, beatings of whites and blacks sitting at lunch counters or riding interstate buses together, threats and even murderous bombings against young children at church. Viewers watched images of the historic Montgomery bus boycott, and those of pernicious voting denials, of peaceful protesters being assaulted with high-pressure hoses and attacked by police dogs, and more. The nation, in recent memory, had been victorious in World War II defending the ideals of democracy overseas, yet there was a huge eyesore within!

Thea knew the "inside story" of racism as well as anyone. In 1954 civil rights pioneer Medgar Evers, a black man, had been the focus of an NAACP campaign to desegregate University of Mississippi ("Ole Miss") Law School, only 150 miles from Canton. After his World War II service in Normandy, he spent years leading all manner of civil rights actions that drew national attention, becoming the first state leader of the NAACP in Mississippi. Evers led the effort to have black student James Meredith enrolled in the University of Mississippi in 1962. Shockingly, Evers was assassinated by white supremacists in 1963, further drawing national attention to a by-then burgeoning civil rights cause. He was succeeded in Mississippi NAACP leadership by his brother, Charles.

Thea's hometown was only a hundred miles from Money, Mississippi, where Emmett Till was slain in 1955 (while Thea was in postulancy in Wisconsin). The broadly publicized torture and murder of Till, a black Chicago teen (about Thea's age) in Mississippi visiting relatives, had sparked civil rights actions into a broad-based civil rights movement. (The incident was painfully reminiscent of the shooting of a black teen near the Bowman home some years earlier, mentioned in chapter 5.)

Fifty-seven miles east of Canton is Philadelphia, Mississippi, site of the internationally infamous murders of three civil rights workers in 1964, during "Freedom Summer," at the peak of the movement. There was one period in the 1960s when Canton itself was a focus of the civil rights movement. Canton, the county seat, and Madison County were chosen for this high-energy activity because of a high concentration of African Americans. Nearly thirty thousand people lived in Madison County; almost 70 percent (twenty-one thousand) of the residents were black. At that time, however, fewer than two hundred blacks in the entire county were registered to vote.

Flonzie Brown, Thea's elementary school classmate at Holy Child Jesus, joined the movement as an activist and eventually led voter-registration efforts. She recalled that "Canton became a melting pot" for activists, "where all major organizations established their presence." She recalls that when the Meredith march came through town, led by Dr. Martin Luther King Jr. in 1966, she was called upon to find housing for everyone. Dr. King himself had called her, and she, with the help of Holy Child Jesus mission, found places to sleep for three thousand marchers in the school gym, the rectory, and elsewhere in the community.[1]

What the southern whites referred to as "the mess" was telecast in American homes on network news night after night. In Canton, black and some white leaders from religious, business, and civic sectors set the standards for courageous involvement with the local black population. Black families opened their homes to civil rights workers, black and white, from the North, who could not easily find housing in southern white lodging facilities. Black churches were havens as generally safe meeting places. However, a few of them "accidentally" burned to the ground — clearly the criminal target of white supremacists.

Bulletins with articles challenging the civil rights coverage in the local newspapers circulated widely among the black community. These flyers carried announcements of meetings and events pertaining to the movement. Many blacks in Canton, knowing their cause was just, also realized that they were in danger of reprisal from southern white officials. They continued their actions in spite of personal danger.

Flonzie Brown later documented her work in the 1994 book *Looking Back to Move Ahead*. In that book she included a reprint from the 1964 *Madison County Citizen* about the Reverend James F. McRee, headlined, "McRee Urges Greater Participation":

> Today we are in the midst of a struggle for the dignity of man. Never before in the history of this great country has so much been said about a problem facing us and yet so little accomplished. We have heard it said time after time that this is only a racial problem; it is a human problem that affects all freedom loving people.
>
> We have been accused of a number of things, but one thing we have never been accused of and that is seeking freedom. Our city, county, and state have made a mockery of Constitutional government, crying for states rights and not human rights. We are having these mass meetings in order for you to be informed about the truth.
>
> You read the daily press and you only get the view that the local power structure wants you to have. In a court order it was said that there had been no effort on the part of the Negro community to discuss these problems.
>
> We mailed two letters to local officials and received no reply. We have Negro teachers in our public schools who have finished our

so-called equal state colleges and some have master's degrees. Yet, they cannot vote. Why? We are asking you to come to St. Paul AME Zion Church on Monday night at 7 PM and let the power structure know you are dissatisfied and you are not going to move away but stay here and fight for human dignity. — Rev. J. F. McRee[2]

The examples all point to this: Thea grew up in a world surrounded both by blatant, systemic racism and by historic civil rights events. Much of the civil rights movement in Mississippi, however, Thea missed while she was in La Crosse, but she remained "very connected mentally and socially," recalls Flonzie. "When she would come home, she'd talk to the elders about the stories. She kept up, whether it was through the newspapers, the television, or her own family, her mom and dad." She experienced the movement, sometimes from afar, says Flonzie, "but she knew about the movement. She kept up with it, she wrote about it; when she was there she participated."[3] So Thea — marking a path that would define her future ministry — as she prepared to move back home to where the civil rights movement was exploding, set about educating her sisters in Wisconsin about the experience of her own African American people.

For a course in American Literature during the summer before Sister Thea returned to Mississippi (1961) she wrote a telling essay called "The Concept of Negro in American Literature." She researched major writers of American literature, cataloging their ideas about African Americans. The investigation deepened her understanding of discrimination against her folk written by, in Thea's words, "those who shaped American mentality."

She begins, "Current activities of organizations such as Freedom Riders, Freedom Writers, C.O.R.E, N.A.A.C.P., National Catholic Interracial Council, and the U.S. Commission on Civil Rights are forcing present-day Americans to formulate definitely their acceptance or denial of the theory of the equality of man.... I have attempted by research to ascertain and in this paper to demonstrate the concept of the Negro as portrayed by masters in the American literary field."

In her paper she went from Emerson to Hemingway, retracing the writers whom she had studied in her American Masterpieces course that semester: Emerson, Hawthorne, Poe, Thoreau, Melville, Whitman, Dickinson, Twain, James, Faulkner, Frost, Eliot, and Hemingway. A look at some of her insights shows how, in her studies, she began developing an intellectual framework for her nascent intercultural ministry.[4]

After presenting some quotes from Emerson's work on racial inequality, she traced the development of his thinking from the time of the Abolitionist movement. "He professed the belief that all slaves should be brought up and liberated," wrote Thea. "He canonized John Brown" in the poem "Ichabod," she wrote, and detailed several other of his writings.

About Nathaniel Hawthorne, she wrote, "He had definite convictions concerning slavery. He felt that it was wrong, but saw no wisdom in the wild views and violent remedies of the abolitionists." Then she chronicled some of Hawthorne's writings that proved her point.

Her next subject, Edgar Allan Poe, "seems to represent the typical southern gentleman of the nineteenth century," wrote Thea. "In a review for the *Southern Messenger* he expressed his own defensive attitude toward slavery, endorsing the institution.... He regarded the Abolition Movement as an envious attack on rights of property. In defense of the Southerners' position he wrote that the South despised all forms of cruelty to slaves, felt they deserved to be treated with kindness and even affection, regretted that they must of necessity at times be forcibly disciplined." She went on to chronicle how in Poe's story of a freed slave, "The Gold Bug," his ideal conception of the relationship between Negro and White is described: "His master is a friend, a child, and a father whom he serves with unaffected love."

Thoreau, Thea noted, had a far different attitude, taking a "violent stand against slavery, against citizens who did not share his militant abolitionist spirit, and against the Mexican War, which he envisioned as a battle for acquisition of slave territory." She quotes *Civil Disobedience* at length, including, " . . . When a sixth of the population of a nation which has undertaken to be the refuge of liberty are slaves, and a whole country is unjustly overrun and conquered by a foreign army, and subjected to military law, I think that it is not too soon for honest men to rebel and revolutionize."

Thea documents Thoreau's advice to abolitionists, including the acts of civil disobedience that were a necessary part of that movement, as well as several other of Thoreau's key writings on slavery.

Next was Herman Melville, "an ardent sympathizer with the Negro cause and a man much concerned with the abolition of slavery, which he regarded as a foul crime." Thea writes about characters in his story

"Confidence Man," who leave "a humorous, though somewhat ironic expression of racial equality." His *Battle Pieces and Aspects of War,* a collection of Civil War poems, expressed, she wrote, "his appreciation for the justice of the Northern cause, his natural repugnance to slavery, and his concern for slavery's abolition."

Thea wrote with startling authority for a college student: "We note his admiration for the colossal form of Atufal, his return to the fact that in his own land this man was king, his acknowledgment of the Negro's 'great gift of good-humor,' cheerfulness, harmony, 'as though God had set the whole Negro to some pleasant tune.'"

In Walt Whitman, Thea saw a "firm believer in the absolute essential equality of man. To him all men were one." She quotes several of his poems demonstrating the fact, including "Passage to India," and "Song of Myself." Wrote Thea, "Whitman ever expressed a particular affection for and admiration of the black man, whom he regarded as an integral part of the American scene." She documents Whitman's immersion in the Abolitionist cause, including his firsthand reports in which "he shocked America by revealing the horrors that he had personally witnessed while traveling incognito aboard an American slaver."

She treats Emily Dickinson very briefly, but reveals Thea's own tenacity, noting, "She was a recluse from her sixteenth year, and so far as I have been able to ascertain, she expressed no public opinion on public affairs. In reading her 1,750 poems and fragments as well as many of her published letters, I found only one reference to the Negro."

Mark Twain, of course, was richer territory. "Samuel Langhorne Clemens was reared a southerner and was familiar with slaves as well as with the ideas and ideals of slave-holders, yet in his attitude toward the Negro, he seems diametrically opposed to the typical, nineteenth-century, southern-white notion of white-supremacy, Negro-subjection. He contrasts his own reaction to slavery with that of the woman he loved best—his own mother."

He notes that his mother had been in touch daily with slavery for sixty years. Yet, Thea quotes Twain, "kindhearted and compassionate as she was, I think she was not conscious that slavery was a bald, grotesque and unwarranted usurpation. She had never heard it assailed in any pulpit, but had heard it sanctified and defended in a thousand; her ears were familiar with Bible texts that approved it, but if there were any that disapproved it, they had not been quoted by her pastors; the good and the holy were unanimous in the conviction that slavery was righteous, right, sacred, the peculiar pet of the Deity, and a condition which the slave himself ought to be daily and nightly thankful for. Manifestly, training and association can accomplish strange miracles."

Thea observes that Twain's familiarity with the details of slave life show "a genuine appreciation for Negro humor, poetry, song." Twain, she notes, "poked fun at the Negro, just as he poked fun at everyone else."

Surveying a number of Twain's written works, Thea writes, "Twain glamorizes the Negroes he creates — and he loves them. Twain usually glorifies, leaves hard unpleasantnesses outside his writings. Yet in his treatment of racism, he is stingingly ironic, even bitter."

She then turns to Henry James, who, like Dickinson, had little concern for Negroes. "When treating the American scene, his concern was with people of wealth, prestige, and high personal rectitude." She reviews his apparent disdain for the fanaticism of Abolitionism in his "Bostonians and the Mississippian."

Like James, Robert Frost "has little to say about racial equity," writes Thea: "He takes it for granted." She does, however, show how Frost expresses his beliefs about equality in his poem "The Black Cottage":

> White was the only race she ever knew.
> Black she had scarcely seen, and yellow never.
> But how could they be made so very unlike
> By the same hand working in the same stuff?
> She had supposed the war decided that.

T. S. Eliot, though, didn't have a lot to say about racism; he "is a man, esoteric in his tastes, who writes intellectually for intellectuals." She treats him briefly, then moves on to an author to whom she would devote much of her academic career: fellow Mississippian William Faulkner.

"William Faulkner writes as no native-born, white Mississippian has ever dared to write," declares Thea, "and as a result of his freedom with the pen, he was virtually ostracized from his home state, after death praised.... Faulkner idealizes neither whites nor blacks, neither the whites who had a code of honor, justice, decency, and kindness, but did not extend that code to cover social inferiors or Negroes beyond a patronizing condescension, nor the Negroes, slaves, servants, sharecroppers, menials doing manual labor and domestic service in and around his ancestral home. Since Faulkner's many writings are, despite diversity of plot, one in region, character (Negroes, Snopeses and Sartorises), and situation, and since they have in common a sympathetic, enlightened, and objective approach to Negro character, a keen awareness of Southern white mentality, a tremendous emphasis on the brotherhood of man concept, and a scathing condemnation of grasping, materialistic aggressiveness, I shall in this paper limit my attention to five books that give glimpses into Faulkner's little world."

One can sense the relish as her essay unfolds. She treats some of Faulkner's themes in each of *Intruder in the Dust, The Sound and the Fury, Light in August, Absalom, Absalom!* and *The Big Woods,* noting that they "are based in a single reality." She quotes Faulkner scholar Hyatt Waggoner's words, that Faulkner "made a provincial Mississippi county courthouse into the focal point of the perceptible universe."

Some of Faulkner's themes that caught her eye: "condemnation of racism, violence, and the activities of 'White Supremacy' groups"; "the South must solve its own race problems by itself and without advice or interference from outsiders"; the dignity of blacks; the "difference of values in Negro and white"; people of mixed racial heritage; "the values of the wilderness where rank and merit are assigned to knowledge, virtue, and achievement rather than to race or family, wealth or power." Thea would explore these themes and more in the years to come.

She concludes her survey with a look at Ernest Hemingway, who "treats his Negroes crudely. He calls them 'niggers'; brings to the fore and mocks their ignorance, childishness, obsequiousness. But Hemingway touches all humanity with that same objective, piercing, and naturalistic crudity. He does not lie." She notes that Hemingway's are not typed characters: "They are individuals who think, plan, act, and react as individuals."

Thea summarizes her lengthy paper:

More recent writers showed an increasing tendency to regard the Negro as an individual rather than a type, yet insofar as specific, distinguishing tendencies can be ascribed to the members of any racial group, they characterized him (correctly, I think), as spontaneous, happy, content, revealing the feel of African jungle in his love of rhythm, color, and song, normally docile and cooperative, but morose, bitter or savagely vindictive when pushed to the wall by overwhelming misery or injustice.

As for our contemporaries, Faulkner and Hemingway, they demonstrate a new progression, development, and enlightenment in their approach to Negro character. The Negro is to them no longer an object of mere pity, kindness, and affection. They show him as pressured by segregation, prejudice, servitude, and other forms of social injustice. Beneath these pressures, sometimes he falls, but often he rises to real dignity, nobility, and heroism.

Having finished her course in American masters, building critical foundations in the world of literature, Thea now set her sights on returning to Mississippi.

Chapter 11

HOME AGAIN

Moving back to the Magnolia State was a joy! After completing her summer in 1961 at Viterbo College in Wisconsin, Sister Thea, in spirit at least, danced all the way to Mississippi. Now, at age twenty-three, she was again in Canton, near her parents, the Holy Child Jesus priests and Franciscan sisters, near her childhood friends. She was in balmy weather with down-home cooking. She took up residence with the other Franciscan missionaries at Holy Child Jesus Convent, where she would live, during the academic year, until 1968. Summers would be spent pursuing her degree back at Viterbo College and later at Catholic University in Washington, D.C.

While it was wonderful to be in Mississippi, the contrast between La Crosse's Blessed Sacrament parish and Canton's Holy Child Jesus mission parish was sharp. At the Canton mission school, material needs were great. Furniture, equipment, and books were often secondhand. Fundraising was an ongoing priority. But it was a treat to have the opportunity to teach in her hometown, at the treasured school where she received her elementary education.

A popular annual fundraising event for Holy Child Jesus Mission was the all-community bazaar. Parishioners, relatives, parents, locals, and friends from out of town gathered items, clothing, household goods, school supplies, and toys, for sale each year. Some years Blanche Klein, FSPA, later novice director, traveled by car from La Crosse to Canton, taking the novices to volunteer their services for the bazaar. Sister Marcella Marie Dreikosen, classmate of Sister Dorothy Ann Kundinger, who was teaching at Holy Child Jesus School, accompanied them and helped with the activities. Cantonites who did not have the opportunity or dollars to visit shopping centers looked forward to the bazaar each year. It was a festive occasion with picnics on the green. People could purchase necessary products for lower-than-store prices. Everyone had a good time helping to raise money for a good cause. Holy Child Jesus was able to meet its expenses for another year.

All of this was happening in the midst of the civil rights movement. Years later, Thea recalled to her friend, the renowned African American author Margaret Walker:

> We were very conscious of the hostility of the [local] Southern white community and their objections to a black nun living with white nuns in Canton. When I was riding with the white nuns, I would duck down in the car when we passed white people in the streets or on the roads — and especially when we passed the white police.
>
> We talked a great deal about segregation and racism and worked hard for voter registration to combat these evils.
>
> One of the things we talked about was the new black consciousness. I think the new black consciousness, in a sense, had its beginning and was developed in my time.... the seven years [August 1961 to August 1968] I was in Mississippi, the civil rights movement was reaching its intensity. That was in the early sixties, when Charles Evers was here. When the people were involved in voter registration.
>
> Medgar Evers was first to come here, but I never knew him. I did know Charles Evers. It was when the Freedom School and the Freedom Houses were in Canton — when so many of our people were making decisions about the extent to which they wanted to get involved in the movement and more and more people were taking a stand. So I was very much conscious of the civil rights movement.[1]

Conscious she would be, but not always near her Mississippi home. In 1962, with the onset of the Second Vatican Council (1962–65), renewal was afoot in the Catholic Church worldwide. That year the Franciscan Sisters of Perpetual Adoration changed from six to five the number of years required for sisters in temporary profession. Thea's class, the profession class of 1958, initiated the new temporary profession plan. To accomplish the change, they remained on mission in towns and cities where Franciscan sisters ministered. On designated weekends during the 1962–63 academic year they commuted to La Crosse (a major time commitment for travel from Mississippi) for formation classes with Sister Charitina Craigen, FSPA, joining the Class of 1957, all stationed at the motherhouse.

Because of this transition, Sister Thea was in La Crosse the entire summer of 1963 to attend Viterbo. While in La Crosse, though, she was invited to speak about the civil rights movement from her unique perspective. The local newspaper, the *La Crosse Tribune,* on Sunday, July 28, 1963, published an account of the presentation Sister Thea gave at Viterbo College. "Negro Needs Understanding" was the headline of the article. A striking full-length photo of Sister Thea, taken inside the main entrance to Viterbo College, accompanied the article. The speech was well received, and by popular demand Sister Thea repeated it a second time two days later. Many of Thea's insights ring true today, though even in 1963 the reporter referred to Thea as "the colored nun." "Minimize the evil—develop the good" was Thea's message, described by the newspaper as her solution to "the Negro problem":

> The racial problem is really a problem of attitude, as the speaker sees it, and it is hard for people outside the Negro race to understand....Interpreting the matter through her knowledge about happenings in her home state of Mississippi, Sister Thea stated, "Prior to 1863, Mississippi was a wealthy land. The wealth was cotton, and all the wealth was in the hands of twenty families. They owned the money, the land and the slaves, thus controlled Mississippi politics. All other whites were dependent on these first families."[2]

The reporter went on to tell the details of Thea's lesson to her audience: the size of plantations, the price of slaves, the various relations among slaves and masters:

> Some owners were good to their slaves, so the plantation went along well even after a master was called into service. "My grandfather was treated kindly," the colored nun remarked. But some slave owners were cruel, and their slaves escaped, if they could, when the Civil War came — they escaped to the Union Army.... Sherman destroyed Mississippi. It was left undefended because its men thought all the fighting would be in Kentucky and Tennessee, and that's where they were engaged in combat. Millions of dollars were wasted.[3]

The writer goes on with Sister Thea's lesson about the differences among the slaves, and hence differing views of whites, that endured in the black community. "Naturally whites fear change, and they also are

afraid the Negro will weaken American culture. These fears are not artificial, they are founded on facts. Negroes fear white dominance because
they have experienced it. They fear rejection. They are barred from
advancement. They cannot fulfill their basic needs."

She spoke of the Franciscan sisters in Canton's black community and
the prejudices against these white women young Bertha had to overcome.
Then she told her audience what African Americans want: "Jobs —
they're the key to advancement; education — it's the key to opportunity;
integration — it means equality; acceptance, but not necessarily mixing;
a high school diploma — not necessarily as a body of knowledge, but as
a right to go ahead."

During a question-and-answer session, the *Tribune* reported, she
expressed that Dr. Martin Luther King Jr. had performed a service, but
cautioned that "the demonstrations must not go too far," and dismissed
Communist accusations against King as inspired by white supremacists.
She also dismissed the Black Muslim movement as basically unpopular
among blacks.[4]

The Viterbo community was abuzz with the frank assessment that
Sister Thea gave. The diocesan paper, the *Times Review*, printed the
transcript of the speech the following week, along with a full-length
photo of Sister Thea on the front page.[5]

After a week's retreat with her classmates, on August 10, 1963, Sister
Thea professed perpetual vows in Mary of the Angels Chapel. Fifty-five
sisters took part in the joyous, memorable ceremony, a combined class
due to the aforementioned transition in the formation program. The
Bowmans, along with many other parents, came for the great occasion
celebrating their daughter's new stage of life and consecration to service
for the church.

Sister Thea returned to Canton in August 1963 as a full-fledged,
perpetually professed Franciscan Sister of Perpetual Adoration.

Her high school students were less enthusiastic about academic learning than Thea's grade-schoolers at Holy Child Jesus had been two years
earlier. However, her new status as a nun with final vows wearing the
distinctive FSPA medal emboldened her confidence. She taught better,
she sang better, she blissfully proclaimed, "Black is beautiful." Nothing,
after all, makes people more beautiful than the belief that they are beautiful. Thea often said she was beautiful because she knew it to be true.
She knew her spirit was beautiful. She spent the rest of her life teaching
people that they, too, are beautiful.

Teaching high school was a challenge. Thea could not understand why some of her students did not approach learning English, history, science, and math with the enthusiasm she had.

The Holy Child Jesus students, however, shared Thea's love of music. So that's where she focused her energies. Her singing groups were talented, and she molded them into performers. Here, now, was a mission fundraiser! Within a few years, the fifty-member high school choir cut an LP record called *The Voice of Negro America*. Sister Thea directed. Mr. C. W. Saulsbury was the accompanist who helped advise the project. The album was a strong seller among those in any way connected to the school.

The choir dedicated the record to "the promotion of brotherhood and universal peace." Between songs on the recording, Sister Thea spoke the message she was coming to own:

> Listen! Hear us! While the world is full of hate, strife, vengeance, we sing songs of love, laughter, worship, wisdom, justice, and peace because we are free. Though our forefathers bent to bear the heat of the sun, the strike of the lash, the chain of slavery, we are free. No man can enslave us. We are too strong, too unafraid. America needs our strength, our voices to drown out her sorrows, the clatter of war.... Listen! Hear us! We are the voice of negro America.[6]

The album cover featured a striking photo of the choir members, with each member's name listed — quite a thrill for any group of school kids in the 1960s, but all the more for these African American Mississippians! The record and its publicity were an impressive achievement for them, and Thea was thrilled with her students. The record featured fourteen Negro spirituals, including such classics as "Steal Away," "Deep River," "Go Down, Moses" and others. Needless to say, it became a family treasure for everyone involved.[7]

Summer 1964 saw the familiar pattern repeating: back to Viterbo College. Thea took advantage of her time to hone her already highly developed communication skills. At summer school in 1964 for an English assignment she wrote a piece about the art of literature that shows her thought evolving on her way to becoming a master communicator.

"Words are not docile," wrote Thea, "they will not serve the man who abuses or does not know them. But he who masters them can use them as he wills, can discipline them to exactitude and make them instruments of science, can make them art by using them as medium to express the intuition of beauty, radiant order, apprehended by his own soul."[8]

She went on to discuss the various uses of language, in science, in art, in literature, quoting John Henry Newman at length: "The language of literature is most successful when most pregnant with human meaning, thought and aspiration, for literature consists in the enunciations and teachings of those who have a right to speak as representatives of their kind [human kind], and in whose words their brethren find an interpretation of their sentiments, a record of their own experience, and a suggestion for their own judgments."[9]

"An author selects from the total wealth of his experience," wrote Thea. "He creates a vision of reality, a vision that is his own, personal, original, governed by his laws, product of all the influences that have made him himself, subjective, yet if great, universal and true."[10]

She also quotes Jacques Maritain, a seminal Catholic thinker of the time. "Maritain defines art as 'the faculty of producing, not of course *ex nihilo,* but out of a pre-existing matter, a new creature, an original being capable in its turn of moving a human soul." She also cites Ezra Pound's definition of literature: "language charged with meaning to the utmost possible degree."[11]

Thea concludes her reflection with the same quote from *Alice in Wonderland* that she had opened with: " 'The question is,' said Alice, 'whether you can make words mean so many different things.' 'The question is,' said Humpty Dumpty, 'which is to be master, that's all.' "[12]

Back in Canton, during the academic year, Sister Thea knew that her experience of teaching at Holy Child Jesus School was vastly different from that of other Franciscan Sisters of Perpetual Adoration. Thea had grown up in that community. She knew the black people of Canton. She enthusiastically did her best to be as fine a teacher as she could possibly be, and the students loved her. No one doubted her outstanding teaching ability.

What surprised many was how she could be so loving and at the same time so demanding. Sister Thea wanted her students to achieve academically. She also wanted them to be happy, self-assured, well-adjusted human beings because, despite the message of segregation (that was finally beginning to change). They were good, they were the beloved children of God. She encouraged her students to exert maximum effort in all areas.

Father Charles D. Burns, Thea's cousin, but also a friend and young priest in the Society of the Divine Word, describes how Sister Thea and Father Luke Mikschl, ST, pastor at Holy Child Jesus Mission from 1960 to 1979, masterfully served the people of Canton during the heady, turbulent sixties. In 1965 Burns wrote an article for the *Divine Word Messenger* describing her work.

In the article, Mikschl calls Thea a "one-in-a-thousand" find for the Franciscan Sisters of Perpetual Adoration — time would prove this to be an underestimate. After providing some basic biographical information, Burns writes of her philosophy, quoting Sister Thea's work itself:

She has written, "The Negro really is different from the white man. He has a different way of thinking, a different kind of endurance. But differences should not cause conflict; they should complement each other. And so it is wise that we do not destroy what is good in Negro culture, but develop it, harmonize it with other traditions. In this way we build a new and better way of life. What is the motto on our currency? . . . *e pluribus unum,* from many comes the one great nation."

Then he discusses how Thea gained perspective:

Leaving Mississippi temporarily was a blessing for Sister Thea. Her own social and racial concepts were broadened. She could write: "I never hated the white man because my mother wouldn't let me." She had great insight. She knew that hatred was crippling, and she let me know in no uncertain terms that it is just as bad for a Negro to be prejudiced as for a white man. Still I bore a deep mistrust. It has been erased by time, experience, and the open-hearted generosity of the many, non-prejudiced whites with whom I have associated.

"As a ten-year-old, I had my first real meeting with people who were white — the priest and sisters at Canton. At first I mistrusted them; but when I got to know them, I learned to love them. Ten years later, I entered a religious community in which most of the one thousand five hundred members are white. In my early years of teaching as a sister I really got to know white children for the first time. I worked closely with them and their parents, and my attitude toward the white man was altogether changed.

"When I went back South, I still had a modicum of fear and mistrust — not for the white man in general but for the Southern white. Here in the South, I first got to know the clergy and religious who were from the South. I went to a neighboring region where there was one sister who was from Mississippi. When I learned that she was from Mississippi, I thought, 'Let me out of here.' I was sure there was going to be trouble. However, this particular sister was wonderful and made a special point of introducing me to all the priests and brothers and sisters in the area that were from the South. I learned volumes that weekend!"

Father Burns, after reflecting in his article on the racially tense situation in Canton, quotes Thea again: "Cannot Americans, many and different, join hands in unity, live in celestial harmony, establish a new and better world? For those who are members of the Church, the Mystical Body of Christ, this sharing of life is a spiritual obligation. The very word 'catholic' means 'all.' Jesus loved all men — and true love always tends to bring people together."[13]

In July 1965 Sister Thea completed course work for her bachelor's degree in English at Viterbo. Thea, the tuberculosis survivor, had finally graduated.

Part Three

Thea in Washington, D.C.

Chapter 12

SISTER THEA
GOES TO WASHINGTON

In June 1966 Thea traveled to Washington, D.C., to begin graduate studies at Catholic University of America during summer school sessions. Her worldview expanded exponentially.

With other FSPA sisters studying at Catholic University, Thea lived in northeast Washington several blocks east of the campus. The sisters boarded in a convent at 1234 Monroe Street, NE, run by a French-Canadian congregation of sisters who had not embraced the Vatican II changes of lifestyles and worship practices affecting most religious communities in the United States.

Besides classes and assignments, residing in community consumed hours. Sister Thea often commented on her lack of time during this initial period of graduate study. The matter of morning and evening meals, the matter of prayer in common with the sisters, walking several blocks to and from campus each day, the matter of some evening recreation before retreating to study took hours she would have preferred to devote to graduate work. She longed for time to accept invitations to homes of new friends. She found classes enjoyable and challenging. Professors encouraged her, and other students contributed intellectual provocation. Her excellent intellect loved the stimulation of advanced study.

Thea's curiosity about all things black, all things African, was constantly whetted. In her hometown, during the early years of the civil rights movement, she was more than aware of the demand for integration, for voting rights and civil rights for blacks. During college at Viterbo, she had been studying her people's history. She had researched black folk literature, music, and culture. Returning to Canton, she had taught black literature and black music at Holy Child Jesus School. All of this had been leading her toward her life's direction. She was becoming aware of a growing black consciousness in herself and in the country.

Now, during her years in Washington, Thea grew into what she would later call her "fully functioning," black self.

Two Washington experiences affected her deeply, she would tell interviewers later in life. First, she was introduced and welcomed into the black Catholic community of clergy, sisters, brothers, and laity. Second, in cosmopolitan Washington and on the university campus, she met many members of the international black community.[1] She met American blacks who were successful professionals, as well as many blacks from the Caribbean, the Middle East, and countries in Africa. Before Washington, the only native African she had ever been near was Canton's Mr. Flowers, whom she never had actually known. Washington was a different story.

At age twenty-eight, for the first time, she had the opportunity to visit the White House, the United States Capitol, and other U.S. landmarks. To her surprise, she encountered blacks in national positions of professional responsibility. This was all new to her. Thea had learned from her doctor-father and her teacher-vocalist mother, from her earliest moments, that she was beautiful. Her black consciousness was naturally high and naturally proud. But living in Wisconsin in the 1950s she learned to behave, as some would observe, "properly, like a good sister in a Franciscan white community way,"[2] a way that repressed her natural exuberance, her natural lively joy, her natural soul.

In Washington she witnessed a newly emerging black consciousness. In the 1960s, years when many African countries shook off colonization, Africans studying abroad increased. In Washington Thea saw American blacks, Caribbean blacks and African blacks being themselves, telling their stories, and moving to their music, dining in restaurants featuring developing-world cuisines. She began to see life differently.

When she began year-round, full-time study during the academic year in 1968, Sister Thea moved to Shields Hall, a residence hall for graduate students conveniently located on Michigan Avenue, directly across from the main campus. There she had another experience that would shape her future ministry. An African friend of Thea's committed suicide. Her friend had tried to share the confusion, the pain with Thea. But Thea was not awake to the power of listening to people's words and, perhaps more important, to their silences. The suicide shocked and saddened Thea. From that point on, she told interviewer Margaret Walker Alexander, she put herself on a disciplined program, one that, along with her reclaimed cultural identity, directed the rest of her life.[3]

She decided to use her natural empathetic gifts to listen closely to each person. Following the events of 1968, the personal tragedy in the midst of social turmoil, she made conscious decision to surround people with her natural warmth, her natural joy. She became increasingly observant, more and more empathetic.

Besides training to teach college students, she developed healing skills that later touched thousands. She began the practice of paying acute attention to her friends and acquaintances. She began not turning from a plea for counsel, for comfort, for guidance. She made a conscious decision to be what some would call a "soul person," reclaiming hers and others' "feelings, passions and emotions and intensities."[4]

She experienced an awakening. She had believed that, because of her profession of vows, she should not be intimately involved in others' lives, even the lives of her parents, but now she took take a different tack. She would be herself. She would integrate her natural soul into all her relationships. She decided not to be separate from others. She decided to be as bold as she had been as a child in Canton, to be daring, to have fun. She was a Franciscan who began to appreciate that St. Francis preached joy. During these Catholic University years, Thea became the expressive, joyful, fully functioning Franciscan Thea. She connected.

People who studied at Catholic University with Sister Thea tell stories about memorable times with her. Dr. Joseph Sendry, for example, an English faculty member today who was just getting started in the 1960s when Thea was a student, remembers her "vividly." Once, he recalls, she gave a talk for graduate students on rhetoric, using her studies of Sir (Saint to Catholics) Thomas More as a springboard. "In her presentation she dressed up in the robe that she would have worn as a Gospel singer and did a performance of some Gospel music. Then she analyzed rhetorically each of the gestures she made and each of the intonations." Her presentation was a complete rhetorical analysis of the songs, and their performance. Sendry also notes that Thea, in the early 1970s, taught the first black studies course at Catholic University, a course in black literature.[5]

Father Robert Dalton, a Glenmary priest who was then a Catholic University student and dormitory chaplain, recalled in 2008 many mornings in the 1960s when he and Sister Thea, both early risers, had breakfast together in the cafeteria. "She was one of those characters who was bigger than life," recalls Dalton. "You would not forget her." He remembers her, too, singing at chapel liturgies.[6]

Then there were the Franciscan sisters with whom she lived. Decades later, in 2000, at a "Theafest" event at the motherhouse and Viterbo College in La Crosse, marking the tenth anniversary of Thea's death from cancer, several sisters gave testimony. Among them was Sister Rochelle Potaracke, FSPA, Viterbo professor of education. She told those gathered:

> It was a time of racial unrest. One night there was a hootenanny on the university campus. (For those of you who are too young to know this word, it was a gathering on the campus with a few guitarists, and lots of singing.) We went to join the fun, taking our blankets to spread on the lawn. It wasn't long into the evening when the emcee was asking for volunteers to perform. Thea took the microphone. Now, these were the days when taking center stage was not a part of Thea's life experience. She began to mesmerize the audience by telling them her grandmother was a slave and a hog caller.[7] She then proceeded to give out the loudest, shrillest hog call that surprised everyone — especially us FSPAs. She shared some stories about her folks in Mississippi and sang a few spirituals, "Old Man River," "Father Abraham Had Seven Sons," and so forth. After that evening, the group of us attending Catholic U were no longer known as "FSPAs," but as "Thea's community."

Within these broader cultural movements, organizations were forming to channel the energy of people who were living in an increasingly open society, finding one another and seeking to work together in solidarity.

As the other black women and men religious and clergy began to meet and reflect on their role in the church, Thea quickly assumed a leadership role, at first among the women. Before that, though, came a gathering of black clergy, the National Black Catholic Clergy Caucus (NBCCC) held in Detroit, in April 1968, in reaction to the assassination of Dr. Martin Luther King Jr. Things moved with urgency. Father Clarence Williams, of the Society of Precious Blood (CPPS), remembers the summer of 1968 well. "It began right after the assassination of Dr. King in April. [The black priests] met in Detroit, and, as they said, the Negro mood had changed. That's when the Negro priests got together and formed the National Black Catholic Clergy Caucus" (a caucus of the National Catholic Conference for Interracial Justice). They assembled each evening for discussion, and eventually "came out with the famous statement 'The Catholic Church Is a White Racist Institution.' That went around the world, and that began the Black Catholic Movement," he recalls.[8]

The first task of the movement was to "work on our black identity, because we were all Negro.... With the assassination of Dr. King and the more self-determining tone, we were determining 'can we stay in the Catholic Church?'" That was a question, says Williams, because "we were in seminaries and convents where people accepted us as experiments usually because most places didn't know if we could *have* black priests or black sisters." Black congregants had struggled to blend into the dominant white culture of the various congregations: "you were trying to be a credit to your race, you were trying to be as white as possible in your diction, in your conduct."[9]

With the changed mood of 1968, as blacks struggled to discover and discern their identity, some people switched to more welcoming religious orders, some quit altogether, as did many white members, for their own reasons. "It was really an intense time of support and affirmation," recalls Williams. "A lot of these priests and sisters were young because they were just a new experiment of the new time. There was a lot of energy, a lot of praising God, and a lot of partying, and then we were coming out of habits too, so it was a very, very challenging time and a good time."[10]

Sister Martin de Porres (née Patricia Muriel) Grey, a Mercy Sister (RSM), attended the National Black Catholic Clergy Caucus that summer as the sole woman guest. But there was no place for black Catholic Sisters at that table, recalls Williams, himself a black Catholic priest: Grey was advised by black priests that their newly founded National Black Clergy Caucus would not be a good place for women to organize. Sister Antona Ebo, a Franciscan Sister of Mary (Missouri), recalls, "The men treated her [Sister Martin de Porres] the same way the rest of the guys in the hierarchy treated us. They told her she did not belong in their gathering and that it would be best for her to go back to her convent and then call together black sisters. That's what she did."[11]

She left with a heightened awareness of a pressing demand. Black religious needed to address themselves to the urgent need for the Catholic Church in America either to develop greater relevancy for black folk or to risk losing credibility. She was determined to call all black women religious to share in a task that would be carried out only by black women religious acting together, fully free, and joyously, especially in the black community, for the "coming of the kingdom."[12]

Ebo recalls that Grey sent letters to all of the religious orders in the United States, inviting them to send any black sister to Carlow College (now University), in Pittsburgh, run by Grey's community, the Sisters of Mercy. The result was the National Black Sisters Conference, founded a few months after the sisters were shunned at Detroit.

Thea is counted among those founding women of the National Black Sisters Conference. She quickly became a catalyst and mentor in the group. A photo of Thea singing went out to Catholic papers across the country and on the National Catholic News wire when she performed a Gospel hymn at the founding conference. Her audience was about 150 fellow black religious sisters, representing seventy-six religious communities. In the words of Antona, "I truly believe that is where Thea took wings and flew away."[13]

There had never been any gathering quite like it. Here were women, many who had been small minorities in their religious communities, meeting to discover what giftedness they brought to the church as black women, vowed to celibate service within the church. A new, broader sense of community was developing.

Williams recalls: "In 1969 groups met [separately], and then in 1970 the National Black Catholic Seminarians Association and the National Black Catholic Lay Caucus were founded, and that began the whole National Black Catholic movement. So we would meet each year together. We'd meet separately as priests, sisters, seminarians, laity, and then would have meetings in unison with one another, liturgies and what have you. That is where I met Sister Thea."[14]

Sister Antona Ebo recalls that the meetings initially were at the end of summer on college campuses. "Then it finally got to the point that we really actually had to meet in hotels." She was seen as another of the leading figures, a kind of elder among the sisters, but the situation was ambivalent to Antona: "There were many times that everybody else knew that Thea was there and people would come to me and say 'Sister Thea wants to know where Sister Ebo is....' I never felt on the 'in group' with her," although the two would become fast friends over the years.[15]

Oldenburg Franciscan Sister Francesca Thompson remembers the early days of the black Catholic sisters' group, but much to Thea's dismay, Francesca quit attending: "I thought that perhaps that I did not agree with all of the objectives of the conference after we started," she recalls. She had been a vice president at the beginning, but things changed; it moved toward what she then perceived as a "militant wavelength" that she did not share. "I felt that I had very little to offer after a certain period," she says.[16]

At that time Francesca didn't share the views of many of the black Catholic sisters. After being asked by her predominantly white community to attend the initial conference, she recalls, "I left her [the superior's] office thinking to myself, 'Why on earth would black nuns be getting together?' Shows you how stupid I am, I didn't understand what they would be discussing! When they got up and told their stories, I just I think I lived in a state of disbelief for the first couple of days.

"There was one sister who was told by her reverend mother, 'You know, sister, I just don't think you belong with us. I think you belong with your own kind.'" The sister, a member of one of many Sisters of Charity communities, replied, recalls Thompson, "'Sister, I thought you *were* my kind, since you're the sisters of *Charity*.'" Says Sister Francesca, "I am just floored — I just can't imagine people being treated like that." Her family had been part of the beginning of the black theater movement in the United States, and her great-grandfather had initiated one of the Midwest's first black-owned newspapers. "So there was always talk of pride. I never ever heard anything that ever made me feel that I was not as good as anybody else."

Why was Thea comfortable with a stronger message? Thompson reflects, "I think that Thea — certainly not in an ugly way — but Thea had suffered much more of what many of the other sisters had suffered, and she could resonate. She could feel a big attraction to what they had gone through."

Looking back forty years later, Thompson says of Martin de Porres Grey and the founding of the black sisters' conference, "I think that she was way ahead of her time.... It was such a brilliant idea of hers." Francesca herself had moved on to become a popular speaker on the presence of racism in Catholic institutions. "Thea never stopped trying to convince me to come back" to the conference, she recalls. But she had found a different forum for her own work.[17]

The conference flourished in the following years, meeting alongside the National Black Clergy Caucus and National Black Catholic Seminarians Association. Together they supported and advocated for participation by black clergy and religious in the decision-making agencies of the Catholic Church. The conferences became a clearinghouse where black sisters, priests, and brothers shared their hopes, dreams, issues, problems, and solutions and where the younger members came for advice from experienced elders.

Thea's growing awareness of black consciousness pushed her toward becoming expert in black music, black poetry and literature, black history, the black oral tradition. She was invited to speak on "Negro Spirituals and the Oral Literature Tradition" for several groups in the East. Later she lectured on that subject on the Catholic University campus. Eventually, while she was completing her studies, she was invited to teach black literature at the university. In 1968 Thea gave a talk at Washington's Howard University that reveals her developing articulation of themes key to the development of her people. This long, substantive speech merits being read in its entirety.

The Negro in Education

Distinguished Faculty, Students —

I am very grateful for the opportunity to speak to you today, for you are the elite. You are men and women of education. You are the hope for our future. You are the future and security of our race. Yes. If black power, black dignity, and black achievement are to exist in America, they must and they shall exist in you.

The idea of Negro word power as black power is as old as the history of the Negro in America. Our forebears divined with instincts true that a man with knowledge is free, that his wisdom and his skills are his integral and sole defense, that the man who is unable to give his humanity voice is in ignorance, remains a slave. History points up the white racists' fear of the educated Negro, of the "smart nigger with letters in his head," of the "nigger with book learning." It likewise emphasizes the burning determination of the Negro people to acquire education and to speak out for themselves in spite of adversity of circumstances and seemingly insurmountable obstacles.

For more than a thousand years my people have walked the hard way. But they haven't been daunted. History reveals them rising at four, working all day in the fields or mines or docks, learning their ABCs at night by firelight — working, walking, begging their way to school to seek for knowledge.

Negro writing in America begins when Briton Hammon, in 1760, published *A Narrative of Uncommon Sufferings.* Jupiter Hammon wrote poetry and prose. Phyllis Wheatley was published.

In the 1800s, the Constitution pronounced a Negro slave equal to three-fifths fraction of a man. After Phyllis Wheatley and Jupiter Hammon published, a hiatus occurred as a result of the passage of laws against reading, writing, and assembly-ing by slaves in the South. In the North, there appeared the literature of abolition. In the South, activities of the underground railroad and ex-slave narratives. Frederick Douglass then appeared on the scene.

In 1892, Julie K. Wetherill wrote of the Negro, "His fine ear for rhythm should be useful to him as regards poetry, and it is an unquestionable fact that he possesses the story-telling gift.... But is uncapable of 'didactic and polemical or intellectual effort.' "

In 1826, thirty-seven years before the Emancipation Proclamation, the first Negro graduated from college in Bowdoin, Maine.

In 1833, when Miss Prudence Crandall opened her school for Negro girls, girls flocked there from Boston, Philadelphia, New York, Maine, New Hampshire, in spite of the fact that under Connecticut vagrancy laws any girl caught going to or from this school was flogged ten lashes on her bare back.

In 1861, Hampton Institute was founded.

In 1865, Shaw University.

In 1867, Talladega, Morehouse, Howard, Virginia University.

In 1869, Clark College.

In 1871 Alcan A & M, the oldest land grant college in the United States.

In 1881, Tuskegee Institute.

By 1913, 70 percent of Negro people were literate, a net gain of 65 percent in fifty years. And in spite of segregation, in spite of discrimination, in spite of the fact that Negroes were accorded positions of inferiority in some northern schools. In spite of that, and the fact that Negro colleges and universities were understaffed, underequipped, and fed by students graduating from high schools that were third- or fourth- or fifth-rate because understaffed, overcrowded, and under-equipped, the first half of the twentieth century produced Marian Anderson, Mary Bethune, James Weldon Johnson, George Washington Carver, Walter White, Paul Robeson,

Langston Hughes, and so on and on and on. Negroes — underprivileged, underpaid, segregated, often underfed — achieved success and fame in every field. No one could hold them down. No one could keep them back.

Just as no one can thwart you once you have elected to pay the price of success.

The Negro was not satisfied. He began to tell the white man, as Dick Gregory likes to put it, "What ever you've got, that's what we want."

In 1935, the first Negro entered Maryland law school.

In 1950, the University of Tennessee, the University of Louisiana.

1954 saw the Supreme Court decision that in the field of public education separate but equal has no place.

1957. Soldiers of the 101st Airborne Division escorted nine Negro children into Little Rock Central High School.

1962. In Albany, Georgia, fifteen Negro teenagers were arrested and dragged away in an attempt to integrate Carnegie Library.

1963, James Meredith integrated Old Miss. Medgar Evers was in the forefront of the struggle to integrate the University of Mississippi. Part of the reason why in the spring of 1963, he got his bullet. That same year Kennedy maneuvered the forced registration of two Negro students at the University of Alabama. Not much later, Kennedy got his bullet.

Negroes' right to education has been secured, but only at the price of blood. Negroes and whites have risked life, liberty, business, to secure your right to the best thinking the world has to offer. If we do not use our rights, we betray our forefathers and foremothers.

It used to be said that opportunity knocks but once and passes on. Thanks to courageous and determined people who have pioneered, you have it different. Your road is opened — with scholarships, grants, fellowships and loans available, with talent recognized wherever it is found, you have it made. Opportunity doesn't knock and pass on. It stays around and begs to be accepted.

Recently, I went to a political meeting. Speakers were all black, excellent men. Aim of the meeting was to get Negroes into politics in our country.

Before, speakers couldn't talk. Born in old days when average Negro had a third- to fifth-grade education. Broke few verbs; had trouble expressing themselves. Excellent men, uneducated, unable to express themselves. Want to go ahead. Want to work for their people.

Dr. Martin Luther King minimized his educational achievements. He had a discipline, he was a philosopher, a thinker, a golden-tongued orator. He led his people. He was hailed as a martyr, prophet, hero. But Martin Luther King — Doctor Martin Luther King — is dead. And we need a leader who has the energy of youth and the wisdom of the intellectual. We, your people, need you.

The American Negro has come a long way in the last fifty years, in the last fifteen years, in the last five years, in the last five months. But our lot will not continue to improve unless we as a people assert ourselves.

By our achievement. By our accomplishment. By our success we give the lie to those who argue for white superiority and supremacy.

By our achievement, our accomplishment, our success we prove to America that black power is responsible, productive, progressive. Black power is one of her most treasured assets that she can no longer afford — in the words of Frederick Douglass — to let her strong black arm hang helpless at her side.

I know that the younger generation is ready to do something for civil rights. Our young people have risked their lives to attend meetings, to march, to boycott, to demonstrate, to sit in. These things are useful and good. But I'm asking our young people for something better and something bigger. How many of you the educated, the elite, are willing to prepare yourselves to lead?

To write for your people? To speak for your people? To represent us in the courtroom? To see that justice is done?

Martin Luther King is dead. Will you speak for us, write for us, organize, lead? Will you lead us into the Promised Land?[18]

Sister Thea's talk was well received at Howard University, and invitations to speak for other groups soon followed.

With the completion of the academic year 1968–69, Sister Thea was awarded a master of arts degree in English by the Graduate School of Arts and Sciences at Catholic University. In January 1969 she submitted "A Complete Explication and Critical Analysis of the 'Ruful Lamentacio of the Deth of Quene Elisabeth' by Sir Thomas More" for her master's thesis. She must have been delighted to read a glowing review of her work, written by one of her professors, Abbé Germain Marc'hadour, in the literary magazine *Moreana* the next June.

In the review, he praises several aspects of the work, including, "Sister even treats us to a phonetic transcript of the whole poem: vowel sounds are important for assessing the wealth of assonance (pp. 46–47). What she says of More as versifier sometimes strikes one as true of More the man and citizen: 'He works freely and creatively within an established tradition,' and his life like his verse is 'rising in direction.' "[19]

During the next academic years, 1969 to 1972, Thea continued graduate study; and writing. For her doctoral dissertation she returned again to her early fascination with Sir Thomas More, this man of deepest principle. While a student at Viterbo College, when given assignments to write analytical papers in history or philosophy, she had "wiggled and waggled," as she said, to research and study Thomas More.[20] She knew more about his life, his family, his work, his philosophy, his writings than she knew about most acquaintances. She even admitted that she knew him better than she knew many of her friends. His utopian sociology attracted her. The famous Hans Holbein portrait of More as Lord Chancellor of England hung in her office or in her home through the years.

Erasmus, More's contemporary, was the first to style him "a man for all seasons." More was noble, honorable, scholarly, and witty and a splendid statesman. Everything about his spirit came alive for Thea. His intellectualism, his humor, his discipline, his devotion to family, his attitude toward suffering, his defense of truth were characteristics she emulated. He had become one of her heroes.

Thea said she had not chosen in advance to write her doctoral dissertation on More. It happened because she really liked one of his last works, a book written while he spent the last fifteen months of his life in the Tower of London, before his execution on July 6, 1535. He was condemned to death because he refused to grant Henry VIII a divorce from Katherine of Aragon.

A Dyalogue of Comforte Agaynste Tribulacyon appealed to Thea's wise, empathetic spirit. She saw in it More's attempt to comfort his family, his friends, and himself while at the same time explaining how suffering is necessary sometimes to get what we want. Fortunately for Thea, *A Dyalogue of Comforte Agaynste Tribulacyon* had not previously been the subject of much scholarly analysis.

Thea was fascinated by the content of More's *Dyalogue* because in the work, More logically — and sometimes humorously — explained the power of choosing right even if it meant grief for oneself and loved ones. Thea likewise was elated with the rhetoric More used in the book. She incorporated Morian techniques of exposition, logic, and persuasion into her own subsequent writing, teaching, and speaking. To emphasize his points and keep his readers' attention, More used repetition, clarity, vivid words and examples, logic, order, and arrangement in a natural progression. Thea followed this example. She became, like More, a skilled communicator. He was fond of the adjective *merrie;* Thea often ended letters to intimates, "Pray for me as I will for thee, until we meet merrily in heaven."[21]

In April 1972, Thea successfully defended and published her dissertation. She titled it: "The Relationship of Pathos and Style in *A Dyalogue of Comforte Agaynste Tribulacyon:* A Rhetorical Study." In what her professors found to be a generally brilliant work, Sister Thea explores how Thomas More used pathos — "essaying to move the will by confronting each passion with its proper object"[22] to comfort his family and friends while imprisoned and awaiting execution in the Tower of London. It is a deep, technical and enlightening study, inspired, in part, by her early preoccupation with More.

Throughout the dissertation, with scholarly distinction, Thea eloquently explains More's superior rhetoric to inform, persuade, comfort his readers as he prepared them to face his fate. Again and again, in subsequent years, Thea used More's rhetorical techniques of ethos, logos, pathos as she again dazzled her various publics. Pathos, feeling, rhythm, repetition, were part of her. She divined that emotion, supported with logical intelligence, could guide her approach to life.

At the end of the dissertation, Thea wrote:

In *A Dyalogue of Comforte,* More leaves "not onelye one suche goode woorde or twayne: but a gret heape therof, to stable and strength the walles of our heartes." The naturalness, spontaneity, vigor, enthusiasm, and intimacy of his prose; the variety and *copia* of his arguments; the attraction and inspiration of his character and example; and the *pathos* of his unflagging effort to reach out to and contact the beloved audience whom he expects momentarily to leave by death are undeniably moving. More died in physical poverty and in worldly disgrace. In *A Dyalogue,* he left his last testament and the last legacy of his wisdom and comfort. From its pages More still reaches out to us, urging enduring solutions to perennially recurrent human problems, and seeking by verbal means, by pathos, to stir the affections of our hearts.[23]

Sir Thomas More would be a source of example and inspiration for Thea in the years to come.

Chapter 13

AN EMERGING AWARENESS

What do we make of young Sister Thea? In the midst of unfolding opportunities for the ever-energetic woman, some themes are emerging. For one thing, in addition to completing her doctoral studies, she had become an effective public speaker and performer. The recognition of that was emerging during the 1971–72 academic year, when Sister Thea spent time in La Crosse teaching at Viterbo College while she finished her doctoral dissertation and prepared its oral defense. She also initiated the Hallelujah Singers. A story in the college newspaper notes the group's "successful debut" on October 25 in the university's Coffee House Club, and noted the idea for the group, "emerged last year when Sister Thea Bowman came to Viterbo to lecture on "Negro Spirituals and the Oral Literature Tradition."[1]

People at Viterbo College, as well as her new multicultural friends at Catholic University, recognized Thea's speaking and singing abilities and invited her to give presentations and performances about black culture, literature, poetry, song. She emerged in a very dynamic and visible way at both Viterbo and Catholic University as an educator about the culture she came from in Mississippi.

This was due in some part to a new openness within the Roman Catholic community. Since the Second Vatican Council, the Roman Catholic Church had become expressly open to cultural expression of non-European traditions. Priest and cultural worker Clarence Williams says that the openness created a space for a fuller expression of African American spirituality: "We weren't just spiritual beings imprisoned in the body," as he puts it. As for Catholic sisters, who moved into community-based work, he says, "As they came out of their habits to embrace their personhood, to embrace their femininity, they realized that they had so much more to offer — I think *that* is how they broke out of the convent. It represented confinement." Once their spirits were set free, he says, "you couldn't stop them."[2]

113

That theme of self-confidence would be key for Thea. She appreciated that her parents had raised her to be a self-confident child. In her work *In Search of Belief* spiritual writer Joan Chittister, a Benedictine sister, reflects on the dynamic that any "only child" encounters.

> When you are an "only" child, I knew, you are the center of the universe, the one carrier of all the hope in the family, the one mirror of a parent's life, the only complete picture of themselves that a parent has. At the same time, not only do you get all of their attention, but you give your parents all of yours, as well. The only child lives in an adult world and takes on adult interests and adult concerns and adult lifestyles and adult perspectives. Nothing distracts the only child from becoming a carbon copy of the one model before them, the adult one, the parental one, the one for whom life has already waxed well and whole. The only child becomes both parents: the father's "son" as well as his little girl, the "mother's little helper" as well as her daughter. In its "onlyness" alone lies its specialness.[3]

But her self-confidence had been buried. When Thea entered the convent there was a good amount of regimentation, even rigidity. In those years, in an environment that emphasized uniformity, she, who was from such a different culture than were her Franciscan sisters, gradually hid some of her original self-confidence.

At Catholic University and in the Washington, D.C., community during the 1960s, she had gained self-confidence back in wide measure and lived life to the full. "This Little Light of Mine," a song from her past that she now again sang with gusto, became her way of life. "This little light of mine, I'm gonna let it shine," became Thea's signature song.[4]

The Franciscan theme blossomed for Thea. As best she could, she imitated Francis of Assisi closely. As had Francis, she loved all creation as her neighbors. People black, brown, yellow, red, and white all were important to her. She loved trees, plants, and flowers, especially magnolias, crepe myrtles, honeysuckle, roses, camellias. She paid close attention to animals — mammals, fish, and fowl. Her fondness for birdsong became legendary among her friends. Freely she sang and talked with her free birds. She joked that if she ever came back it would be as a mockingbird! Thea was attracted to all creation, she would quip — especially where the climate was warm![5]

Besides her growing comfort with her expressive self, in the spirit of St. Francis and in her own cultural heritage, Thea also had been tuning in to movements roiling in the American 1960s. There was the civil rights movement, of course, to be followed by the women's movement. There were major changes in the Catholic Church, worldwide. Thea capitalized on all of these things. It was an exciting time to be black, Catholic, and a woman. To many, Thea included, it looked as if things were taking a turn for the better.

Thea, raised in the cradle of a spirited, expressive African American Christianity, was finding an emerging openness for that type of expression in the Catholic Church. In convening Vatican Council II, Pope John XXIII had urged the church to open the window to "let in the fresh air" of new ideas. Pope John had directed the bishops to help him begin a spiritual reformation within the church, including reaching out to other Christians, and to other religions.

In the church, there had been periods in history when there was more emphasis on feeling, on passion about life, God, relationships. Francis and Clare of Assisi, in the thirteenth century, John of the Cross and Teresa of Avila in the sixteenth century, are excellent examples of emotional expression. For example, Francis is credited as being the first to enact the birth of Jesus with his live nativity dramas in Greccio, Italy (precursor to our modern Christmas-crib customs), and also the first to enact the fourteen stations of the Cross, a now-universal Lenten practice of meditating on various moments in the passion and death of Jesus. He preached being in touch with Jesus of Nazareth as a human being. In those medieval and Renaissance days, many church people went on pilgrimages. They were concerned about getting their souls into heaven, about moving their own lives toward God. Mystery and morality dramas, festivals and processions — it seems most everything in the church was dramatized.

In the following centuries, though, really until the twentieth century, Catholics in Western Europe, enlightened and industrialized, moved toward acting, at the official level, as if emotion were not a good thing. Though it was swept by pious European-born expressions like, for example, devotion to the Sacred Heart, the Catholic Church was not a welcoming place for richly expressive, African American spirituality. The 1960s began to see a change in that. As the church opened itself up to new experiences in the 1960s and 1970s, Thea embraced the new possibilities.

One of these new possibilities was the Charismatic movement, begun in the Episcopal Church and spread to other mainstream, predominantly white, churches in the early 1960s. The movement's worship emphasized expressing the gifts of the Holy Spirit described in the New Testament, such as faith healing, speaking in tongues, prophesying. This, to Thea, was not far from some of her early faith experiences back in Mississippi. But, as she would see, there are differences.

Thea wrote of a time when she made a Catholic Charismatic Retreat. During the first conference the directors set up the idea of feeling free and expressing themselves. She remembered someone said something, and she responded, "Hallelujah!" People around her looked at her as if she had two heads![6] Black people, of course, have been shouting and dancing in church for centuries. She realized that she had been charismatic all her life! She came to see that her new religious life had effectively weaned her to a type of spirituality devoid of soul. From the 1960s onward, Thea worked to reclaim her heritage — and to help others do the same.

Starting with her popular talk, "What the Negro Wants," given in La Crosse in 1963, in the coming years Thea was frequently invited to speak on black culture in general, black Catholics, and Negro spirituals. She was a most engaging speaker, often sprinkling her presentations with her own soulful performance of Gospel music. She was meeting a growing interest in many U.S. cities for insights into African American culture.

A newspaper notice for a talk she gave in New Haven, Connecticut, gives a picture of that interest, and, dry as it is, gives a feel for how foreign Thea's culture must have seemed to the dominant culture: "Her program entitled 'Negro Spirituals and the Oral Literary Tradition' will express through lecture and song the folk tradition of the blacks during the days of slavery in America. She will sing and explain the songs that portrayed the joys and sorrows, ideals and religious depth of the Black Man in America for four hundred years. She will show the relationship between Negro spirituals and other oral literature, and compare it with similar traditions of European culture."[7] Her work was cut out for her.

Part Four

Thea at Viterbo

TO EUROPE

For graduation, Dr. and Mrs. Bowman gave the new Doctor Sister Thea Bowman, FSPA, a trip abroad. Celebrating the completion of her studies, Thea joined several sisters who had been selected for that summer's Viterbo College faculty study tour to Europe. Thea would tour various parts of Europe and then culminate the experience with a three-week seminar in English literature at Oxford University. Thea capitalized on every offering during the European adventure.

After four intense years of graduate study at Catholic University, interspersed with teaching stints back at Viterbo, Sister Thea was exuberant at her good fortune, traveling abroad for the first time. She was thrilled with her parents' graduation gift. In return, Dr. and Mrs. Bowman asked Thea to send them postcards.

Dutiful daughter complied. Through Thea's detailed descriptions, the proud parents read, accompanied in spirit, and treasured the trip. They mounted each postcard with Thea's detailed descriptions into an album. The Bowmans probably had to read the cards with a magnifying glass, because Thea made the absolute most of every inch of postcard space. Single-spaced, unusually tiny (for Thea) handwriting covers the cards. Extrovert Thea occasionally wrote lines on the front of the cards, too. She reserved space only for her parents' mailing address and required postage. The few cards Thea filled full were mailed in envelopes. They comprise a daily personal record of the European trip.[1] Besides obviously thrilling with travel abroad, Thea also focused single-mindedly on gleaning learnings she could use in future literature teaching.

It was raining in La Crosse the Wednesday afternoon on June 20, 1972, when the Viterbo delegation sent the FSPA travelers off. Thea was surprised she actually made it to the airport on time, because until nine o'clock that morning she was putting finishing touches on a paper she would present upon her eventual arrival (July 15) at Oxford University.

119

She tasked her colleague and friend Sister Charlotte Bonneville to help with typing the paper, then mailing it to Oxford.

On the trip to Europe with Thea were three other persons from Viterbo: Sister Mynette Gross, academic dean; Sister Ladonna Kassmeyer, comptroller, business office, and, after June 26, Sister Annarose Glum, music faculty. In Frankfurt they planned to connect with Sister Annarose Glum, who at the time was in Europe with a Viterbo College singing group. Major driving responsibilities during the tour were assumed by Sister Ladonna, housing by Sister Annarose, event planning by Mynette. Thea was in charge of purchasing food supplies for breakfast and lunch each day.

The trio flew from La Crosse via Madison, then Janesville and, finally, Chicago, where they boarded a Lufthansa 747 headed east to Germany. Thea wrote, "I am seated for the great ocean-crossing." With that expression, she may well have been mindful of the brutal ocean-crossings her slave ancestors from Africa were forced to endure.

The flights were exciting for Thea, though uneventful by flight standards. Arriving in Frankfurt two hours late, they missed their connection to Cologne and had to wait a few hours. Thea amused herself in the spacious modern Frankfurt airport, marveling at the myriad shops and moving walkways.

In Cologne, the hotel where they spent their first night in Europe, was quaint, small, partially destroyed in the war, and just around the corner from the magnificent Cathedral of Cologne. Thea started documenting her trip on postcards to her parents; "Construction of this greatest German cathedral started in the Middle Ages around 1248 and completed in only six hundred and thirty-two years," Thea wrote. From Cologne they set off on the popular Rhine River to Mainz excursion, where they cruised past many ruins dating to medieval times. In one of her early messages to her parents, Thea remarked, "Sisters Ladonna and Mynette were diary-ing...but since I am writing the news to you each day, I don't feel the need to do a diary. This way I have descriptions and pictures too — the 'diary' is yours." After only two days, she wrote, "I feel I have learned volumes."

Thea's personal and up-close, on-site education continued throughout the trip. From her study of literature she had been aware of medieval city, castle, and village systems. Seeing them she was amazed how widespread they were. After an overnight in Frankfurt, they picked up a rental car and drove to Wurzburg, Nurnberg, Stuttgart, Heidelberg, Darmburg, and back to Frankfurt, stopping at places of interest along the way. They especially enjoyed the mountains and toured a huge castle in "The Student Prince" city, attended a Mass in the chapel at the University of Heidelberg, then stopped for a snack at the Red Ox, a student gathering place for centuries, since the earliest days of the university.

Though everybody else around drank beer, Thea ordered an ice cream. A teetotaler (common among religious southerners), she noted that beer was everywhere and the locals drank beer as she drank water. In Frankfurt they toured the cathedral, though years later Thea told an interviewer that the church sites were not her strongest interest.[2] Goethe's house drew her. Inauspicious as it was from the outside, the inside of the house, Goethe's study, his wife's bedroom, family portraits, the music room delighted the literature teacher in her. Thea, no doubt, was already mentally scheming how she could use her Frankfurt days when she taught "Faust."

Highlighting their return to Frankfurt was their meeting up with Sister Annarose Glum and the "Viterbo Marianettes" singing group, homeward-bound after their United Service Organizations (U.S.O.) European tour. One of Thea's students from Holy Child Jesus School, Nola Jo Starling, was now a Viterbo student and a U.S.O. tour member. Nola Jo had been a soloist with the Holy Child Jesus High School Choir on the aforementioned album, *The Voice of Negro America,* which Thea had directed when she taught high school in Canton. All the far-away-from-home Viterbo College students were elated to see three La Crosse Franciscans they knew.

Thea exulted in all she was seeing and what she was learning from excellent tour guides. She claimed she saw a castle in Aschaffenberg that was as big as all of Canton! Her upcoming world literature classes would be enriched with details she gleaned in Germany. In fact she wondered how any professor of world history or world literature could teach those courses without having visited the sites. What she was experiencing with little effort would be impossible to gain by reading books, she wrote to her parents.

Germany also interested Thea because here she could learn something of the culture that spawned the Franciscan Sisters of Perpetual Adoration. The FSPA congregation was founded by a group of six Franciscan (Third Order Secular) women from Ettenbeuren, Bavaria, in southern Germany. Until she actually went to Germany, Thea's impression of the German work ethic and Germans was that they were serious, efficient, dour, somewhat off-putting, frugal, emotionally unexpressive. The clash of her own southern upbringing upon entering a primarily German community had been, in some respects, piercing. Meeting actual Germans in their homeland afforded her an entirely different perspective. With their friendliness, warmth, gaiety, exuberant personalities, the German locals enthralled her.

In Germany, June 27 through June 29, they traveled to Augsburg, Munich, and Dachau. The stop in Augsburg was memorable because they toured the famous Fuggerei, a walled "Town with a Town," founded in 1516 by Jacob Fugger the Rich and his brothers as the world's first social settlement for hardworking, yet still poor who were Catholic. Monthly rent when Thea visited was one deutschemark, noted Thea "the same as a price of a postcard."

With Sister Ladonna Kassmeyer at the wheel, they next drove to Dachau. At the concentration camp they viewed a picture/slide study of the horror. Thea did not purchase postcards or slides of Dachau because the "memories of what I have seen are awful enough." Arriving in Munich, they stopped to visit the National Deutsche Museum with its world class collection of artifacts dating from 1100 to 1800, and they toured the site of the upcoming 1972 Summer Olympics. After Munich, they drove into Austria, to Salzburg. Here they had their first close-up view of the snow-covered Alps. "Breathtaking," Thea wrote. In Salzburg, Maria von Trapp's Nunnery of Nonnberg and the six-thousand-foot Untersberg mountain, over which the von Trapps escaped from the Nazis, attracted the tourists. (The Von Trapp story, immortalized in *The Sound of Music*, had recently become a cultural sensation in the United States and a production at Viterbo.)

The FSPAs enjoyed all things Mozart, including a performance of Mozart's "Don Giovanni," albeit in a marionette theater. Thea commented she would have thought the marionettes were real people, so life-like did they seem. They enjoyed the opera, as well. She liked her time in Salzburg so much that she wrote home, "I love the mountain lakes and castles. If you were here, I'd like to stay a year or two."

She was charmed by the Bavarians and the Austrians, many of whom wore attire similar to the attire worn in La Crosse during Oktoberfest each autumn. Only one night did it rain while they were in Germany and Austria; otherwise the sun shone bright each day. If there was any problem for the new PhD on the trip it was the fact that she had been in Europe for over a week and had not received any letter from her parents.

The first thing Thea did at each hotel where they stayed was to inquire after mail and messages. But letters from Canton, Mississippi, would not catch up with them for a few days, until the travelers would arrive in Assisi, Italy, historic hometown of St. Francis and St. Clare, and of the Franciscan movement.

But first came Germany and Austria. As with many people who visit World War II concentration camps, for several days after, Thea could not get Dachau out of her thoughts. "I still think of the pictures, the sights we saw at Dachau — rooms built for sixty into which four hundred Jews were crowded, whipping block, public square for roll call and punishment, pictures of prisoners hanged by their wrists or forced to stand for hours in the sun or during slave labor, or going to a gas chamber, or so starved they looked like skeletons, used as human guinea pigs, thrown into open mass graves, piles of dead naked bodies, fillings ripped from teeth. I think I'll never forget it."

In Innsbruck they visited the University of Innsbruck Library. Here Thea was particularly interested in exploring the large collections from the Middle Ages and the Renaissance. From there they drove through the famous Brenner Pass descending foot-by-scenic-foot into Italy. Their first Italian night was in Balzano, the gateway city between German-speaking Austria and the Italian-speaking Trentino region. "Balzano exhibits a Tyrolean atmosphere," penned Thea. On the drive she was refreshed by the Alpine streams and waterfalls, the snowcapped mountains, mountain forests, and crags.

The fact that Italy was considerably warmer the lower down the mountains they descended made her southern heart happy. Driving through Trent they got into a traffic jam, which was not uncommon there because the highway from Innsbruck south to Trent, to Verona to Bologna was then, as it is now, one of the busiest in Europe. Holiday-bound travelers frequent the area, especially in the summer.

From June 30 to July 5 their journey featured stops in Verona, Bologna, Florence, Assisi, and Rome, briefly. In each Italian city, the Viterbo sisters arranged to take a city tour. Verona was fascinating because of its Roman ruins, its massive first-century Roman arena, its impressive St. Zeno church, and because it is the locale of two Shakespearean plays, *Two Gentlemen* and *Romeo and Juliet*.

Thea had her own picture taken by the statue of Juliet, as she had by many major literary, art, and scholarly sites. She bought several slides of

Verona and its attractions the better to enliven her teaching of Shake-speare. She also bought a slim two-foot long baguette loaf, the kind the locals toted under their arms as they pedaled their bicycles around town. Sister Ladonna received a letter from her family while in Verona. Thea looked in the mail to no avail. She wondered if her parents were getting the postcards she sent.

A guided tour in Florence revealed most of the city's riches in the morning. During their afternoon in Florence, the quartet strolled through the compact city to sites they wanted to revisit: the Duomo, the Ponte Vecchio, Dante's house, Michelangelo's David, tombs of Michelangelo, Machiavelli, Galileo, and Dante in the church of San Croce, paintings by Botticelli, Da Vinci, "The Madonna of the Chair" by Raphael, paint-ings by Titian, Van Dyke, and many more. They did some shopping in Florence. Though Thea disliked shopping, she was intent on finding in Europe just the right sweater for her dad.

On the next day, July 2, they drove to Assisi, the spiritual home of every Franciscan. To add to her Franciscan joy in Assisi, a letter from the Bowmans mailed June 27 was waiting for her at the hotel desk. Connecting with her family was always paramount for Thea: Now she could relax. Mail from Wisconsin had come regularly. She wondered what the issue was with letters mailed in Mississippi. At any rate, she was happy her parents were accompanying her on her European trip via her daily postcards.

Receiving news from home definitely buoyed her spirit. She was bet-ter able to soak in every aspect of sacred Assisi. There is San Damiano, where Francis heard a voice telling him to "repair God's church"; the Basilica di Santa Chiara, where St. Clare's incorrupt body is honored, and Duomo San Rufino where Francis was baptized. There is Tem-pio di Minerva, dating from the Roman Empire, and the Basilica di San Francesco, with world-renowned paintings by Cimabue and Giotto and where St. Francis is entombed. At the highest elevation is for-tress Rocca Magiore from which one has an unobstructed view of this beautiful medieval town, and more. Sister Thea purchased an Assisi hand-embroidered linen dress for her mama, whom she knew would appreciate the fine needlework.

A major delight was to see the famous Umbrian larks and hear their song. Francis had been charmed by the ancestors of these very larks. Though larks are considered morning birds, the evening Francis died, when the friars escorted his body to Assisi, singing larks are said to have accompanied the procession. The FSPAs were elated to tread the same narrow streets Francis and Clare had trod. The group taxied up nearby Mount Subasio. From the summit the panoramic view of the Umbrian countryside was a marvel.

In Florence Thea had been happy to carry on a conversation with an Italian, albeit in French. She purchased freshly baked black bread, which the travelers later enjoyed on the drive through Perugia. In Assisi, when Thea shopped for lunch supplies she took pleasure in being able to make herself understood in the various small markets and boutiques, once again, *en français*.

On the drive to Rome July 3, they stopped at the huge Maria Angelorum ("St. Mary of the Angels") basilica just outside the walls of Assisi. Enshrined inside this large church is the tiny original Portiuncula ("Little Portion") chapel Francis and his early followers used. It is a key foundation spot for the Franciscan movement in its many forms — brothers, sisters, priests, and lay.

The first order of business on July 4 in Rome was a tour of Vatican City. Thea wrote that the Carceri in Assisi, a hilltop retreat where Francis prayed, was more inspiring. She also thought many of the churches they had already seen were more beautiful than St. Peter's. That basilica reminded her of San Croce in Florence with the tombs of Michelangelo, Machiavelli, Galileo, and Dante. St. Peter's, though, sported many more tombs. They prayed at the tombs of Peter, Pius XII, John XXIII. Though Thea was not overly impressed with the huge church, she was impressed that the Vatican had been the center of Catholicism, and for centuries the center of much of Christianity. While at the Vatican, they toured the libraries, the Sistine Chapel, and the museums, and enjoyed a public audience with Pope Paul VI. They made a final stop at the Vatican Post Office to purchase stamps and mail cards from Vatican City.

On their second day in Rome, the Viterbo Four took a deluxe tour. The bus drove past historic site after historic site: the Vatican, the Borghese Palace, Gallery, and Gardens, the Pantheon, Castel Sant' Angelo, major churches, the Tiber River, the Spanish Steps, the Forums, the Colosseum, the Victor Emmanuel Monument. It was a field day for a budding college teacher. All in all, the city of Rome was thrilling to this sister who had been raised Protestant.

After a late afternoon dinner, with the family of a young Italian, Rino, whom Sister Charlotte Bonneville had taught English, Sisters Thea and Annarose flew to Athens. Sisters Mynette and Ladonna departed for

Spain to visit the University of Valencia, where Viterbo students were
having a Spanish immersion experience. The four travelers planned to
connect again in Rome a few days later.

The days of July 5, 6, 7, and 8 in Greece were chief highlights of Thea's
European tour. Their early evening flight from Rome, over the Aegean
Sea, was beautiful. From the plane, Thea marveled at the view of the
Grecian peninsula and island formations. Greece was different from the
other countries they had visited; it was seemingly more foreign. Radio
stations played only Greek music, none of the American music they heard
in other places. Thea wrote that the Greek folk music was especially
enjoyable to the two sisters, both musically trained. They checked into
their hotel and then strolled around a few blocks. Thea was charmed by
copper work etched with antique Greek motifs and an old man hawking
roast corn.

Thea and Annarose had difficulty sleeping the first night in Athens.
A sort of demonstration lasted into the wee hours, including shouting, singing, horn honking, general jubilation. Streets around the hotel
swarmed with policemen and locals. Several men were rounded up and
hauled away in a huge paddy wagon. The next morning the yawning
travelers discovered the noise did not signal a revolution; rather Greece
had been victorious in an important soccer game!

Their first day in Greece included a commercial tour of Athens: the
Parthenon, the Acropolis, the Temples of Zeus and the Winged Victory,
the Forum, several churches, the Tomb of the Unknown Soldier, the
Temple of Dionysius. In the evening they went to a sound and light
show of several Athenian historic sites. It was followed by a Greek folk
dancing group who performed well past midnight. Thea was cheered
to meet a black opera soprano who was there with a German opera
company.

On the second Grecian day they traveled to Thebes, Delphi, past the
Battlefield of Marathon, the place where Dionysius was supposedly born,
the place where Oedipus was exposed, where Agamemnon is said to have
sacrificed Iphigenia, and where the Greek forces met to depart for Troy.
In addition to many ancient historic sites, wrote Thea, they saw lots of
gypsy teams; they saw cotton and tobacco fields, goats, donkeys.

At Delphi, goat cheese was a luncheon treat after they climbed part
way up Mount Parnassus to visit the Temple of Apollo. Later they viewed
the Temple of Athena and her gymnasium. Trekking in the world of

ancient Greek literature Thea knew well was a joy. The days in Greece were made complete when a letter from Dr. and Mrs. Bowman arrived.

Their Grecian sojourn over, the traveling Viterbo duo flew to Rome on July 8, to meet Sisters Mynette and Ladonna. In their rental car the next day, they headed north, stopping to visit Viterbo, the city after which the FSPA college was named. After all the venerable Grecian sites laced with literary references, the drive to Viterbo was a tad bland. Thea noted the flight from Athens to Rome took an hour and forty-five minutes. The car ride from Rome to Viterbo was ninety minutes. In Viterbo, a city of fifty thousand, they visited the Church of St. Rose of Viterbo (the young Franciscan after whom the FSPA motherhouse and Viterbo College are named) and viewed the incorrupt body of the young Franciscan.

Now four again, they went on to Siena to visit the Duomo, one of Italy's greatest cathedrals. Travel guides describe Siena as Italy's prettiest medieval town. The weather was wonderfully warm. Thea was in her element, though her companions reported the visit less enthusiastically. Thea noticed after attending several Masses in Italian, and after hearing the locals speak, she better understood why Italy produces great poets. With her trained singer's ear, she noted with delight the Italian language had a "multi-plasticity of final vowels and generally a beautiful vocalic quality that is naturally musical."

Because the cathedral they wanted to see in Siena was locked, they drove northeast past Florence, through Bologna, to Parma, the home of Parmigiano-Reggiano cheese and Parma ham, prosciutto. Ahead of schedule, they decided to bypass Genoa and press on to Milan to visit La Scala and Milanese museums displaying Verdi and Chopin artifacts, and then go to Paris the next day.

In Milan, the guide promised anyone who wished could sing from the stage at La Scala. Thea was excited, then deflated, when an unscheduled rehearsal took precedence! The Milan tour took them to Napoleon's Arch of Triumph (now called the Arch of Peace), the Sforza castles she'd studied in sixteenth-century literature, and the famous pink marble cathedral. Milan was the most progressive city they visited. Because the temperature was hot, because the sightseeing had been strenuous the whole trip, the Viterbo quartet splurged on an air-conditioned hotel (an extravagant fourteen dollars per person) in Milan, where they savored a sirloin steak dinner that evening.

Flying from Milan took Thea and Mynette over the Alps and prepared them for the beauty they found in the City of Lights. Paris did not disappoint. All the famous places manifested before their eyes. City Island, the Seine, Notre Dame Cathedral, the Sorbonne. At the Louvre, Thea was particularly interested in the Greek and Roman sculpture and paintings by Raphael, Rembrandt, Giotto, Delacroix, Van Dyke, and Rubens, she wrote. They also took in the Tuileries Gardens, the Opera House, the Champs-Élysées, the Arc de Triomphe, the Arc du Carrousel. Thea wrote that she had felt most at home in Italy, though her French was much better than her Italian. She wrote she would really like to get a teaching position some summer in France or in Italy. "Wish you were here," she wrote to her parents. Thea was falling in love with Europe.

The travelers planned four commercial tours of Paris and its environs, plus a Parisian sound-and-light show. They went to Versailles and Chartres, which was smaller than Thea had imagined but exquisitely beautiful, more beautiful, she wrote, than Notre Dame. Taking a night tour, they marveled at the illuminated sites they had seen by day. "How fun to read and immediately comprehend French menus," she noted on a card.

After morning Mass on July 14, before Sister Thea and Sister Mynette flew to England, they experienced the pomp and circumstance of the Bastille Day celebration in the streets of Paris. It was exciting, soldiers in full-dress uniform, prancing horses, government officials and Bastille Day royalty waving to the crowds from convertibles, a canine corps, motorcycles, more than seventy armored tanks, helicopters and jets flying overhead. Sister Mynette returned to the United States a few days later, while Sister Thea danced toward Oxford. Sister Ladonna and Sister Annarose had gone from Milan to Switzerland and Germany, joining Mynette and Thea in London, before heading back to the United States.

Thea felt at home in London. Having studied English literature in depth, she was now delighted to actually see many of the places storied in literature. Almost immediately upon arrival, viewing only white, tall, imposing Buckingham Palace and a few monuments, she boarded a train, sitting in an opened-window compartment for four, to Oxford. A young Irish soldier sat next to her. Striking up a conversation, they talked about religion, education, parachuting, and his family. He gallantly carried her bags off the train, up three flights of stairs, then secured a cab to Wellington Square for her.

In Oxford, Thea moved into student mode, drinking in the history of Oxford and England. Here was the town for which the beloved college town in Mississippi, home of William Faulkner, whose work she had studied deeply, was named. She would also take a promised excursion to Stratford-upon-Avon, the home of another writer she revered, of course, William Shakespeare.

Now Thea enrolled in the Oxford University Department for External Studies to take courses during the July 15 to August 5, 1972, summer school for adult students. She lived at Rewley House at Wellington Square. That facility housed the center for the Department for External Studies, and included lecture and teaching rooms, a library, common rooms, a bar and housing for fifty residents.

Ensconced in her room, Thea picked up the essay Sister Charlotte Bonneville had forwarded, then met with her study group tutor. After a first session of class, she joined fellow students for dinner, followed by an informal reception for students and faculty. Everything went smoothly. Thea was thoroughly at home in the academic environment. Meeting the faculty and students from several countries was invigorating.

Thea took a two-week course, "The Individual in the Novel," with six other students. Jane Austen was her focus. Seminar classes met daily, including weekends, usually at 11:30 a.m. under the tutelage of Peter Preston, M.A. In addition, students attended three programmed lectures, were assigned a fifteen-hundred-word paper each week, and had two individual meetings per week with the tutor.

For many, the best part of the summer session were all the side trips, on-site tours of various colleges, the Bodleian libraries, city tours, tours to Stratford, plays, concerts featuring all things English. Thea repeated wrote to her parents, "Wish you were here."

Seeing places she had been studying years previous was thrilling, she wrote. In the main her classes seemed less challenging than many she had taken at Catholic University. She experienced less pressure in the English classrooms. She relaxed and felt free to take part in all planned extracurricular activities.

She remembered her first breakfast in England on July 15: ham, eggs, red beans, tomatoes, orange juice, milk, and toast. Thea observed how England differed from the countries she visited on the continent. First of all, everyone spoke English. Second, it seemed strangely like what she had experienced in northeastern United States. The second round (after the Spanish in the Southwest) of America's European settlers, of course, were from England. Washington, D.C., and New England were full of Federal Period architecture and furnishings. She had little to adjust to — perhaps only morning and afternoon tea.

Her roommate, Barbara, a German student who during the year studied English and French at the University of Fribourg, arrived on July 16. She too was enrolled in the "Individual in the Novel" course. A few days later Barbara's boyfriend wrote he was glad she was rooming with a nun!

Two students joined Thea at Office (Prayer of the Hours, prayed at various times during the day) and Mass at Blackfriars Priory on Sunday. The priory is a community of Dominican friars living a common life of prayer, study, and preaching in the center of Oxford. Daily, the public is welcome to join the black-cloaked friars for Mass and the Divine Office in the priory church.

That first night of the summer school session several students went pubbing. Oxford boasts over sixty pubs on campus. Thea declined: She was sound asleep when her roommate returned.

The weather in England continued sunny and warm, as it often had been on the continent. There were no fabled English rains or fog. The laid-back, relaxed pace at Oxford appealed to Thea. Students were encouraged to soak in the sights and sounds and history, to take side trips. Oxford was proving to be vastly different from her experience at Catholic University. That campus and city hosted comparable events, but graduate student Thea had felt guilty if she attended them. Her coursework at Catholic University, unlike that at summer classes in Oxford, had demanded intensive and extensive study.

She rejoiced in the diversity of students at Oxford. In her program were English, Welsh, Scots, Swiss, Germans, Norwegians, Americans, and Austrians, of many persuasions: Catholics, Anglicans, Episcopalians, Unitarians, Methodists, and, she mentioned, one vegetarian. The youngest was twenty-one, the oldest, over seventy. It was "a real polyglot group," Thea said.

A tour of Churchill's birthplace, Bleinheim Palace, was memorable. The estate is still in the family of the Duke of Marlborough, Winston Churchill's family. Thea was enchanted with the world's longest library room, the world's largest private collection recorded and the golden dinner service in the state dining room. One evening with her fellow students she enjoyed a performance of *The Importance of Being Earnest*. Thea found it "funnier and more understandable" seeing it with people from its native country. Many of the local allusions she had not noticed the many times she had seen the play seemed enormously funny in England. She had not thought of Oscar Wilde as a local-color writer. One evening the group engaged in a discussion led by an Oxford scholar on the future of marriage and the family. Another highlight was the evening that distinguished scholar Noam Chomsky came to give a lecture on linguistics.

The summer session proceeded smoothly. Oxford administrators and faculty were kind. Regular letters from home added to Thea's bliss. On a rare free day, Thea practiced singing because she had volunteered to sing spirituals at a group party. The party was lively; Thea's singing was beyond anyone's expectations. For her efforts she was presented with a dozen red roses and two larges posters of Oxford. Not surprisingly, the group invited her to perform at the farewell party at the end of the term. She also continued serious sweater shopping, aiming to purchase just the right sweater for her dear dad.

Making friends was easy at Oxford. The "polyglot group" members were fascinating, intelligent, and spirited. Rudy from Germany took Thea under his wing during her time in England. His wife met them when the summer session ended. Together they spent two days sightseeing in London. Thea went to Mass and the vesper service each weekday evening at Blackfriars with friend and fellow student Karen Cox.

Friends advised Thea where to stay in London during her last two days in England. She confirmed reservations at the Hotel Winchester. However, the Winchester was six miles from center city London, it was pricey, and Thea did not know her way around. After deliberation she accepted an invitation to stay at the home of Rosemary, another fellow student. Rosemary also offered to drive her to Heathrow Airport to meet the flight to New York City. After more deliberations, it was decided Thea would stay at a German Catholic mission several of the German students knew.

Still drinking in the exhilaration at Oxford, though not at the pubs with her "gang," a highlight for Thea was just meandering about campus. Her goal was to visit each of the thirty-nine Oxford colleges. She mused that the medieval town was similar to when Sir Thomas More was there. She paused at Oriel College, where Cardinal John Newman went to school. She visited the site of the martyrdom of Anglican churchmen Thomas Cranmer, Hugh Latimer, and Nicholas Ridley, who were tried for heresy and burned at the stake. During a walking tour of the university, her group visited Christ Church, Magdalen College (where Cardinal Wolsey, John Lyly, Joseph Addison, and Oscar Wilde went to school), Merton College, Queen's College, and the Shelley monument.

At Oxford, Thea discovered punting. A punt is an open flat-bottom boat with squared ends, used in shallow waters and usually propelled by a long pole. Some of her class enjoyed a punting tour of the Thames while Thea joined others who strolled along the river bank.

On July 25 the "polyglots" took a chartered bus to long-awaited Stratford-upon-Avon, a place Thea truly wanted to see. (*Avon* is an old Celtic word for "river," so Stratford-upon-Avon means "the road crossing the river.") Shakespeare's lovely town lived up to expectations. The Avon, the swans, the flowers, the houses, Shakespeare's garden, his grave, the theater, the spirit of Shakespeare was everywhere. *Coriolanus* was the featured production the day they visited. Thea wrote that most thought the interpretation was more avant garde than expected in Shakespeare's hometown, but everyone enjoyed the performance.

Finishing her final paper, attending final classes, having a final session with the tutors, packing and going to the farewell party — all these filled her closing days at Oxford. Then there were the good-byes to be said to many new friends, a few from the United States, others from Germany, Norway, Switzerland, Austria, and England. Everything accomplished, the group enjoyed a dinner celebration, entertainment with Thea singing, and a farewell party at which Thea managed to stay until 11:00 p.m. Her roommate returned at 2:15 a.m. and commented that the party was still in full swing.

The next morning Karen and Barbara got up early to see Thea off after breakfast. First order of business after the sixty-mile trip into London was to book an all-day tour. What a day she had! "Yesterday was one of the most exciting days of my trip," she wrote to her parents on July 30, 1972.

That day had been chock-full of new experiences for the first-time London tourist. Thea visited Westminster Abbey with graves of Chaucer, Dryden, Dickens, Byron, Handel, Edmund Spenser. Then there were busts of other old friends in the Poets' Corner, the hall Henry VIII used; the Houses of Parliament, No. 10 Downing Street, a London home of Charles Dickens, Big Ben, London University, the Bank of England, Hyde Park, the London School of Economics (where John F. Kennedy had studied), the Mall, the Inns of Court, St. Paul's Cathedral (where Donne was rector), the oldest Elizabethan domestic dwelling in England, and more.

"Biggest thrill was visiting the Tower," she wrote. "Hadn't realized that it was formerly a huge fortified complex of mostly towers. Saw Gate — Traitors' Gate — through which More entered the Tower, also the tower where Raleigh, Lady Grey, and Anne Boleyn were imprisoned. Also saw block place where Anne and other royal personages were privately executed. Visited crown jewels. Saw diamond as big as a fifty cent piece." Thea looked in amazement at the Beefeaters who guard the tower in colorful uniforms dating from before Thomas More's time. Though she missed her Oxford polyglots, she was having a splendid time touring London.

Later that evening Rudy took Thea out to dinner. Afterward they ambled over to view the place of public execution where Thomas More died. "I stood on the block place," she said simply. Rudy met his wife, Nerate, at the train station later. At the German Catholic mission they told the director to petition Thea to sing at Mass the next evening.

Thea went with Nerate and Rudy to the outdoor Petticoat Markets on her last day in London. Goods of every kind were offered: food, live monkeys, sweaters! Later Thea went alone to Chelsea, took the underground to Beaufort Street to see Reparatrix Convent at 22 Beaufort Street, built on the spot where More's house stood. In the back yard, she gazed at his mulberry tree near which, according to legend, he received the news that Henry VIII had sentenced him to the Tower of London. She walked along More's section of the Thames, viewed Crosby Hall, and visited the More Chapel in his parish church. She looked at his first wife's tomb and what used to be Margaret More's garden. Then she went to the site of one of More's farmhouses, now a school. She saw some of More's relics in a synagogue and a More monument, thus completing her Morian pilgrimage.

As she had promised, that last night Thea stayed with her fellow student friend, Rosemary, and her family in Beaconsfield, in what Thea had described as a "huge mansion" they had purchased some years ago. Enjoying more luxury and space than they ever had before, Rosemary's family spent time renovating the house and were just ready to put it on the market. Rosemary's four daughters entertained their guest with a Roaring Twenties playlet. The girls sang for Thea, and she sang back to them. Because Thea had a morning flight to New York, everyone retired early. It rained during the night and on the way to the airport. Thea remarked that she was one of the rare persons who stayed eighteen days in England without having been rained upon. As passengers boarded the plane, it poured!

After a smooth passage through customs in New York, she boarded a flight to Chicago and then to La Crosse. In Chicago, she remembered later, it suddenly dawned on Thea that she was back in the United States after forty-five days abroad. Several FSPAs welcomed her home at the La Crosse airport. Thea was happy to be back, and her friends at Viterbo were happy to have her back in town.

Right away she was asked by fellow English Department professor Sister Celestine Cepress if Thea still planned to take her to Canton. Indeed Thea did. Sister Celestine requested "soul" food while she was in the South. Thea wrote to her parents asking them to have ready for Celestine "black-eyed peas and hog jowls, okra, sweet potato pie, grits, pigs feet, skillet cornbread, hoe cake and molasses, corn pone, peach cobbler, hot sausage for breakfast with eggs and grits, Jell-O pound cake, black folks' coconut cake, et cetera." For herself she ordered "pork chops, turkey, American cheese, grapefruit, spinach, string beans, cantaloupe, beef roast, steak, hamburger, carrots, wieners, ham, cottage cheese, et cetera." The food in Europe had been good, often tasty, but the southern palate was seeking home cooking.

Thea looked at the slides that Sister Ladonna had taken, wrote thanks again to her parents for the trip, spent a brief re-entry time, attended an FSPA assembly, had some minor fibroid surgery, went home with Sister Celestine to Canton and then returned to La Crosse to enter wholeheartedly into her teaching career at Viterbo College. Glory days were about to be hers at Viterbo.

As usual, her activities were published in the *Madison County Herald*: "Sister Thea Bowman, FSPA is visiting at the home of her parents. She recently returned from a six-week trip to Europe and an English Seminar Session at Oxford University, a graduation gift from her parents." She taught Black Literature to black and white students while pursuing graduate study [at Catholic University]. She will be teaching English at Viterbo College, La Crosse, Wis., beginning with the fall term."[3]

Needless to say, in the following years she poured European highlights into her teaching at Viterbo College. She returned to Europe with student study tours in 1974 and again in 1976. But now, in 1972, she would return to Viterbo to be on the faculty as professor of English.

Chapter 15

THE MOST POWERFUL WOMAN
ON CAMPUS

"Beware of Thea. She is the most powerful woman on this campus."
A concerned person voiced a warning to the new dean of students at
Viterbo in the summer of 1972. Little did the Cassandra know that
the new dean (one of this book's authors) and Thea had been friends
since their days in formation with the Franciscan Sisters of Perpetual
Adoration!

The "warner" was correct about Thea's voltage. She was a powerhouse. She had been popular on the small campus during her ten-year
stint as a student there — interrupted by time away at the tuberculosis
sanatorium and years involved in religious formation and teaching at
Blessed Sacrament and Holy Child Jesus schools. She had been invited
to La Crosse several times as a speaker on black studies and as a vocal
performer. She was now a professor of English, returning to a college
she loved.

At Viterbo, her reputation as a stellar student, a distinguished scholar,
a performance artist, and a much-loved and admired authority on black
literature and Negro history, as well as an authority on Thomas More,
William Shakespeare, William Faulkner, Eudora Welty, and southern
writers in general, was solid. She was equally well-known for her over-
flowing spirit of joy. Her signature song and radiance hovered in the
air around her: "This little light of mine, I'm gonna let it shine." She
reflected good news. Like a magnet she attracted almost everyone she
met. Soon after settling in at Viterbo, Thea pursued many avenues of
interest. Music was a priority. She performed often with the Hallelujah
Singers, which she had organized in 1971 (see chapter 13).

An article in the local paper announced a performance with the La
Crosse Symphony:

Lecturing to La Crosse clubs and school organizations, primarily on the topic of black culture, Sister Thea often refers to the influence of music in the religion of Black America. To emphasize points, she and several of her Viterbo student friends sing Negro spirituals and what she calls Down-home Gospel Hymns. That informal group has developed into the Hallelujah singers. Through their singing this spirited group hopes to preserve the old songs that generations of black Americans used to praise God, to comfort their brothers, and to ease the pain of life's trying situations. Of the two white members of the Hallelujah Singers, Sister Thea smilingly says, "They're a very welcome minority group!"[1]

Besides teaching three classes at Viterbo, auditing four classes at Catholic University, taking oral exams for her doctorate during the academic year, Thea continued as a popular speaker and performer throughout the area around La Crosse known as the Coulee Region. The infectious singing of the Hallelujah Singers, coupled with Thea's communication mastery, captured the public's attention.

Another *Tribune* story, written by a local music professor, Dr. Truman Hayes, describes one of the shows and gives a hint at how novel it was to have a Gospel choir performing in all-white La Crosse:

> "The Hallelujah Singers," directed by Sister Thea Bowman, appeared in dramatic manner rising from the orchestra pit to sing their arrangements of "O Happy Day," "Gonna Live with the Saints," and "In the Morning." With hand-clapping, call-and-response techniques, and a general sort of conversational approach, they suggested the uninhibited joy in music and religion that seems characteristic of many black people.[2]

Sister Thea began her six-year tenure on the Viterbo faculty teaching full-time in the English Department, and eventually she became its chairperson. A master teacher, she induced in her students an infectious love of learning. She was exacting, demanding, and unorthodox, and taking classes from her was the highpoint in college for many Viterbo students. She taught the way she wanted to learn, with soul.

While at Catholic University, Thea had consciously chosen to blend her native black culture with her deep Catholic beliefs. Catholic University strengthened the two important forces in her life: her black heritage and her aspirations as a vowed woman religious. She decided to wed black cultural expression with a life of Franciscan service. As she gave service to people, students, colleagues she sought to serve and to glorify God.

Since she had personally experienced the injustice that crippled the oppressed, she was on fire to lift oppressed people out of ignorance and poverty. Like today's Dalai Lama, who often breaks into laughter, she injected happiness into every situation. Thea imbibed that spirit expressed throughout history by so many memorable religious leaders.

Thea's mind had been molded by her parents, the old folks, and her teachers in beloved Canton, her later teachers in La Crosse, Washington, D.C., and Oxford, and by the tradition of her "holy Father Francis," whose lifestyle all Franciscans try to emulate. All of these teachers beckoned Thea toward happiness, toward the good, the true, the beautiful. When she realized that "being Thea" was enough, she knew she was beautiful. Years later, her friend Father Joseph Nearon, at the Institute for Black Catholic Studies, taught a basic doctrine: what is true is always true and does not change. Sister Thea strove to live and teach that "true truth." She lived her mantra from the Negro Spiritual, "Done made my vow to the Lord, and I never will turn back":

> Done made my vow to the Lord,
> And I never will turn back,
> I will go, I shall go
> To see what the end will be.
> Sometimes I'm up, sometimes I'm down,
> See what the end will be,
> But still my soul is heav'nly bound,
> See what the end will be.... [3]

Though often weary, she never did turn back from her vows and her decision to serve and to do good. The joyful positive attitudes of St. Francis of Assisi (c. 1182–1226) and later St. Thomas More (1478–1535) fascinated and captivated Thea. Francis and Thomas during their lifetimes attracted people of all ages by their merriment and humor — and they still do. Laughter and zeal sustained them as clearly as did prayer, fasting and discipline. Thea followed their example.

Like her grandmother, Thea was a natural teacher. Education was her passion. She communicated her love of learning. Studying the styles of Francis and Thomas More had taught her a lesson: though human beings are communicators, human communication is often difficult;

however, with "sufficient meditation and sufficient care and sufficient skill," people can surmount difficulties. Francis did. Thomas More did. Thea tried to do that, and her students, admirers, and friends attest that she succeeded.

Thea owed much of her spirituality to the Franciscan tradition. She projected an authentic, happy style. To her, the Franciscan rule was simple: follow the Gospel, be a person of prayer, be builders of the church, concentrate on the temples inside people. Be joyful, be peaceful. Reach out; help the poor, the outcasts of society, the sick, the psychologically needy. Divest yourself of possessions and give to the poor. Thea was an inveterate collector, a recycler (far ahead of the modern movement), who, like anyone who had lived around social poverty, knew there were people who could find uses for things others discarded.

St. Francis had loved nature, and, in turn, nature was responsive to Francis in unusual ways. Thea shared this gift. Growing up in the South, where the climate lured people to the outdoors much of the year, Thea had learned to revel in nature. She learned to appreciate Brother Sun, Sister Moon, and Mother Earth, as St. Francis called them. In his spirit, she knew how to treat all of creation as neighbor: love the animals and all sentient beings and they will reflect love back to you. She continued to be fascinated by birds — and enjoyed warbling back to them!

As she told Margaret Walker Alexander, Thea had learned from her Grandpa Ed that an education was necessary for survival: "For years black people in the South had been forbidden to learn reading and writing."[4] She learned the power that came from understanding language and literature. She knew that if a teacher understands literature, that teacher can understand what people mean when they communicate. Literature, then, brought Thea a great sense of joy. Having fun, being merry was a high priority in Thea's life. Above all, she wanted her students to enjoy literature, so she tried to impart a love for it.

When she taught Shakespeare it was not only in the classroom. She took her students to playhouses all over with Shakespearean links: to Madison, Milwaukee, Chicago, Minneapolis, to Stratford (Oregon), Stratford (Connecticut), Stratford (Ontario), even to Stratford-upon-Avon in England. She wanted students to experience joy while learning enduring truths like the audiences at the Globe Theater did when Shakespeare was pouring out plays for the Elizabethans.

When she taught southern writers, often her classes went to Oxford and Jackson (Mississippi) to study William Faulkner and Eudora Welty, to New Orleans to experience the incomparable French, Caribbean, Spanish, Creole, West African amalgam of culture and music in that cosmopolitan city. She had medical experts help students understand Shakespeare's medical terminology; she had her students enact scenes. Home economics students prepared Elizabethan cuisine for her classes; she made her students enthusiastic about learning by giving them memorable experiences.

In freshman composition classes, which she affectionately titled "How to Survive in College," Thea encountered students who thought they could not write. She challenged them with her philosophy: if you can talk, you can write. The students did both. Creative writing and advanced composition students learned to be articulate about literature. In the early part of a semester, freshmen found Thea's written admonition, "More Hemingway, less Henry James" on their papers. By the end of the term like their teacher they understood what writers wrote and they were able to communicate what they wanted to say about what they read. They learned from Thea to take the spoken and written word seriously.

While on the Viterbo faculty, Sister Thea developed and nurtured working relationships and friendships with faculty, administrators, and staff members. During a celebration of memories at Viterbo, one faculty member recalled, "Several years ago I met Sister Thea Bowman, who was a professor in the English Department. Even though our contact was limited, it was always meaningful. She had a profound influence on me and still does to this day. I remember her great welcoming smile and her gorgeous singing voice. I remember hearing the stories from students about their class spring break trips with Sister Thea to Canton, Mississippi. Every student found this experience to be profound and life changing."[5]

One of her Viterbo students, Tim Claussen, had Thea for freshman English class in 1971. He remembered his experience in Thea's class in great detail, and gives a flavor for what it was like for many students to be on the receiving end of Thea's teaching:

In 1971, I landed as a "townie" in Sr. Thea Bowman's first freshman comp and rhetoric class at Viterbo College in La Crosse, Wisconsin. Fresh from her PhD at Catholic University, Thea insisted that we write essays of no more than two double-spaced pages.

When we complained about the restriction, she replied, "If you can write two good pages, you can write two hundred. Or two thousand. Why should I read two hundred, when I can figure out the problems in two?" I fancied myself quite the writer until I got back my first two pages. They were soggy with red ink. Since Thea believed that writing was never finished until it had been reworked (the "labor of the file" she called it), I went to see her. As we reviewed her terse comments, she kept asking me, "Do you understand?" I made the mistake of nodding. After I turned in the revised two pages and received practically the same comments, I admitted, "I guess I don't understand." Thea had no time for bluffing. Either you understood or you didn't — that simple. No shame in not knowing; only a feeling of stupidity for not admitting you didn't. That one lesson alone liberated and structured the rest of my college career.[6]

Claussen remembered the challenge of Sister Thea: "Where do you find that in the text?" or, "How does that prove your idea?" and finally, after vainly defending his approach, "You have a right to any idea you can support." Tim reflects, "I eventually learned to love her cool, pleasant, and maddening method of questioning, but only after I learned to imitate it!" He goes on to pay tribute to his teacher's demanding, yet gracious style: "Thanks to Thea, I think differently. I choose words differently. Not only am I now more sensitive to meaning and nuance, but I like the sounds of words. That's why I still use Thea's pet phrase, "Thank you kindly" in the Midwest where the equivalent is "Thank you very much." I'm sure "kindly" sounds artificial. But to me, the "-ly" is more courtly, more feeling, more gracious, more lovely than the hissing "ch-" tagged onto *much*."[7]

The transition Thea made from doctoral student and European traveler was noted in the La Crosse and Mississippi Delta newspapers. On one occasion Greenville, Mississippi's *Delta Democrat Times* reprinted a story by Janet Gottfresden that had first appeared in the *La Crosse Tribune*. The story, "Woman to Be First Black Instructor at Viterbo" had all the usual details of her qualifications to teach and of the novelty of having a black college professor in La Crosse. In the 1971 story, what was likely Thea's principal message to the reporter is paraphrased: "Sister Thea emphasized that ten years ago it might have been quite an accomplishment for a black person to achieve a position comparable to hers in an all-white community. She now believes that, although it is different to an extent in La Crosse, it is not uncommon for one of her race to be teaching in an all-white community." The story notes that Sister Thea is not the only black instructor in the city: Brenda Randolph had been teaching for several years at La Crosse State University.[8]

Throughout her career at Viterbo, Thea was a powerful, popular teacher, as well as a sought-after speaker. She added to that when she chaired the English Department, attending monthly faculty and administration meetings in addition to regular department meetings. From 1974 to 1982 she was also on the FSPA Southern Province Board of Advisors, which met in the summer and on several weekends annually. Her whirlwind of activity was noticeable, so much so that it even garnered notice in the college newspaper, at the beginning of Thea's fifth year on campus. Terming her a "doer as well as a thinker," the article went on to document her many activities:

> In addition to the long hours spent each day teaching students and correcting papers. Sister Thea indulges in several extracurricular activities. These include speaking appearances, outside-the-classroom enrichment experiences and moderating, as well as actively participating in the Halleluia [*sic*] Singers' programs.
>
> For example, in September, Sister Thea prepared a local group of seventh- and eighth-graders to see the National Players in *Twelfth Night*. She described this as "one of her most enjoyable experiences." She also traveled to Prairie du Chien, first with the Halleluia Singers, and again as speaker to an adult education group on "the black man's approach to God." This past month the mobile Sister Thea spoke to the Wisconsin Library Association in Stevens Point on "media for use in oral ethnic literature." She ushered a group of Shakespeare students to watch *King Lear* at the Milwaukee Performing Arts Center. She also spoke to different groups in Carroll, Iowa, at Holy Trinity Grade School in La Crosse, and at Northland College in Ashland. The Holy Trinity experience was extremely interesting to Sister Thea because she was talking to children about dialects.
>
> November will bring trips to Eau Claire and Viroqua. When asked how she finds time to get so much accomplished, Sister Thea replied, "I think you can do pretty much what you want to do, if you want to do it."[9]

Thea kept an annotated calendar which proves the point further, showing what some would call frenetic activity. There are classical singing engagements as well as Spirituals, from coffee house to symphony. There are black culture weekends, literature backgrounds, and national conference speaking engagements with increasing frequency over her six years on the Viterbo faculty.[10] All the while she fulfilled her routine — and extensive — administrative and faculty duties.

A look at some of her activities in detail tells us something about the person she was becoming, about her deepening cultural identity during the 1970s, and about her newly emerging role. The shock of the 1960s was behind the United States, the war in Vietnam and the turmoil on college campuses were in the past, the post-Watergate skepticism had set in, but the social movement for human dignity was still alive and strong.

Thea often spent energy and time telling firsthand the story of African Americans. One such occasion in 1974 attracted large audiences and repeat performances. " 'We fight the battle of Old Jim Crow, come join us!' was both the rallying cry of Black Culture Week last month at Viterbo College and the main theme of the week's student convocation," reported the *La Crosse Tribune*.

The paper reported the story of the repeat performance of the program, based on "Jerico Jim Crow" by the great African American poet Langston Hughes. It was an hour-long program of music, dance, poetry, and pantomime. "Said Sister Thea Bowman, of the Viterbo English Department, 'Our goal is intercultural understanding. Minority groups here are so few; most La Crosse children have no opportunity for formal daily relations with members of nonwhite ethnic groups. We feel that the most important thing we can do is to actively open channels of communication and enlightenment.' "[11]

Then there were the five study trips to Mississippi, starting in 1974. Billed as the "Faulkner-Welty Study On-Location in Mississippi, Tennessee, and Louisiana" trip, it took place over Easter break. The trips were popular and mind-expanding, as Thea delighted in sharing the South with her northern college students.

The account of the 1974 trip in Viterbo's *Lumen* demonstrates the flavor of soul Thea shared:

After many hours of reading and after several Saturday half-day seminars, forty Viterbo people and their friends set out on April 6 via bus to see the real Faulkner-Welty places and people. From La

Crosse on the Mississippi in Wisconsin to New Orleans in Louisiana over Lake Pontchartrain; from the Delta Land and the Brown Loam Land to the Hill Country of Mississippi State and the dogwood and azalea land of Memphis, Tennessee; from Greenville and Canton to Jackson, Vicksburg, and Natchez Trace and on to Oxford, it was exciting all the way.

The story goes on to describe the host families, the "folks on the street and in the stores and dance halls, the children and the nuns in HCJ School in Canton, mayors, writers, and the folk in the Canton Hollow."

It was a totally new and mind-stretching experience for the northern pilgrims. "Eudora Welty's 'Delta Wedding' and 'Losing Battles' really came alive for me as we drove through the Delta territory," offered one student. "And we actually walked along the Beale Street of Faulkner's *Light in August*." In those days when regional foods stayed generally close to their regions, the food was a new experience. But it was the people connecting — Thea's career trademark — that made the biggest impression: "It thrilled me that my mother in La Crosse met my Canton mother over long-distance telephone," offered one student.[12]

Thea's reputation as an informative, educational, spellbinding, unforgettable speaker grew by leaps and bounds. She was often off campus sharing her message with various groups.

Sister Thea, proud to be a teacher, enjoyed speaking to and working with other teachers. After all, she saw education as the best way to lift people out of poverty and ignorance. She said, "Teachers are good people — they give a lot. But we all get into trouble because we foul up communications. Seeing ourselves, we can improve."[13] Having become an expert on a great communicator, St. Thomas More, she was eager to share with educators what she had learned.

It should be noted that Thea had great respect and admiration for the vision of Dr. Martin Luther King Jr., who had been in Canton during the summer of 1964 (with the help of Thea's childhood friend, Flonzie — see chapter 10). His assassination, like those of the other civil rights martyrs, bowed her. Thea wrote a provocative article about Martin Luther King Jr. in April 1978, her last spring as chairman of the English Department at Viterbo. The La Crosse Catholic diocesan paper, *The Times Review*, featured it under the headline, "Dream Is Fading but Isn't Dead." Here are Thea's reflections on Dr. King:

April 4, 1978. I said to my friend, 'That's the tenth anniversary of the death of Martin Luther King. All blacks on campus will wear black,' I said. 'I'll wear black, too' [my friend said]. 'You will?' 'Of course. Why not? I'm wearing green today, and I'm more American than Irish. I'm only three-fourths Irish, and I'm born American. Martin Luther King means more to me that St. Patrick. Martin Luther King has affected my life more than St. Patrick. Martin Luther King doesn't just belong to black people. He belongs to America, and I can wear black to mourn his passing if I want to.' 'All right. All right. No offense.' It made me think.

My Irish friend (three-fourths, that is) saw King's dream not as a dream for one race or people but as one man's interpretation of a Constitutional imperative, as one man's ringing enunciation of the American dream.

It made me remember. Black and white together marching in Montgomery, Selma, Washington, and Jackson. People, black, white, red, brown, yellow, working together.

Protest demonstrations, court trials, boycotts, sit-ins, freedom rides, men and women jailed and killed, Senate debates, exposure by the media, voter registration, new legislation, human rights, constitutional rights, treaty rights, people hearing each other. "God is on our side. We shall overcome." Black, brown, yellow, white, red, together struggling, fighting, even dying for freedom.

But this is supposed to be a sermonette. It sounds more like a memory. Or could it be a meditation.

Oh God, Oh God! Oh God! Ten years later the dream is...I cannot say that it is shattered. I cannot say that it is dead. But I see it fade. I see it recede. "Let freedom ring," said Martin. "Let freedom ring from...." Still ten years later, many in our America are not free.

Blacks, reds, browns, yellows, poor whites, grays, gays, groupies, gangs; the young, the retarded, the handicapped, the unemployed and the unemployable.

The alienated and dispossessed, refugees who take jobs that could be filled by Americans, children who get in the way; the retarded, the slow, the sick, the unwanted; the Irish (if you don't like them). Italians (if you don't understand them).

Those who because they do not think like we do, work like we do, pray like we do, live where we do, love like we do are cramped, confined, discredited, shut out, hemmed in, rejected or ignored, the millions who because they are somehow different are denied (in ways both large and small) the basic right to life, liberty and the pursuit of happiness which our Constitution seems to guarantee. "Now," said Martin, "now is the time to make real the promise of democracy. . . . Now is the time to make justice a reality for all God's children." I have a dream. We have a dream of an America where all the boys and girls and men and women and their countless generations can be free.

On April 4, 1968, MARTIN LUTHER KING was assassinated.

If you hear me, wear black on April 4.

Why? It will remind you and me that the dream has not yet become reality, that we have work to do. It will signify a recommitment under God to freedom and justice for all.

It will signify a willingness to work, to struggle, even to suffer to hasten that day when all God's children red, brown, black, white, and yellow, no longer despised or rejected, dispossessed or set apart, may become: One nation, indivisible, with liberty and justice for all.[14]

Thea's intercultural activities were not limited to blacks and whites. The 1970s were a time of emerging Native American consciousness as well. In 1975 she initiated a Native American literature class for Viterbo students. Thea invited a Winnebago couple, La Vern and Lorraine Carrimon, to assist her in the course. La Vern Carrimon was a World War II veteran of the Army Air Corps, having served in Africa and Italy. Lorraine, on her father's side, is a great-great-grandchild of Black Hawk, chief of the Sauk tribe, which was a force to be reckoned with at the beginning of the nineteenth century, but eventually was slaughtered by the United States army, not far from present-day La Crosse.

The Carrimons felt it a privilege to have the opportunity to meet with the students. La Vern wanted to help give the class a true picture of the American Indian as he was and is. He wanted to change the movie and television versions of the First Americans as drunk, murderous, scalping men. According to Carrimon, much of the Indian culture has been lost "because of government and church schools where the children were not allowed to speak their own language." Carrimon told the *La Crosse Tribune,* among his comments of praise for Thea, "She's trying to get people to understand one another so that we can live in harmony."[15]

The class sponsored a celebration of Native American songs, dances, and poetry in an effort to share their exciting learnings about Indian life and literature with the entire Viterbo community. Grants from the Wisconsin Arts Council and the National Endowment of the Arts made the program possible. First Americans donned ceremonial dress and delighted the audience with their performances of a variety of dances.

Thea's foray into the world of First Americans was typical of everything she did to promote cross-cultural learning. Rather than just reading about a subject, she endeavored to shape the topic three-dimensionally: in memorable, dramatic form. She did all these things with sometimes almost superhuman insouciance, to the delight and sometimes astonishment of her friends. She continued in this style later when she returned to Mississippi.

Flush with triumphs in her teaching career each year at Viterbo, Thea grew more and more cognizant of the declining health of her aging parents. She, as an only child, felt she should move close to her parents and communicated her need to the Franciscan leadership. The Spring of 1978 would be her last at Viterbo.

In a display of her versatility and campus involvement during that last semester she would teach at Viterbo College, Sister Thea thrilled her many friends, students, colleagues, and fans by acting a major role in the April 27–30 production of *Member of the Wedding* by Carson McCullers. Reported the *Tribune*, "Sister Marie Leon La Croix, who directed the production, said, 'The Member of the Wedding concerns itself with adolescence and the strange bond between blacks and whites in the South. McCullers herself has described the play as "unconventional because it is not a literal kind of play. It is an inward play, and the conflicts are inward conflicts. The antagonist is not personified, but is a human condition of life: the sense of moral isolation." ' "[16]

Sister Thea played the part of Bernice Sadie Brown, the family's black cook who "mothers the motherless Frankie."[17] She excelled in her performance and received positive reviews. Having Sister Thea appear in a Viterbo dramatic production increased sales at the box office!

By the end of the semester, Thea had been informed of her new assignment to return to Canton after the summer session (1978) at Viterbo. Starting in the fall, she could be near her increasingly frail parents. The summer before that, though, was a flurry of activity. Speeches, trips, annual retreat, FSPA meetings, summer school teaching, concerts, applying for a new job in her home diocese of Jackson, Mississippi, packing, farewells — all were on the agenda. Thea ended her teaching years at Viterbo and in La Crosse with signature flourishes.

First stop that season was in Canton itself to speak on May 21 to the Holy Child Jesus High School graduating class. From her speech it is evident that Thea enjoyed the invitation to be commencement speaker that Sunday evening. There was no sign of whatever hurt she may have felt when she entered the church, with its front entrance facing away from the street. That was a legacy of the 1960s zoning laws, which forbade having public buildings for blacks opening to a white neighborhood. She spoke with conviction and pride.[18]

Back in Wisconsin, the La Crosse community remained keenly interested in Thea's activities, even the Mississippi high school commencement. In the *La Crosse Times Review* newspaper article, "Thea's Regional Exchange: A Convert Returns," by Debby Smith, we hear Thea tell how she experienced speaking at the Holy Child Jesus commencement. "The thing I really feel in coming back is that I know where a lot of these graduates are coming from," Thea told the reporter. "We have people in that class whose mothers, fathers, grandparents, even aunts and uncles and sisters and brothers have really made sacrifices to see them graduate. And I'm telling them that they've made it this far not just by their own effort. They've made it because other people have suffered — some with two or three jobs and in other ways." She spoke to the key of what would become her ministry back in Mississippi: She said she encouraged the thirteen graduates to evaluate what it really means to be successful: "As they make their steps forward, they have to reach back and help."

She also told the reporter something about Mississippi: "You must understand how much more it [graduation] means in a place like this than somewhere where it is just taken for granted that people will go to high school and graduate and automatically go to college." Education is the only way out, she told Smith. "You don't necessarily need a high school diploma or college degree, but you must know how to help yourself. Older black people worked very hard, but it didn't yield any proportionate results. Like capitalism: you have to have money to make money."[19]

After the jubilant commencement celebration, Thea made her way back to La Crosse to complete her Viterbo assignment. During Viterbo College summer session Thea taught a course in Shakespeare. Her class eagerly looked forward to the summer Shakespeare Festival tour to Stratford, Ontario, August 7 to 14. Excursions led by Sister Thea to

Canada or England to see Shakespearean plays were always on the top ten favorite college experience lists.

Thea appeared a bit nostalgic on this last of her Shakespeare tours for Viterbo. Wistfully she strolled through the Stratford gardens enjoying blossoming flowers and plants mentioned in the plays. With her entourage, she soaked in the Canadian productions for the festival: *As You Like It*, *The Merry Wives of Windsor*, and *The Winter's Tale*. She experienced a winter of her own, the end of her years teaching at her beloved college.

Finally after concerts, performances, community meetings, and "Theology in the 70s," an all-FSPA congregation assembly, Thea headed home to care for her aging parents and to pursue ministry in the South. With hoopla, celebrations, farewells, and sadness, yet some joyous anticipation for what lay ahead, she left college teaching at Viterbo to return home.

Part Five

Back to Canton

Chapter 16

SISTER TO THE WORLD

Some would say that the twelve years from 1978 to 1990, when Thea Bowman moved back to Mississippi and engaged in an ever-broader ministry of intercultural awareness, until cancer overtook her, were the most influential years of Sister Thea's life. They certainly were the years during which the world beyond her immediate ministry came to know her.

In this section of the book, themes will interplay in Thea's final, fruitful years. Much like a symphony, or perhaps, more appropriately, like a complex choral piece, her concerns with her native Mississippi, from life with her parents, to life at her home parish, to life in her home diocese, to life in Mississippi's intellectual community, to concerns about Africa, to concerns in her own Franciscan religious community and in the church at large — all of these themes and others reemerge and interplay during these years. Ultimately, her own theological, pastoral reflection on the meaning of suffering and dying over several years of degenerating cancer would be one of her final gifts.

But what drove Sister Thea back to Canton in 1978 were her parents, who needed her help. Care for ailing or aging parents, after all, is seen by the church as a sacred duty. When there are no siblings able to take on this duty, it is not uncommon for parents either to move close to where a religious sister is in ministry, or for the sister to be assigned to an area where she can provide the support that her parents need. In Thea's case, the latter was the right answer.

Thea's mother, Mary Esther, had been ill for many years, but now her father, Dr. Theon Bowman, was too frail to care for her. In a nutshell, then, as Thea later told interviewer Margaret Walker Alexander, "When my father became ill, I came back to Canton."[1]

Her home had been the happy place, a place where tired ones could rest. Her home had been for her a haven of love, nurturing, learning, stimulation, joy, and safety. Now it was her turn to give comfort to her parents in the full measure they had lavished on her during her growing-up years. Father Joseph Dyer, a local pastor, looking back on Thea's life, told an audience that Thea exemplified the Fourth Commandment, "Honor thy father and thy mother," with deeper devotion than most people he knew. From the fall of 1978 until their deaths at the end of 1984, she was lovingly present and assisted her parents according to their needs.

Thea, though, was coming home to the place where her ministry was born, and she needed to stay in active ministry. She came back to Mississippi, a cradle of African American culture, as a spokeswoman for what was emerging nationally as a black Catholic identity movement. The people in Mississippi whom she joined in ministry, led by Bishop Joseph Brunini and, later, Bishop William Houck, were, locally at least, civil rights pioneers.

Joseph Brunini had become the Roman Catholic bishop of all Mississippi in 1966, after serving in parishes and in the administration of the Diocese of Jackson-Natchez for close to thirty years. A native Mississippian, he knew that the Catholic Church, whose members, away from the Gulf Coast, were a scant minority, could serve as a mediating force in the civil rights conflict, a conflict fought most bitterly in Mississippi. He and his minority church played a sometimes important role in improving race relations in the South throughout the civil rights era.

Bishop William Houck, who served with and eventually replaced Brunini, after Brunini's retirement in 1984, recalls of his predecessor: "In those days when it was difficult even for some Catholics to accept this whole matter of integration in the schools, he took a strong stand. He integrated our schools, and he did take criticism for that from some of our own Catholic people, but he was a leader in the city and in the state."[2]

Houck recalls Brunini coming to the defense of blacks during the civil rights era, when burnings of black churches were not uncommon. "It was also at a time when we had the burning of the Jewish Temple here in Jackson." In 1969, in his Christmas homily, "he challenged the religious leaders to come together to put a stop to the religious violence," says Houck.[3] The result was an organization that exists to this day, the Mississippi Religious Leaders Conference.

"Everybody just loved Brunini," recalls Sister Antona Ebo, a hospital administrator who eventually, at Brunini's urging and Thea's invitation, came to work at the University of Mississippi Medical Center, in Jackson.

"He had that little chuckle about him," she says. "I really actually fell in love with the old guy because he reminded me of Bernanos's *The Diary of a Country Priest*. He was a man of multiethnic heritage: his father was Catholic; his mother was Jewish. I think that had a lot to do with his interest in civil rights and those kinds of things," says Ebo.

"You would just walk down the street and black, white, polka dot — and I know that they were not all Catholic because they don't have that many Catholics in Mississippi — but everybody spoke to him," recalls Ebo of her friend. "You know, it was almost like meeting a brother: 'Hi, Bishop, . . . So how are you doing?' 'Well, I'm doing pretty good,' and he had that little giggle. He was just a man of the people," she recalls.[4]

"I think it was Bishop Brunini's idea," says Bishop Houck, speaking of Thea, "that here was a wonderful black woman who was talented, who had her doctorate in English, a native daughter of Holy Child Jesus Parish. . . . Since she was going to be living here, encourage her to join the diocese staff and give her that responsibility of arranging awareness all about people and the cultural diversity in the Church."[5]

Thea admired Brunini's gifts and appreciated his backing. He whole-heartedly supported her plans to improve and foster communications between African American and white Catholics in the diocese and beyond. He joined her in inviting and insisting that African American Catholics be involved in decision making in diocesan agencies, parishes, and institutions. Here was a chance for his church, small as it was in most of Mississippi, to model racial cooperation. To take full advantage of this dynamic woman's presence back in Mississippi, upon her job-seeking visit to the diocesan offices, Bishop Brunini created, and offered to her, the position of Diocesan Consultant for Intercultural Awareness. Within days Thea outlined her vision and aims for the position. She continued as consultant, and later director, in this position, fashioned it in her own image, and soon received regional and then nationwide acclaim through it.

Conducting her unique brand of workshops, lecture-recitals, liturgy-celebrations, seminars, and short courses on intercultural awareness, she began a life that entailed traveling around the diocese and throughout the South. Thea's incandescent presence and the "true truth" message she expounded, an unvarnished, sometimes difficult truth, attracted ever-increasing venues; soon she was on national and international Catholic speaking circuits.

Her scholarly, professional stance is evident in the monthly reports she wrote, detailing for the bishop an account of activities, goals, strategies, and results. A memorandum, "Report of Progress on Inter-Racial and Inter-Cultural Awareness and Exchange," to Bishop Brunini, dated August 31, 1978, the first report prepared by Thea, is substantive and detailed.

She presented her mandate from the bishop: (1) to try to help improve inter-racial relations in the diocese; (2) to try to help the black schools in their self-help programs; and (3) possibly to undertake some activities designed to foster black vocations.

Thea documents the desire for meetings with various diocesan leaders, surely preparing for any questions that might come later from her expansive work across the diocese. Thea explained that her preferred working mode in her new ministry included building familiarity, working through areas of difficulty together, and working together in pursuit of common goals. She reports that she experienced her new colleagues, very few of whom were African American, as responsive, supportive, and eager to cooperate.

Then she articulated her vision for music, a rich part of her cultural tradition that did not find as much expression in the Catholic community as it did in Protestant assemblies: "In September I would like to try to establish a Diocesan Gospel Choir, (1) to sing at liturgies; (2) to promote appreciation of black life and culture; (3) to provide entertainment; (4) to serve as a bonding organization for blacks in the diocese.[6]

The bishop gave Thea a wide range to influence the entire diocese through her unique communication skills to learn about, appreciate, love, and proclaim the beauties, the power of black culture. This she did with deliberate joy and relish. As she had in her teaching in La Crosse, Canton, and Washington, D.C., she paid significant attention to a key educational principle: what youth learn early they carry throughout their lives.

Thea gives a listing of her numerous meetings in July and August with groups, leaders, and individuals focusing on black Catholics and their interactions with the Church in the diocese and the state of Mississippi, specifically in Canton, Clinton, Greenville, Jackson, and Lexington. These activities involved considerable driving to and fro. From Canton to Jackson she drove thirty miles, from Canton to Clinton forty miles, from Canton to Greenville seventy, from Canton to Lexington forty. Her travels pointed to distances she would later traverse from coast to coast and abroad while proclaiming Christianity's Good News. She met with Church staff scattered throughout the state: clergy, sisters, brothers, missionaries, school principals, parish administrators, parish councils, CYO (Catholic Youth Organization) leaders and groups. In addition to all the traveling and meetings, in her first days working at the diocese, she set up an office in the Amite Street chancery in Jackson, formulated a budget, purchased a car, and took part in a press conference on justice issues.[7]

Returning home in the evenings, she was exhilarated and tired. Frequently she attended or led events and meetings in the evenings and on weekends. She was on fire with the challenges her new position presented. She saw much work was needed to help bridge the gap of disparity between whites and blacks. She kept her FSPA sisters in Canton and her parents in the loop about her events. The sisters supported and accompanied Thea on trips when their schedules allowed and when invited. "She was very loyal to Bishop Brunini," recalls her friend Fernand Cheri. "I mean *extremely* loyal to him. I think it was because they shared some of the same values when it came to combating prejudice and racism in Mississippi."[8]

Designing ways to effect significant interracial exchange among black Catholics and white Catholic cohorts was a priority. She understood how to soften single-minded, provincial perspectives. She wove nuanced ideas, promoting equality into dialogues. She stressed looking at all aspects of interracial relations: She emphasized our common humanity, that everyone has human dreams, hopes, feelings, thoughts, goals. These insights were what made her communication successful.

Longtime friend and associate Sister Jamie Phelps notes that Thea dispelled people's negative prejudgments simply by being herself. Thea could transcend racism, recalls Phelps: "I would imagine that Thea's spirit of joy and generosity would dispel most negative expectations of a black girl, a black woman. I think that's what she did." Just to get to know Thea, was to love Thea, she adds.[9]

Thea's friend and coworker in Mississippi, Sister Antona Ebo, explains that it was not always smooth and seamless: "Some people really didn't know Thea personally but they knew of Thea — and some folks didn't really care that much for Thea." Thea came on strong, Ebo explains, and was seen by some as "too forward."[10]

But there was more than all of that. She brought an educator's sense of program and curriculum to her work. In the beginning, she planned a group process with Holy Savior parish, Clinton, Mississippi. The efficacy of her plan was valued and soon networked all over the diocese. The process first involved self-study; examining one's attitudes, deepening one's understanding of minority groups (which, in much of Mississippi, were actually the majority); developing appreciation of one's heritage, values, problems, contributions.

Then there was outreach to the various racial groups: attempting to promote understanding and exchange within the white community; attempting to reconcile and unite; as well as reaching out within the black community, working through black churches, Catholic and non-Catholic.

There was a sharing of pulpits, choirs; planning joint activities for children, adults, seniors; worship services; groups based on common interests (poetry, art, theology, cooking); sharing church bulletins; extending special personal invitations through churches to social events and other public activities; opening formal dialogue for interested persons. At the close of her consultation were procedures to keep the work ongoing: set up a time line; assign definite responsibilities to definite people — in short, set up a system of accountability and evaluation.

Finally, her signature style was to sing Negro Spirituals, and, if possible, include blacks from the local areas in liturgies of the local white Catholic parishes. It was new territory to bring different racial groups together in worship.

Her deep musical knowledge and profound performance skill were integral to her ministry, and, to a point, she played to her audience, as all good performers do. She had inserted Gospel music into her presentations early in her teaching career, and had, in Wisconsin, often invited local musicians and singers to perform with her. Now she continued that practice. As the scope of her ministry later expanded, conference planners all over the United States were amazed at her ability to materialize back-up musicians and singing groups seemingly out of thin air almost anywhere she was invited for presentations.

She used the accessible, entertaining quality of her performance to win her audience over. She had learned that in her bones from her worship experiences as a child and from her studies of rhetoric. Her presence was so powerful, the quality of her music so strong, that she won people over. But there were those on the sidelines — albeit in the minority — who were a bit uneasy. "There were some things that I saw Thea do personally that I didn't care for," says Sister Antona, "but I was a northerner. I was one of those damned Yankees! When she entertained in groups of white people she put on the bandana and went to a more [pause] — at times, I felt that I was sitting through a minstrel show, and I really didn't like it."[11]

Thea, to her pleasure, though, was welcomed everywhere she appeared. She was a woman of the theater and used its methods to her advantage. Word about her planned innovative multicultural projects and inspiring presentations spread. The tall, attractive, talented Franciscan with the down-home flavor was gratified. A part of her, not surprisingly, fed on the appreciation of her audience. She dove into her new work with gusto.

During that first summer of 1978, after a brief Labor Day holiday respite, Thea moved quickly into the thick of things. During September her work multiplied, and she fell, once again, into a tumultuous pattern that was familiar to those who had worked with her in Wisconsin. It would remain so.

Thea's personal datebook contained even more engagements. It included house meetings with the sisters at the convent, medical appointments for her parents, conference calls, etc. Calendar entries listed below from her September 30, 1978, report to Bishop Brunini indicate intense activity. Meetings often started at eight or nine in the morning; her weekends were often booked; there were frequent evening meetings.

September 30, 1978
Memorandum
"Report of progress on Inter-cultural Awareness Efforts"

September 1   Jackson, 2 planning meetings
September 5   Vicksburg, two liturgies at St. Aloysius School, assembly program, poetry readings in English classes, faculty meeting, recommendations to administrators
September 6   Diocesan Office, debriefing, parish council preparations
September 8   Jackson, Meeting with Bishop, separate meetings with two priests, one sister
September 9   Jackson, Diocesan Sisters Council meeting, prep for multiethnic awareness day for council
September 11   Jackson, Vocation Committee meeting
September 14   Diocesan Office, staff meeting, prep for day at Holy Savior Parish, Clinton
September 15   Canton, Meeting to implement Convention resolutions

September 16   Jackson, Diocesan Pastoral Council, CYO Pro-Life
              workshop
September 17   CYO Pro-Life workshop
September 18   Greenville, conduct workshop on multicultural
              pluralism
September 19   Jackson, conduct workshop on multicultural
              pluralism, liturgy music practice
September 20   Jackson, workshop prep, lunch and meeting with
              bishop and others, evening lecture-recital Holy
              Ghost PTA
September 21   Jackson, luncheon meeting, music rehearsal with
              Canton children
September 22   Canton, music rehearsal for Clinton parish
September 23   Jackson, sing at REACH meeting at St. Richard's,
              meetings with deacon candidates, discussed criteria
              and evaluations of deacon program
September 24   Clinton liturgies with children's choir performing
September 25   Renewal Center meetings with Deans for
              Convention follow-up
September 26   Columbus, conduct multicultural pluralism
              workshop
September 29   Jackson, meetings and engagement prep
September 30   Renewal Center, CYO meeting[12]

On September 5, she visited St. Aloysius School (students: 15 black; 265 white) in Vicksburg where she spoke on "Black Music and the Black Man's Approach to God" in an assembly program. She led hymns during two school liturgical celebrations there. Making the most of the occasion, she did poetry readings in English classes and held discussions with the students. In discussions, parents and school personnel expressed concern about the paucity of black students at the school. But, in truth, few black families could afford to send their children to a Catholic school. Sister Thea directed the Gospel choir of fourth-graders from Holy Child Jesus School in Canton at the Mass on September 24 at Holy Savior Parish in Clinton. The choir was invited to sing at the Masses to enable the Clinton parishioners to experience a cultural expression of religious music different from the type to which they were accustomed. To encourage fellowship, with the choir and the parish, a covered-dish dinner followed the Mass.

Thea plunged heart, mind, and spirit, as usual, into everything she did. Most of her professional time she was listening, teaching, encouraging, helping to heal with her spirit-filled presence. She set up dates for a Gospel music liturgy at Mound Bayou, a hundred miles to the north, for December 17. She agreed to do a lecture and recital on "Black Folk Song and Black Approach to God" for the Ladies Auxiliary Reflection Day in Jackson for November 26. She sponsored and planned a colorful multi-ethnic awareness day for the religious sisters ministering in the diocese at Holy Child Jesus Mission, in Canton, on December 2. She planned a workshop with Christ the King faculty in Jackson.[13]

Her extensive academic and professional background was tapped. At a regional or diocesan level, she helped formulate new criteria for evaluation of deacons prior to ordination. She conducted a poetry reading/discussion on pro-life themes including abortion, alienation, drugs, prejudices, and war. Bishop Brunini asked her to take out memberships in Opera South and the Mississippi Arts Commission. She met with Tony Hewitt of the commission on September 21. The bishop also encouraged her to attend the University of Southern Mississippi "Sense of Place" symposium October 5–6 in Hattiesburg. She finalized plans to attend the Conference on Ministries in Southern Black Rural Parishes in Bay St. Louis, two hundred miles south, on the Gulf Coast, October 16–19.[14]

She was fearless in critiquing policies and programs when asked. Her evaluations, wisdom, and input were sought out. Her detailed, constructive evaluation of the 1978 interdiocesan conference on ministries in black rural parishes in dioceses in Louisiana, Mississippi, and Alabama is one such example of how tactfully she could deliver a hard message.

Filled with appreciation for the workshop idea, she nevertheless explained that the publicity did not reflect what participants experienced. "I feel that the results of the workshop were in no wise proportionate to the outlay of money, time, effort, and energy expended by the national offices, the staff, and the participants," she wrote. "Because I realize the pressing needs of rural black parishes, because I realize that blacks and whites in leadership in rural black parishes need help to establish effective programs of self-help, because I appreciate the importance and the dedication of the organizations and the persons who sponsored this workshop, I dare respectfully to submit the following observations and suggestions."

Then she went on to show how the planners could have been more effective. Advance publicity had been unclear, therefore attendees came with widely differing expectations. Attendees were, predictably, frustrated. The frustration, though, had been avoidable. Thea expressed confidence that directors came with skills to "conduct a workshop on the process of leadership within the parishes: how to create effective visions, strategies, and structures of leadership within the parish." Most of the people attending, however, already showed those general skills; they wanted help with specific needs. The National Office of Black Catholics published a vision for rural black parishes that the group had already embraced and had already begun to implement.

Then came the hardest message: Thea noted that some attendees were uneasy with an all-white staff who lacked ministry experience in rural black parishes. Four of the nine participants departed after the second day because the workshop did not meet their expressed expectations or needs. Others who stayed until the workshop ended — prematurely — shared that frustration. The event would have been more satisfactory, suggested Thea, had the workshop facilitators moved quickly from creating a vision to developing strategies to implement goals.

In her gentle, yet firm style, Thea proffered suggestions. This instructive tactic Thea learned early and had honed throughout her college and graduate study years. She had displayed it in classes, FSPA meetings, with her English Department colleagues, and with her friends. When an occasion called for it, she could be maddeningly thorough. She used her critiquing skill with efficacy. By her careful attention students and clients developed and learned more.

Among a list of particular suggestions she suggested more input for future planning: "The difference between input and agenda seemed to imply that we do not know our own needs, that we needed outsiders to decide what and how we should think about ourselves and our situation." Such input would allow the conference to meet some of the special needs of rural black and others from the "grassroots."[15]

One thing that Thea did not challenge overtly was the presence of segregated Catholic parishes in Mississippi communities: in many places there were, and are, historically black parishes and historically white parishes. Sister Antona recalls, "There were times when, after she developed her cancer, I drove her to a couple of different places in Indianola, Mississippi. The Immaculate Conception was practically a brand new church for white people and then St. Benedict the Moor (or 'the black') was for black folks." The black church was a converted house, with worship space in the living room and bedrooms, etc., being used as various classrooms and gathering rooms. "I had said to her several times, 'Thea, something really has to be done about this. I just don't agree with this separation.' Thea would just remain very quiet. It was like Thea knew her call and she really would not go and let me mess around with what she was called to do."[16]

In those early years, word soon got around that Sister Thea Bowman was not only compassionate, she also expected excellence. These traits won her legions of supportive friends and colleagues.

Her musical reach continued to be a key to her success. In November, at Grambling State University, a historically black institution in Louisiana, she told the students not to forget their cultural roots. According to the write-up in the student newspaper, "Thea maintained that if we pay serious attention to the music of the black Church, we will understand black cultural, psychological, and religious history. From their music blacks derive strength for the present and the future." Thea told the crowd, "The old slave songs or spirituals were some of the earliest and most anguished cries of black people for freedom. They fanned the flame of hope and courage. Whether you are a Christian, or an agnostic, or an atheist, if you are a black American, those old songs are part of your roots." True to her style, she broke into song from time to time as she talked.

She knew from her studies and her intuition the physiological and psychological effects that music itself has on the human person. She knew the effect music of the old black church has had on black people through the ages. "Those black spirituals are my roots. Those songs helped my people to survive. They let them express themselves, their joys, their pain, their grief, their longing, their frustrations, their love of God, and their love of each other."[17]

She would move from that type of gathering to something, a few weeks later, as different as a Canon Law Conference, attended by chancery and tribunal officials from the province of New Orleans. Sister Thea directed a "Cultural Awareness" celebration at the conference.

Still only a few months on the job, for the Sunday Mass at Jackson's Cathedral of St. Peter the Apostle on November 29 she coordinated a Gospel music liturgy, directed and soloed with the choirs of grade- and high school students from Immaculate Conception School, Clarksdale, and Holy Child Jesus School, Canton. She helped choreograph an interpretative dance performed during the offertory procession. The liturgy concluded with the choir singing a Negro Spiritual as they moved down the center aisle. "Most dioceses in the South have large black populations," Sister Thea said. "The Gospel-music liturgy was added to the Canon Law conference in an effort to show how the church speaks to other cultures."[18]

Dozens of engagements — public events and other duties — filled the final months of that first year. Travels around the South were punctuated by trips to La Crosse, where Sister Thea served two terms on the FSPA Southern Province Advisory Board (1974 to 1982). This board met frequently, sometimes monthly, sometimes every six weeks.

Bishop Houck remembers Thea's work in the parishes during those years with gratitude: "When I arrived she was her wonderful self, dynamic and lovable . . . and developing as much as we could an awareness of different cultures within the Church, particularly in Mississippi." He remembers her as "tall and stately" and "attractive" and especially focuses on Thea challenging constantly "her own black people to be aware of how good they were and what they can do, and particularly what it meant to them to be faithful to their Catholic faith, in terms of intercultural awareness." That was not limited to black-white relations either, he adds: "We were beginning in those days to see not only the Vietnamese coming in, but also the Hispanic immigration."[19]

In looking back on Thea's early years at home (Houck had come to Jackson as an auxiliary bishop in the late 1970s), he acknowledges the situation that Mississippians were in, coming out of the civil rights movement. "She and I worked together several times, trying to get together pastors of parishes that had been established and were still operating as what I call 'historically black parishes.' " Those black parishes were segregated from nearby white parishes. "She was very challenging to priests," recalls the bishop. The goal: "to get them to know one another better and to see themselves as a Catholic community in that town." Years later, as her fame grew, recalls Houck, "many times I tried to encourage parishes — white parishes especially — to invite her to come in and speak and to share her story."[20]

In addition to all the diocesan activity, Thea closely monitored her aging parents, especially her fragile mother. After all, she was a doctor's daughter. When she could, she drove Mrs. Bowman to the doctor's office in Jackson. On December 29, 1978, she celebrated birthday forty-one.

Chapter 17

BEYOND MISSISSIPPI

After the first heady few months, anyone could see that Sister Thea the dynamo would continue at an intense pace. She was a woman on a mission, and it soon became clear that Mississippi wouldn't contain her as an adult any more than it had when she was a teen. Besides coordinating, participating, rehearsing with singers, and performing in many events, Thea's schedule shows ongoing prepping for future engagements throughout Mississippi and the southern region and increasing travel to national conferences and meetings. She was in demand in cities across the United States, East to West, and in Hawaii, in Canada, in the Caribbean Islands, and eventually even in Africa.

Thea was riding the wave of reform that was rippling through American society via the social movements that followed the civil rights movement, and the wave of reform that was changing the Catholic Church worldwide following the Second Vatican Council. At once there was a movement for black identity in American culture and recognition in the Roman Catholic Church of cultural identity beyond Europe, a movement, within the church at least, that is still unfolding in the twenty-first century.

Part of this movement had been the founding of the black priests,' sisters' and brothers' groups (see chapter 12). By 1979 it was time for the three groups to come South. The invitation came during the 1980 convention in Chicago. The groups were invited by Bishops Joseph Brunini and William Houck to hold one of their conventions in Jackson, Mississippi. Sister Thea served as one of the coordinators for the conference, which finally was held August 7 to 13, 1983.

The local Catholic newspaper depended upon Thea to help its readers understand the significance of the conference coming to Mississippi. Said Thea, "One reason we are meeting in Jackson is because so many of us have roots in the South." She also mentioned "the concerns and gifts" of the area, keeping her practice always to accent the positive, while still being present to the more challenging issues. The conference included an invitation to local black Catholics to "get to know the black clergy, sisters and brothers better."[1]

The conference was a soulful success. Delegates got a firsthand look at Mississippi heritage and hospitality. Mississippi Governor William Winter greeted them when they visited the Old Capitol Museum. Conducted by executive director of the Mississippi NAACP, Robert Walker, the conference participants toured the governor's mansion, the Mississippi Museum of Art, Tougaloo College and Farish Street Historical District, the unofficial center of black culture in Mississippi's capital. It was there that economically successful blacks lived before fanning out to other areas after the end of legal segregation. A banquet at Jackson State University was followed by a public Mass celebrated at Smith Park on Thursday evening.

Cullen Clark wrote for the August 6, 1983, *Clarion-Ledger:*

A "family reunion" of sorts gets underway Sunday when almost two-hundred and fifty Catholic priests, nuns, brothers and seminarians begin gathering in Jackson. The Most Rev. William Houck, auxiliary bishop of the diocese, said hosting the conference symbolizes how all Christians are called to work together. "I think it will raise the consciousness of people in the Jackson diocese about the number of black people involved in the ministry of the church." Sister Bowman compares the annual conference to "a family meeting where everyone is free to openly discuss issues and problems....I always look forward to these conferences. They are renewing for me. It's like a family reunion."[2]

Speaking twenty-five years later, Franciscan Father Fernand Cheri remembers the 1983 conference as "one of the best ones we've had." He was on the planning team for that year. "I got to see a side of her as she spoke passionately about the problems of racism that she faced growing up in Canton, Mississippi, and working at Holy Child School" as well as dealing with racist attitudes among some in her own community and among church people in the Canton area, he says. "We planned that conference with the sense that she was going to showcase black religious for Mississippi." And that's pretty much what they pulled off. "She gave us a taste of the Diocese of Jackson with all its gifts." Unforgettable to him was meeting Margaret Walker in person: "I mean this was an introduction to a black poet, a black writer as well as to African American spirituality.... It was just beautiful — just to see everybody's spirit and openness come together and the beauty of the conference was just wonderful."[3]

Building awareness of the widespread roles of black Catholics in ministry was a continuing theme of Thea's ministry. During the civil rights movement and the years around the Voting Rights Act, Catholic leaders throughout the United States had established black Catholic ministry offices in local dioceses. Thea was called upon by her growing list of friends in the black clergy and black sister groups to speak at events in their dioceses, on their campuses, in their parishes throughout the United States. When she came, she assisted, cajoled, and promoted black culture, including as part of her effort her unforgettable Gospel singing. When she spoke to mainly all-white Catholic groups about welcoming other styles and cultures into Catholic circles, she would often say, "I tried your way [of worship] for thirty-some years; now you, try mine!"[4]

Her audiences grew. A national Catholic Youth Organization convention of thirty-five hundred young Catholics and their leaders, which Thea had first addressed in 1979, became an annual engagement for Thea. Other engagements had similar results: repeat invitations and a loyal base of followers.

Her love of southern literature and her recognized Faulkner scholarship drew her back to Oxford, Mississippi, 150 miles north of her home, where earlier she had toured with Viterbo students. In the campus church in Oxford, she was keynote speaker for Black Awareness Week in February 1980 for the university and Oxford communities. Soon she was invited to speak at the annual Faulkner conferences at the University of Mississippi, another of the places where she would make a lasting mark (see chapter 24). The camaraderie with Faulkner scholars from all over the country renewed Thea's spirit. At other conferences, in different venues, she was a memorable presence. At the "Mission in the 80s" assembly, sponsored in July 1980, by the Franciscan Sisters of Perpetual Adoration in La Crosse, she was a Gospel proclaimer at the liturgy. Invited to the assembly were laity, priests, and bishops from areas where the FSPA ministered. Keynote presenters had missionary experiences around the world.

The "go where we have never been before" theme propelled Thea as she promoted integration among diverse cultures. She encouraged people of all colors to "walk together, talk together, pray together, sing together, suffer together, laugh together," to embrace differences. She taught people they would find they are more alike than different through those acts.

She continued to combine her speaking and singing talents, charming audiences with experiences of cultures different from theirs — especially if the audience was mostly non–African American. She liked to recount the story about a young Puerto Rican woman who lived for some time with a community of sisters in Mississippi. She ate their food for four weeks, but the fifth week, when she prepared some Puerto Rican cuisine, the sisters complained about its strangeness. Then Thea asked, "When do I stand against oppression in my world? After all, that is the only world I can change."[5]

As she matured in the intercultural awareness consultant role, she insisted that black Catholics enrich the church with their unique gift of black culture. Black spirituality was a glory that she taught skillfully. What are its unique gifts? Thea taught that the four major characteristics of African spirituality — holistic, communitarian, contemplative, Eucharistic — could enhance Catholic worship services, could give them soul and vitality.

Thea, along with Bishop Brunini and Bishop Houck, convened a meeting in Jackson of the new Organization of Black Catholics, following the U.S. bishops' conference goal to establish offices for ministry to black Catholics in each diocese. Thea had promoted this idea in Jackson, and took part eagerly in initial stages of its development. Nine parishes sent representatives to the steering committee meeting held at Holy Child Jesus Parish, Canton, on July 12, 1980.

The new black Catholic organization had these goals: to work with the black community to identify needs of the black Catholics and the larger black community; to serve as an advisory body to the diocese; to help sensitize blacks and those serving the black community regarding the needs of blacks and needs of the whole human family; to ensure involvement of blacks in the decision-making process of the diocese; to share resources and to ensure mutual support.

Planners included a picnic and liturgy (sponsored by the black Catholic fraternal group Knights of St. Peter Claver) to take place later in the summer. Officers were elected and, with the bishops, they made plans to attend the first National Office of Black Catholics Conference in Chicago, August 6–9. A liturgy workshop was scheduled for November in Greenville.[6]

Then there was the Institute for Black Catholic Studies (IBCS), a new program at Xavier University of Louisiana, a historically black university founded in 1915 by Katharine Drexel (canonized by Pope John Paul II in 2000). The institute, whose pilot program began in 1980, would grow into the major center of the black Catholic movement in the United States. An article in the *San Francisco Monitor* (a Catholic newspaper), reported on the beginnings of the IBCS idea, to make a permanent institution of what had, up to that time, been occasional college courses on black Catholicism: "There is no place in this country specifically geared to the Black Catholic clergy, the Black community and their needs," the paper quoted institute founders Father Joseph R. Nearon, SSS (Congregation of the Blessed Sacrament) of Cleveland; Father Thaddeus Posey, OFM Cap (Order of Friars Minor, Capuchin), of Kansas City; and Sister Toinette Eugene, PBVM (Presentation of the Blessed Virgin Mary), of San Francisco.

These founding members outlined their hopes for the institute, which would include graduate-level classes and an archival research center. The need was a for a place that would specialize in "the ways, methods, and means for reaching black Catholics," Sister Eugene told the paper.[7]

Sister Thea kept her eye on and heart in the developing institute from its beginning. It was she who was instrumental in encouraging the Black Catholic Symposiums, predecessor to the IBCS, according to Franciscan Father Fernand Cheri.[8] She had supported the founding of IBCS with Joseph Nearon, who, in the years before his sudden death in 1984, insisted on the "true truth," that is, the deepest truth, without polish. Then she was invited to serve as a charter faculty member, says Cheri,[9] a position she joyfully held from 1980 to 1988. Her specialty was training clergy, sisters, and brothers who ministered in black parishes and black communities in liturgical worship and in preaching. She also taught a popular course on the spirituality of black literature with Jesuit Father Joseph A. Brown. Brown recounted later how he first met Thea:

[At a reception for a gathering of the National Black Catholic Administrators], while I had been enthusiastically renewing old acquaintances with colleagues and friends, I noticed the arrival of a strange looking woman who seemed to be navigating her progress along the fringe of the gathering. A tall, dark-skinned person, she was dressed for maximum warmth in the Chicago-area November cold. A long coat, a head-wrap, gloves and boots gave her the appearance of someone who took my grandmother's admonition seriously: "In the winter, if you have to choose between being pretty and being warm, choose warm." This tall stranger was carrying two shopping bags and had an intense gaze that seemed more disturbing than inviting.

I was soon called back from the peripheral notice that I had given to her, and my friends and I made our way to the chapel. Just as the crowd fell into that universal quieting down that occurs at the beginning of every church service I have ever attended, a loud and raw moaning began in the back of the chapel. I could not help but turn to see what was erupting at that solemn moment. The same tall, dark-skinned woman who had disconcerted me at the reception was sitting in the last row of the congregants, rocking from side to side and uttering a truly unsettling vocalise. I asked one of my friends, "Who is that woman? She's dressed like a bag lady off the streets, and she looks half crazy to me."

The response given me by Father J-Glenn Murray was a look of disbelief and shock. "Do you mean you don't know who she is?" "No. I've never seen her before in my life." "That's Sister Thea Bowman," J-Glenn told me. He went on, whispering, "I thought everybody in the world knew Thea by now. People either love her or loathe her," he said. "I decided it was altogether easier to love her. So I do."[10]

At that first meeting, both Joseph and Thea were on the program for the conference of the National Association of Black Catholic Administrators in Techny, Illinois, in 1986. He was the keynote speaker; she led the prayer services — albeit in a way that was not typical, at the time, for such gatherings! The following spring, she invited him to come to the Institute for Black Catholic Studies and teach with her. "That really began our collaboration and friendship," he recalls.[11] It was one that included conducting workshops together occasionally, and teaching summer courses at the institute.

In spite of her commanding dramatic presence, Brown says he regrets that Thea was not a writer. Pioneering black theologian Cyprian Davis, OSB, he recalls, commented that, according to Brown, "people don't pay attention to how smart she was. When they do talk about how smart she was they move back into the Renaissance literature, PhD and all that." But that's not the point, says Brown. "The point is that she came to the

Catholic Church with a fully formed spirituality, prayer, and theology." You start with the spirituals, full tradition, and community speech, "and you build your theology off of that." That's how she could be so radically honest, he says. "She never gave up her roots in order to fit in. So she never had to defend or explain herself. She just was."

This is in the midst of European dominance, he decries, with black theologians applying European insights to black theology. "Her teaching and her entire way of preaching was a form of black theology that you don't often see in the Catholic Church," this Jesuit observes. She had an "incredibly strong and organic" understanding of black theology.

What stood out most about her, Brown says, is that, first, "Thea Bowman told the truth in all circumstances," and, second, "that her humility was her strongest attribute, because as a humble person she really didn't show a lot of fear." She could face whatever was in front of her, he says. "Some people would call that courage or prophetic behavior but I call it humility, in the sense that she was completely grounded in who she was." And she didn't make airs about it, he adds: "She did it as a person who simply had the truth to say and that she was going to be responsible to the truth." [12]

At the beginning of the 1980s Thea's speaking, singing, and teaching ministry beyond Jackson and Madison County continued to grow. San Francisco, Houston, Oxford (Mississippi), Minneapolis, San Francisco again, La Crosse, Cleveland, Chicago, Louisville — she spoke at workshops in all of these cities during the first 10 months of 1980, in addition to her duties in the Diocese of Jackson. Her dynamic, scholarly, spell-binding, provocative, infectious, challenging presentations made her attractive for invitations from everywhere.

Yet, along the way, talented as she was, she was no prima donna. She made friends as she went, and reached out to all manner of people. Maryknoll Sister Norma Angel recalls her shared friendship among herself, Thea, and Sister Julian Griffin, all three African American Catholic sisters. Thea had drawn all three together as a kind of mutual support in their cultural diversity work. "I want you to meet another sister who can be a support to you," Thea told Norma. "There was a place of struggle for me, coming to the States [from Latin America], and whatever assumptions people had about who people were who were in this package being black skinned," says Norma. "So there was just this comfortable hominess, you know really being in a place where I didn't feel at home." Both Thea and Julian became like "big sisters" to Norma, she recalls.[13]

These close personal friendships were a key to Thea's ongoing work. There were a handful of close, personal friends over the years, and certainly a long list of acquaintances who, as one person said, claimed her as a "best friend." Thea was able to communicate a sense of personal closeness to many people. Those who could truly count her as a personal friend thought of her as a "soul sister, in every sense of the word," says Sister Francesca Thompson, who clearly was one of them.[14]

Addie Lorraine Walker, at the time of this writing Dallas provincial leader of the School Sisters of Notre Dame, describes Thea as a "soul mate." She often was mistaken either for Thea or for her nonexistent birth sister, since they shared a similar style of ministry, were look-alikes, and eventually were best friends. Common friend John Ford, ST, would tell Addie, "When you meet her, you'll know her from the inside out . . . when you meet her you are going to meet yourself," recalls Addie. When they finally met, staying at the same residence hall during a 1980 conference, recalls Addie, "It was really kind of frightening . . . and I think it was kind of scary for her, too, initially." Eventually, she says, we "realized that we were sisters."

Both from the Deep South, they shared much in common. "Like Thea," she says, I "grew up in the black community with the old folks teaching us the songs . . . so I learned all the songs all the way through the Bible. She was the only other Catholic person I knew who did that." Both, as adult Catholic Sisters (though in different religious communities) taught Sunday school, vacation Bible school, using the body, song, and so on: "It was a modality for teaching and looked at black ways of living and black ways of teaching, and black ways of praying and there's the Gospel and song as a continuum of the expression of this spirit embodied in black people, the spirit of God, in the body of black people."[15]

Friendships with Addie, Francesca, and a handful of other women and men would feed Thea's spirit as her ministry unfolded.

Chapter 18

LET FREEDOM RING

Invitations from near and far, from both within and outside of Mississippi poured into the diocesan office and Holy Child Jesus Convent. Sister Thea's extraordinary speaking and presentation skills captivated audiences. People in her workshops and seminars acclaimed her message and mission. As she sang, again and again, "This little light of mine, I'm gonna' let it shine," her little light could not be hidden under any basket.

In November 1983 the Congressional bill to honor the memory and martyrdom of Dr. Martin Luther King Jr. was signed into law by President Ronald Reagan. Fifteen years after the assassination of King, the United States government, prodded by civil rights leaders, supported by a grassroots campaign of people who had struggled for years, institutionalized King's memory. The civil rights movement and its leader would be always remembered for fighting — even to death — to make equally available to all citizens the rights promised in the Declaration of Independence.

An early proponent of Dr. King's message, Sister Thea helped promote King's legacy. In January 1983 she traveled to Selma, Alabama, with her close friend Sister Antona Ebo. In 1983 Sister Antona was ministering as chaplain at the University of Mississippi Medical Center in Jackson and worked closely with Thea in the early organizing years of the National Black Sisters Conference, as discussed earlier, in chapter 12. Sister Antona had participated in the historic 1965 Selma marches, a civil rights protest story told in the 2007 public television documentary, "Sisters of Selma."

Flying from St. Louis to Alabama with two planeloads of fifty-four sisters, priests, ministers, and rabbis, Sister Antona was the only black religious sister in the group. "I was frightened. I did not know then that the whole world would be watching," she said.[1] An early attempt to stage a civil rights march from Selma to Montgomery, fifty miles to the east, had been repressed by a brutal horse-mounted racist attack by local law enforcement. Antona had been part of one of many attempts to march after that "Bloody Sunday," which, due to the national publicity garnered by the rapid involvement of supporters like Sister Antona, finally resulted in presidentially directed federal protection for a march several weeks later. The night they returned from Alabama, in the midst of those preliminary march attempts, religious sisters from the group were guests on the fifty-thousand-watt KMOX St. Louis talk radio. Word of the courageous protest was broadcast throughout the South and Midwest.

The "Selma marchers," suffering at the hands of legally sanctioned racists, and their eventual successful march, led by Dr. King and protected by President Lyndon Johnson, became one of the lasting symbols of the civil rights movement.

Now, all these years later, Sister Thea was invited to offer the keynote speech at the Martin Luther King celebration at the Queen of Peace Catholic Church, with her friend Sister Antona close by. The *Selma Times Journal*, on January 16, 1983, published an account of Thea and Antona's time in Selma. Jean Martin wrote,

> In her work, Sister Thea promotes activities "to help people to a better understanding and appreciation of their own heritage, the values and ways of thinking that made them who they are. With this understanding, a greater willingness to appreciate the cultures of other people is created. I try to help the ethnic groups understand each other better and work together more easily." Using cultural sharing as a basic approach, the tall nun who moves like the dancer she is — "a folk dancer," she disclaims, "not a professional" — works with schools, children, colleges, and universities. And she takes as her most useful tool, her own understanding "as a black person, of my history and heritage, the way my people saw life and celebrated it to share its treasures": the art, the music, the food, the dance, the song. "I try to get people of all cultures together to share their giftedness."[2]

The writer went on to describe Thea's talk about Dr. King: "She talked about the kind of person Dr. King was, the kind of things he did, particularly in Selma. She asked them to remember his dream of freedom and liberty for all people, his nonviolent approach to solve conflict and effect change, and his valuing spirituality over material things."

Thea also talked to her Selma audience about King's radical simplicity as he matured, "the need for everyone to work together to ensure dignity and equality of all people," practical things we overlooked such as the opportunity to work and earn a living, the injustice of people wasting food when people are hungry. She then, reported Martin, challenged her audience with a question to everyone listening: "What am I doing in order to bring freedom to the reality where I live, to help somebody create the world that is really an American dream?" It was a challenge against apathy.[3]

This talk of Thea's was in a long line of talks she had given, each year, since the 1968 assassination of Dr. King, and would continue to give. Sometimes she found it odd that white friends did not realize his importance to the black community. For King's birthday commemoration in 1984 she spoke in Indianola, Mississippi. In 1986 she led a rousing King celebration at the University of Wisconsin–La Crosse. The final time she was keynote speaker for a Martin Luther King celebration was in 1988 in Milwaukee. She captivated the Wisconsin city with her inspiring account of King's remarkable leadership in the civil rights movement. That occasion, due to cancer's recurrence, was the last time she was able to stand during a presentation.

Antona bemoans the fact that Thea's work in Mississippi in the early 1980s increasingly took a back seat to her out-of-state engagements. During that time, Antona recalls telling Thea, "Why don't we get at least the parish councils of the various black Catholic churches in the Jackson and Canton area to organize a workshop on what our black bishops say about what we have seen and heard." (She is referring to the 1984 call for evangelization from the ten black U.S. bishops of that time, issued as a document called *What We Have Seen and Heard*.) "We managed to pull that off." They invited Father John Ford, a friend and leading black Catholic priest, to speak.

Antona's next project, she says, was to get Thea, in her role as director of intercultural ministry, to get out to the parishes and publicize her work, that is, "tell people that we are around." The two black sisters were conducting programs together. "My problem," recalls Antona, "was getting the parish councils of the predominately black parishes to come together. Their problem was they didn't want to be called black and they could not understand why they had to come together as black people." It was the persistent problem of racially divided communities of worship.[4]

Besides working and speaking in Mississippi in those early 1980s, during February and March 1983, Sister Thea traveled to Iowa, Texas,

Washington, and Wisconsin. The trip to Wisconsin to the city of Stevens Point was memorable, as it had been the site of her sanatorium stay and many visits in later years as a Viterbo professor. Now she was invited back to receive a newly created La Crosse Diocesan Justice and Peace Award.

At that time, in the 1980s, much of the justice-consciousness of the U.S. Church had turned toward Latin America. True to her universal, Catholic vision, Thea could see the need afar as much as she could the need in her own back yard. She designated the $1,000 award for an orphanage in Zaragoza, El Salvador. "The village is the home of some 2000 children who have been orphaned by the armed violence in El Salvador," Sister Thea said, according to a newspaper account. She then went on to explain the connection between the orphanage and the recently murdered missioners in El Salvador. The Diocese of Cleveland sponsored both the orphanage and two of the martyrs, Sister Dorothy Kazel and layworker Jean Donovan.[5]

The year 1983 was memorable also because it was Thea's twenty-fifth anniversary as a professed sister, still the only black member of the Franciscan Sisters of Perpetual Adoration. In June Thea returned to La Crosse to celebrate with her profession class. The daylong reunion and celebration was a joyous event, although Thea's parents, by then, were too frail to attend. A similar day of festivities happened back in Canton some weeks after Thea's return. In La Crosse, she had worn a black suit and black blouse; here, at home, Thea donned African attire.

It was a high celebration. Music including, "My Faith Looks Up to Thee," "We Have Come into His House," "I Surrender All," and "O Make a Joyful Noise," was by the congregation. Ms. Girtie Saddler and Sister Patricia Haley, SCN, did the readings, Rev. Joseph Nearon, SSS, proclaimed the Gospel; Rev. Fernand J. Cheri, OFM, delivered the homily.

Five years later, living precariously with cancer, Thea spoke in detail to interviewer Margaret Walker Alexander about some of the themes of gratitude she had begun to name at her anniversary. Thea recalled thoughts about being who she was, an old folks' child, a black woman religious from the South, a Franciscan Sister of Perpetual Adoration:

> I dream that by walking and talking and working and praying and playing together we can create a better world for all of us. I dream

that we can form the kinds of families and churches and communities in which we share faith — faith in God, faith in ourselves and faith in another but also faith in hope and in joy and in love. I dream of a family, of a church, of a community in which we teach one another and we learn to respect one another and to hope with one another and that we find joy and meaning in helping and passing on the gifts that have been given to us.

I dream of the kind of community in which we find our work in sharing our gifts and really building up the body that is the body of Christ. As I have traveled thousands of miles promoting inter-cultural understanding, I don't know what persons, places, experiences have impacted the most on my life. I feel like Alfred Tennyson's speaker, you know, "I am a part of all that I have met," and that thousands of people, places, and experiences have helped to form who I am and who I try to be. I think of my parents, I think of my grandfather, the community of faith into which I was born and into which I was enculturated, I think of some of my early teachers, of the priests, brothers and sisters who taught me when I was young, of special people that I met when I came to St. Rose and came to Viterbo, of people I've met on the travel circuit....

I was profoundly influenced by the place that I was born and grew up in, Mississippi, where so many of the struggles of life almost capsulated me.

The experience of teaching has impacted the most on my life. Teaching in grade school, high school, college, and university. I realized as I have lived longer, how many of my own personal and emotional needs have been met in the classroom and how much I've learned from my students.

The "still point" for steadying me on my journey (for which I search) is God within. The older I grow the more I realize the importance of trying to be a centered person and of trying to act out of a committed — what my people call a "convicted" — life. So the moment of silence, the moment of forethought, the moment of prayer, the moment of communication with friends who have helped me to see myself and to see my life and to see my God and to see other people have been still points that have steadied me on the journey.

The question has been asked me, "In what way have the letters FSPA enabled you to 'glow in fire' on your Christian journey?"

When I think FSPA, actually I think of people who have enabled me. I think of some of the early FSPAs who came to my hometown, Canton, Mississippi, as missionaries — Sister Mildred Burger, Sister Eleanor Naumann, Sister Judith Quinn, Sister Genedine Melder, Sister Theone Beres. They came into my world and showed me the possibility for life and growth that I had not ever dreamed of. The showed me that people from different races and cultures could work together and could enjoy it.

Sister Charlotte Bonneville was very special in my life. She believed in me and trusted me when I didn't believe in myself or trust myself. I hesitate to name the names because there have been so many FSPAs who have loved me and who have believed in me; who have encouraged me and supported me, who have challenged me to do and be my best, who have walked with me when times were troubled, who have understood — these Sisters have enabled me and actually that is what FSPA has meant in my life.

I would like to say from my heart: thank you to all the people who have been so good to me. I'd like to say I'm sorry for the times when I haven't connected properly. I'd like to say that there is still hope that we still can have good news and that we can still be good news for one another and that I think it's worth the effort.[6]

Chapter 19

AN EMPOWERING MISSION

In 1984 Thea was just developing as a known figure in the ministry of intercultural awareness across the United States. As noted earlier, this openness to intercultural awareness, in the church at least, was influenced deeply by the 1960s Second Vatican Council. Intercultural awareness, in the church, is the work of building bridges across cultures in a community that, for many hundreds of years, had seen the western European way as the only way. This was the Roman Catholic Church, which expected conformity and uniformity.

True, throughout two thousand years of church history, local cultures had a way of taking root in the Catholic Church wherever it landed. But as the European church strengthened, as European culture became dominant in the Western world, including in the United States, those cultures of Europe came to be seen as the normative look of the church. This had happened in many colonial areas around the world: the culture of the colonizer became the norm to which the colonized — and in this case, the "evangelized" — had to conform. The Second Vatican Council caused the church to name that dynamic. People worldwide in the following decades set about growing expressions of the church that incorporated more strongly the gifts and insights, the ways of being human, of local cultures.

Thea became a key leader of that movement among African Americans. On the days around All Saints' Day, November 1, 1984, one of the authors of this book spent a few days in Canton, Mississippi, interviewing Thea for a freelance article in *St. Anthony Messenger,* while attending a unique conference on Catholic ministry in southern minority communities. Thea spoke freely about her role as a cultural agent.[1]

She talked first about how her approach in the schools was to encourage teachers to use "family style" education, where the older students work with the younger ones in the typically small schools. "We try to work with the family model," Thea told the interviewer. "That's the way we were raised." Then she talked about what had gone wrong in the colonial model: "A lot of people of my generation, in an effort to be accepted, adopted what I would call 'white Caucasian ways,' and some of our traditional ways are better than what we adopted." Her plea was to go back and "claim the values and wholesome practices of our heritage."

She described the Nigerian robe that she was wearing for her presentations to schoolchildren and teachers on All Saints' Day, whose striking black-checkered pattern gave an air of command as Thea stood before a sleepy-eyed group of schoolchildren at 8:00 a.m., imploring them to break into song. She liked the outfit, she said at first, because it was "easy care" (easy to iron) and "comfortable." Then she reached a little deeper: "I'm different! The clothes are an expression of my personality, an expression of my values, and expression of my history and culture, and my tradition. I'm a black, traditional person."

When asked about how her intercultural ministry connects with her commitment to the Franciscan community, she homed in on the joyousness of St. Francis of Assisi. "Black people, in ages past, have traditional ways of teaching the children to rejoice in grief, in adversity, in oppression, in slavery — it's that kind of joy that helps a person keep going in faith." She admitted that some of the children would not grow to share joy as she did, but "any way that I can share love and joy with you will help you to share love and joy with other people." As we arrived by car at a rural school, she waved to a group of children, excited at her arrival. "Nobody stops to play with a lot of these kids," she said. Stopping to wave and carry on, she said, is what St. Francis was all about.

In the wide-ranging interview, that took place around various events over the course of a weekend, she talked about the perspective she gained by leaving Mississippi as a girl. "I began to see that some of the stuff that had been held up to us as ideals by the 'Great White Race' were crazy." She went on to give examples of the black community caring for a pregnant teen and her baby, where the white community would more typically shun the girl or encourage an abortion. Thea shared her ideas about being a follower of St. Francis, surely a key to understanding Thea's entire life. "Some of what I try to share is what I learned from the poor and oppressed. It's like what Francis learned from the lepers. To me, it's the only way to work with our people."

She spoke of reaching into her own tradition as a source of strength and courage. Using the example of the spiritual, "Children, Go Where I

Send Thee," which she had taught the children at the school that morning, she asked, "Did you notice a lot of memory work in that song?" (The children's song, in a series of verse repetitions, each one longer than the previous, recounts some key moments in "salvation history" — Noah, Old Testament prophets, etc.) She bemoaned the fact that many of these same children, whose intellectual skills are written off as non-existent, easily memorize complex pop songs. "Part of what I try to do is to get the methodology that comes out of where they are, and do what *I* want to do with it!"

Asked about why she had become Catholic, she recounted the story of the Franciscan sisters' commitment to health care, to "sharing the Good News in ways that were concrete and real. I was not attracted to the church per se so much as I was attracted to Christian people giving real Christian witness. I gave up a lot, in terms of our whole worship tradition, in order to be Catholic. I wanted to be associated with those people!" A whole town changed because of those sisters, she added. Then she commented, tellingly, "I thought *all* nuns were like that."

She cautioned the interviewer that this might not be the right message for a Catholic magazine (an intended outlet for this interview) but, in her view, "I don't believe that everyone's got to be Catholic." She became Catholic because of the witness of Catholic people, she said, and felt called to Catholicism, and stayed Catholic because it is the Church of St. Peter, "but I believe God leads people in different ways."

Speaking to a small group of teachers at the rural school in Camden, out from the county seat of Canton, on All Saints' Day, she told a story from her own childhood: "I think about my grandfather, who was a slave, and he talked to us about his slavery. He said if we didn't know about slavery, we wouldn't know about freedom." Of her grandfather, she said, "My grandfather walked from New Orleans, Louisiana, to Memphis, Tennessee, one time because he thought he was going to get a job. He didn't get a job, but he learned."[2]

Later, during an interview, she reached into her experience for another example, this one from her music. She had been leading the classic Negro Spiritual "Walk Together Children," with the Camden schoolchildren before her teachers' workshop began. With its plea to do such things together as walk, talk, sing, pray, work, and more, Thea described the song as "the recipe for a good faculty, assembly, school, church, community . . . " and so on. "The old folks used to say, you walk together and you may get tired, but you *don't* get weary."

Then she appealed to a shared value of her people: "We are a singing people. And if we, as black people, lose our gift of song, we lose one of our treasures. Our history, our memory, our old people, our future — all are in our songs. We've got to sing together to play together." Observing a trend that would only become more pronounced in future decades, she said, "If we played more with our children, our children wouldn't be playing some of the destructive games they are now."

Her appreciation for the gifts of each culture — not only black culture — was part of Thea's appeal everywhere. During the interview she recalled the time she had worked with cross-cultural groups back in Wisconsin. "I won't tell you what we called it, but it was a show," she said, with a mischievous glance. The idea was that each participant would share some personal information, whether history, culture, or traditions, that would be followed by cultural sharing, in this case "virtuoso sharing or participatory sharing." There was Thai dancing, Native American hoop dancing, or rain dancing. All would join in and then there would be a sharing of food. Thea had repeated that formula for intercultural sharing in many settings over the years.

During that interview Thea answered a question of whether or not she would have returned to Mississippi if it weren't for her parents' failing health. Indeed, as we'll see later in this chapter, understanding Thea's parents is a key to understanding Thea. She answered the question with a quick affirmative: "When I was in training in Wisconsin, when I first went there, I thought it was the only place to be, and I had some very good years there. But then I was ready to do something else. I was homesick for the South."

Asked how she would describe the heart of her ministry, she stated simply, "I would hope I would describe it as building the Kingdom — in other words, to love the Lord your God with your whole heart, with your whole soul, with your whole mind, and to love your neighbor as yourself." She added, "Then you get into some even heavier stuff, where Jesus says, 'Love one another, as I have loved you;' and 'Greater love nobody has than to lay down your life for the one you love' — that's what I think the Kingdom is all about."

It all comes down to, she said, "loving in practical ways," serving the poor, so that "everybody can be *somebody*. I say, 'Everybody wants good news.' Did you ever find anybody who *didn't* want good news?" she quipped.

"I do what I can to help people," she said more seriously. And because she had experienced more cross-cultural situations than most people, a black woman becoming good friends with Anglo-Americans, Winnebagos, Asian Ameicans, and others, that became the locus of her work. "If we can start with our little children," she said, "and lead them by the hand, and teach them to be comfortable with people who are different than they are" to clean a room together, or cook a meal together, "that is something."

She concluded with her thoughts on being black and Catholic: "I say the Church needs folks like me, to 'liven it up' from being 'so dull.' There has always been a place for blacks in Catholic worship, she insisted, and "now there is a movement of black people who are saying, 'We're tired of this. It's okay for you, but don't impose it on *me!*' "

Black Catholics, she said, "are at the cutting edge of Catholicism: you know, the majority of the people in the world are *not* white Europeans!" That church may have plenty of right ideas, "but the expression comes across as incomplete, because a lot of churches try to do the headtrip, the intellectual thing, without feeling, movement, or color. That's not life. The nuns don't like clapping in church, so nobody claps. If you don't understand the importance of culture, you don't understand the importance of this."

Outside of the interview, Thea had even more challenging words for the organizers of the "Mutuality in Mission" conference that was happening nearby.

That conference, sponsored by the Catholic Committee of the South, whose name belied its small, ad hoc character in the 1980s, was a weekend get-together for members of Catholic religious communities from various parts of the United States who had been assigned to work among poor communities, primarily black, in the South, and members of those local communities, from across the region. For this event, nationally well-known speakers such as Riverside Theological Seminary professor James L. Washington and civil rights pioneer L. C. Dorsey were flown in from afar. When Thea heard that this was going on in her own back yard, she made sure she was added to the schedule![3]

At one point, Thea took the floor and talked to the small assembly of perhaps fifty. She, after all, had given many talks over the years on the very theme of intercultural sensitivity. Her first observation was that the group had self-segregated into black and white for social time the evening before: "Why do you do that?" she probed, admitting that it was a common occurrence. Then she dug in to her main point: "It's not an example of mutuality. I'm different; you're different. And we can come to one another with full hands as gifts that are *real*. Your gift is real, but it's not mine."

Her main point was that people need to admit and own their cultural differences; that lays the foundation for mutual respect. "When I say, 'we're all alike,' I'm copping out. If I say we're all alike, I'm saying, 'I don't need you. You know what I know, and I know what you know, and I don't need you. But we're different. We don't look alike, we don't walk alike, we don't talk alike, we don't play alike; we don't see life alike, we come from a different history, a different past, a different experience." The solution: "Come to each other in our diversity, carrying one another, giving and receiving."

She added that white missioners will have more influence in changing racist attitudes of their own communities than perhaps anything else — not a message that people may have expected to hear: "I can change my organizations because they are mine, they are of me," she said. "And when I bring my organization into conformity with that Church ideal, then my organization becomes a living witness to the possibility, to the hope, to the faith and the love."

She implored the group to find ways to desegregate while they are in the black community. So many times, she observed, whites come in to do service, but then go off unto themselves for worship and social time. "If you don't pray with me, I will suspect that you do not love me. If you come to me and serve me and don't walk with me and talk with me and stand with me, you serve me but you end up being the power in my community, and you play me like a button! And when the times get tough, you go home. But if you walk with me, then we can build. We can build a kingdom."

Finally, she hit on a raw nerve: the sharing — or nonsharing — of power that is a dynamic in cross-cultural, and particularly, in cross-class, situations. "How many have had the experience of folk who want to help?" she asked, to an assent from members of local black communities. "They have their agendas and plans, their strategies, and their programs, and they have allocated the budget — and then they come in and want to talk to you?"

It happens all the time, she observed. "It may be your money," Thea scolded the religious communities, "but don't come and say it's me!

Include me in the planning from the first." That approach would yield a *true* mutuality in mission, she added.

Along the way she picked up on an example of a social worker who spoke of stepping out from behind her desk to join clients on the bench to help put them at ease. That, Thea said, would be an excellent analogy for the very mission of the church.

During these years, Thea was challenging not only to whites in ministry in the black community. Sister Norma Angel tells of how Thea challenged and encouraged her to remain committed to her own calling (Norma is the Maryknoll sister first mentioned in chapter 7). "There came a point that I actually felt that the challenges were just too much," recalls Norma. "She said to me, 'If you ever feel like you want to leave your community, I strongly encourage you to call me before you make that decision.'" Norma, a native of Cacao, Venezuela, who grew up in the Netherlands, had, as previously mentioned, encountered her own share of discrimination from within her community.

The day came when she just couldn't take it anymore. As she says, "I had my bags packed." Then she called Thea. "I had sort of this naïve way of looking at life," expecting that religious communities wouldn't mimic society. "She was the one who really had a way of just explaining things," recalls Norma. Thea talked over with Norma why Norma had joined Maryknoll: the motivation to work for social justice, "from the perspective of faith." Then she challenged her: "Then that's where you need to grow," said Thea. "In your perspective of faith, because I can tell you today, there will be circumstances wherever you go." Confused, Norma asked, "What do you mean?" Thea replied, "Wherever you are, people are going to bring who they are with them. If your vocation is dependent on who is around you, then it will not sustain itself. Your job is to make a decision that you want to grow in your commitment and live it. If you choose to be distracted by circumstances then I think you need to leave." That conversation helped Norma to make a shift in her thinking, she recalls, one that made all the difference to her. In short, she says, Thea's direction was deeply empowering, helping her to sort out a deeper meaning in cross-cultural ministry.[4]

That is not to say that, over the years, Thea did not have her own moments of doubt. She told Sister Addie Lorraine Walker, who counts herself as one of Thea's best friends, "You lose footing, and you just have to regain footing — it's part of living," says Walker of Thea. In the earlier years, as Thea went through her metamorphosis in Washington, D.C., "she lost footing and no longer identified with the FSPA. She began to search. Should I go somewhere else? To another congregation?....Do I still fit as a religious?" With the help of her friends, she weathered her storms, and remained a Franciscan Sister.[5]

The freedom from circumstance that she counseled to Sister Norma perhaps says much about why Thea stayed her own course, as well. She seemed to have an innate faith that, in spite of adversity, things would work out. During the interview with one of this book's authors (John), back in 1984, Thea had told the story of the man everyone in Canton had called "the Chinaman." A shopkeeper, he was the only Chinese-American who stayed in Canton after the children were expelled from the public school during World War II anti-Asian discrimination (see chapter 5). When the civil rights movement happened, during a boycott of white-owned stores, the "Chinaman" prospered, as his became the only store the blacks would do business with.[6] It was that kind of stubbornness — or, as some might say, *faithfulness* — that kept Thea going.

◆ ◆ ◆

At the beginning of our story, we heard of Thea's parents' background, a mixture of the oppression experienced by all black people in the United States, most bitterly in the southern states, and the experience of being part of a black middle class that grew up in some urban areas after the Civil War and Reconstruction. Now they were at the end of their lives.

Her father, as she told an interviewer in *Sr. Thea: Her Own Story*, a 1991 film documentary[7] produced by Edward J. Murray and Clarence Williams, was not encouraged by his family to come to Canton. He could have done much better financially, she said, but there were no doctors for the black community there, and he felt called to serve. Her mother had been a successful teacher in Greenville, but had supported her husband's desire to serve where he was most needed. It was growing up in this household of serving parents that prepared young Bertha to become the woman who Sister Thea became.

Thea loved her parents with a daughter's strong love. She recounted their last years in an interview with Margaret Walker Alexander. Here is a significant excerpt from that interview:

My parents experienced much suffering before they died. My mother was ill for twenty years. My father was strong, and he was a stubborn man. My father had pain and he had discomfort, but he just keep on going. He would say any day where you can be up and around is a good day. As long as my mother was alive, he, no matter how sick he was, wanted to be up; he wanted to put on his clothes and his tie and sit in his chair.

In 1984, I was diagnosed with breast cancer and I had a modified radical mastectomy. I guess my first reaction was concern for my parents. How could I keep them from being traumatized by what was happening to me? I discovered the lump one day and went to the doctor the next. By six o'clock that evening he said I had to have a biopsy, and he explained what the outcome might be. Later, the doctor found metastasis in my lymph nodes, so I was put on chemotherapy. I was not happy, not pleased. But I had been reared in a community where people faced illness. My response was: This is my condition. How do I deal with it?

At the time, I was told there was a 20 percent probability the chemotherapy would lead to remission, so I tried it. I was on chemotherapy for a year. I stopped it in February [1985] and in March [1985] I had another cancerous tumor in another lymph node. That was removed and I went on a series of therapies — radiation, diet, and megavitamin. In addition, during 1985 I had two tumors in my chest wall that faded spontaneously.

I was diagnosed in 1984 [March]. When I had my first cancer surgery, my mother had been in the hospital for about six weeks. I was in the room next to her and I remember, by that time my mother was not speaking — so I went in to tell her that they had discovered a lump and I was going to have a biopsy and that if the biopsy showed malignancy, I was going to have surgery. I told her I was in the room next to her, and as soon as I got out of surgery, I would come and see her. Her blood pressure shot up. That told me she understood what I had said. I went to surgery and as soon as I got back, I wanted to see my mother. They would not let me go see her until my doctor said, "Let her go."

So I went over to see her, and then she started calming down. Her blood pressure went back down again. All three of us were sick and suffering. There was interaction and a definite spiritual connection.

In November 1984, when my mother was dying, my father's nurse, a white woman who was in home health care, did not believe that Daddy knew his wife was dying. My father was a doctor and had practiced medicine for fifty-four years. The nurse thought we should tell him, and I agreed.

We sat in the living room and the nurse told him she thought my mother was dying. My father sat there, his face did not change, and he said, "Thank you." He said, "You have been very kind and I know that you have done everything you could do." That was all he said. Even then, the nurse did not think my father understood. I knew he did — that would be the way my father would respond. Wouldn't that be a typical way for a gentleman to respond?[8]

The next day Thea's father had a stroke. "He let us know that for him life without Mama was not worth living; he wanted to die," wrote Thea a few months later. On November 15, 1984, at age eighty-one, her mother died. Her father was in the hospital and could not go to the funeral. By year's end, he, too had died, at age ninety. He died in his home on December 16, 1984, tended to day and night by family friend Doris O'Leary.

Doris was a childhood friend of Thea's who actually had lived in the Bowman home for a period after her own home had burned. Going later to California to raise her family and work in the health care field, she stayed in touch with her friend. She flew to Canton for Mrs. Bowman's funeral and stayed with Thea to help take care of Dr. Bowman, sleeping on a cot in his bedroom. Doris was with him when he died peacefully in his sleep.

At her mother's funeral, by her mother's request, Thea had sung, "I've Done My Work." Part of a verse goes,

> He guides my steps, and He knows best,
> He will not harm where He is blest.
> And so goodnight, I'll take my rest,
> Where sweet wild roses grow.[9]

She sang it again for her father's funeral. Both parents were buried in historic Elmwood Cemetery, Memphis, Tennessee.

Thea was surprised he died so soon after his wife's passing. With some melancholy, in her first "form" letter dated February 7, 1985, Thea wrote,

I miss them, truly, but I trust, believe, know they are happy together with God and with so many loved ones who have gone before.

Through it all, rightly or wrongly, God knows, I've tried to walk and work on as if my world was steady, working for the Diocese of Jackson and appearing spasmodically from coast to coast. And God has/will make a way.... Right now I am trying to reorganize the pieces and journey onward.[10]

Resuming a grueling schedule on her now-national speaker's circuit, later Thea wrote several form letters to legions of friends recounting how she coped with what would become in few short years her increasingly undependable body. Her spirit, mind, and voice would remain strong and her life would go on, full tilt, until January of 1988, when her cancer would return. But much would happen during her three-year reprieve.

Chapter 20

FAMILIES,
BLACK AND CATHOLIC

In responding to one of her growing number of interviewers in April 1985, Thea said of her battle against cancer, "You have to decide what you really want in life, what's important." Those words speak the theme that had emerged in Thea's life since the onset of cancer. Tireless she always had been; in the aftermath of her first cancer treatment and the death of her parents she became urgently focused on her mission of promoting cultural identity. The cancer, she knew, could return.

Thea was being interviewed by journalist Julie Horgan for the La Crosse Catholic newspaper, the *Times Review,* after receiving the prestigious John XXIII Award from Viterbo College. The award recognizes outstanding leadership and exemplification of the spirit of Pope John XXIII, who stood strongly for world peace and, by convening Vatican Council II, opened the door to sweeping modernization of the Roman Catholic Church. At her acceptance speech, reported Horgan, Thea spoke of courage: " 'Courage, in fact, is what is often needed to overcome barriers between people of different racial, religious, or ethnic backgrounds,' [Sister Thea] noted. She said she believes that a 'fear of the unknown' creates those barriers. 'You have to learn to work through the fear,' she said. 'So often, when we're fearful of one another, we tend to avoid each other.' "

Thea spoke then also of the need to openly embrace differences, rather than mistakenly think that people are all alike: "People who make such assumptions profess to be free of prejudice, but at the same time they show little appreciation for the qualities that make people different," she said. "It is through this lack of respect for unique qualities that people miss out," she added. "It means that you're deprived of my experience and I'm deprived of yours, and we're both probably hurting."

Among other things, Thea explained why she homed in on music to help promote her message: " 'Music,' wrote Horgan, 'gets us in touch with feeling and demands a kind of involvement that nothing else demands,' she said. As she tries to encourage intercultural awareness, it is important for her to put people in touch with one another at levels deeper than just the cognitive."[1]

Thea shared with that journalist examples of two very different people who had come in tears to her after performances — one a Welshman being reminded of his mother's folk songs, the other a Jewish woman who reconnected with memories of surviving one of Hitler's Austrian concentration camps — as demonstration of how universally music can touch. Dan Rooney, Hall of Fame Pittsburgh Steelers football team owner who also received that John XXIII Award from Viterbo that night, remembers that "hers was a hard act to follow!"[2] Thea had Viterbo College choral singers positioned in the second- and third-tier balconies in the Fine Arts Center. Her talk was rousing, her singing soared. When the chorale and the audience joined in the choruses, seemingly everyone in the window-walled center lobby became ecstatic. Rooney and Sister Thea became friends that April evening in Wisconsin. (A few years later, after cancer's return, when Thea was no longer able to walk, Rooney gave her a wheelchair, which Thea christened her "Steeler-mobile.")

At that time, in 1985, Sister Thea was occupied with coordinating and editing articles from black and other scholars and community leaders for what would become an important book in some circles. The bishops' agency, U. S. Catholic Conference, commissioned Thea to compile a book for ministers and others who worked in the black Catholic community.

Entitled *Families: Black and Catholic, Catholic and Black,* the book caught on and was widely used within the black Catholic community. The paraliturgical celebration of the *Nguzo Saba,* the "Black Value System," for example, written by Fernand J. Cheri, OFM, and Toni Balot, has been used all over the United States at conferences on the subject of cross-cultural awareness. In their piece, Cheri and Balot develop the idea that by living the values of their ancestors, pray-ers participate in the creation of a new people. Their reflection was based on an academic work that Cheri had written for his theological studies.

Cheri recalls, "There were seven Black values based on the study done by black political scientist [and Kwanzaa founder] Ron Karenga. He picked seven values that were reflected on both continents, as Karenga put it."[3] Those values are: unity, self-determination, collective work and responsibility, cooperative economics, purpose, creativity, and faith as the black ancestors' legacy.

The articles in the book, along with many of the charts and activities, stimulated discussions in Catholic dioceses that promoted ministry to blacks and other minority groups. People who heard Thea speak used the book to help grow her message in their daily lives and work.

Thea wrote in the book's Introduction, "It assumes that the Black family is alive and well. It assumes further that we as a people need to find ways old and new to walk and talk together; to bond more surely; to extend family more widely and effectively, so that no one is fatherless, motherless, sisterless, or brotherless; so that no one lacks the life-sustaining human support of family."[4]

The book includes the thoughts and concerns of black folks of various faiths and perspectives who have thought deeply about the plight and potential of the black family; reflections of black Catholics on black family and faith, black family and Catholicism, the church and the salvation of the family, black families and the salvation of the church; and a treasure trove of resources, including facts, people, graphics, articles for reflection. All of that is followed by a more interactive offering: songs to sing and poems for meditation; activities, images, and ideas for family-building activities.

It received critical acclaim in the broader Catholic community, when it started to circulate the next year, perhaps most succinctly expressed in Peter Mara's review in *Mississippi Today*:

> The social sciences spend countless hours on the problems of black family life, which are quite real, but the results of such study have been meager. Those who did the research too often ignored the persistent strengths of the black community, including the strength of faith.
>
> In this book, every problem is honestly faced, but in a different, positive spirit, confident not just that a solution must exist somewhere but that mature Christian black people themselves will supply it.
>
> Likewise, American Catholics often regret the seeming weakness of the Catholic Church among black people, or boast of achievements some of which are in truth no better than lukewarm.

Sister Bowman's work is a cause for celebration. Just the variety and depth of the insights provided by her many authors will be informative and upbuilding for most of us.[5]

Sister Addie Lorraine Walker, SSND, recalls that these themes were the core of Sister Thea's teaching in her many intercultural workshops. "The teaching strategies cut across learning styles," says Walker. "If they don't get it this way, I'll do it this way," she explains, "but it's got to be the same message so that, when they all leave, they will all have the same message — even though they receive it in the environment in a different kind of way."

It was that approach that she would share with other black educators at various gatherings, and especially at Xavier University's Institute for Black Catholic Studies. "It's the one thing, it's the integrated thing so that she could take the very life of the black community, black Christians, in any age, in every age and kind of tease out for people," says Walker, "or hold up the spirituality for people. In essence, it was the only thing worth being about: walking and talking and living with God so that you walked the walk, and talked the talk, prayed the prayer, lit the fire, and lived the passion of a life for Jesus Christ." That was key for her, says Walker: "She could reconnect you with your spirituality rather than have you try to replicate *somebody else's* spirituality."

At the Institute for Black Catholic Studies, Thea taught a course entitled "Black Theology and the Arts," in which she would put this all into an academic context. "She could do it in literature from Shakespeare to James Baldwin," recalls Walker. "She could help us to see how the songs of Zion or the slave songs were songs for freedom that could facilitate that same freedom in our context today."

"That's what resonated with people," says Walker, "even with the [Catholic] bishops. She called their stuff on them — forced them to look at themselves and what they said about what they want to live — to say, 'You have to put up or shut up.'"

She would challenge people, including church leaders, says Walker: "She would take their words or the words of the Gospel and hold them up for them, or sing the words for them, or pray them or preach them. In her presence your phoniness would have to fall away."[6]

Karen Horace, who then was an administrator in the Chicago public schools and a lay minister at her own parish, St. Felicitas, on Chicago's southeast side, attended the institute during summers in New Orleans, beginning in 1986, when the program was well underway. She recalls the tremendous influence that Thea wielded as a mentor. "We just took to each other and became friends," she recalls. "One thing Thea taught me is how to critique programs without critiquing the individual," she recalls. Then there was Thea's constant urging toward reform: "She challenged things and didn't just accept the status quo," says Horace. "She challenged it and challenged you to challenge it." As Horace says, "She shot from the shoulder, but she did it all with love."

Horace also recalls that Thea always encouraged both a spirit of inclusion and one of inquiry. "She taught me to make sure that I solicited advice and opinions and didn't just run roughshod over people." Those are all things that Thea did that became a major influence on how Horace acted back at her Chicago parish.

She recalls a particular incident in one of Thea's classes that illustrates her point. During the course, Thea would ask the students to self-evaluate; to give themselves a grade. "She would look at the grade and would ask you why you did it." If a student either overrated or underrated herself, recalls Horace, Thea would gently tell the student and wrest out a more accurate evaluation. "She didn't accept wrong," says Horace, "whether it was wrong on whichever end."

Much of Thea's work centered on tooling these churchworkers for effective presentation in their educational programs. Horace gives, for example, an exercise from Thea's class Spirituality of Black Literature. "We had to take a story — either create a story of our own or take a story that was already written — and we had to reenact the story with an audience. We had to go out and get an audience of children, if we wanted children, or adults. We couldn't just do it for the class. We had to actually import an audience, but we had to act it," she recalls. Everybody learned their parts and conducted a performance, which Thea would critique with the student at the end. The goal was for the student to be able go home and do likewise in his or her parish.

"Anytime I have to do anything publicly or for someone else's consumption," says Horace, "I look back on the lessons learned from Thea, even to the physical presence. . . . When hunting for words, I look at Thea as my inspiration. She inspired me to do things that I didn't think I could do."

Thea insisted on inclusion in her classes. Horace remembers one time when everyone somewhat naturally gravitated toward a segregated seating arrangement (there were both black and white students). "She made everybody get up and move," recalls Horace. Thea told them, without doubt, "That's not acceptable." Thea also worked with the class on preparing prayer services. "There was a standard that had to be kept," explains Horace. "If you didn't meet the standard she'd let you know about it. You really didn't want to be at the brunt of her evaluation if you didn't do it right!"[7]

Chapter 21

TO MOTHER AFRICA

The Institute for Black Catholic Studies and the book on being black and Catholic weren't the only big things on Thea's burner in 1985. Thea's friends had decided early in the year to send her to Africa for the International Eucharistic Congress, an occasional weeklong multi-cultural gathering, held in various locations worldwide, and celebrating Catholic spirituality, especially as it is expressed in the Eucharist.

It was an offering of healing, in the wake of her cancer and her parents' deaths, from the many whom Thea had brought a deeper sense of their own personhood. Bishops Joseph Francis (Newark, N.J.) and Bishop James Lyke (Cleveland, Ohio) endorsed a fundraising effort to make the trip happen. In a letter to "Friends of Thea," friends John Davis and Father Charles Burns, SVD, wrote:

> Over the years many of us have shared the gifts of Sr. Thea Bowman through song, poetry, narrative, and dance. As recipient, we have heard her express only one heartfelt desire — to go to the mother country! 1984 has been a painful year for Thea. Mother Africa in the presence of friends will provide much healing.[1]

The gravity of her personal situation was compounded by the sudden death of her dear friend Edmundite Father Joseph Nearon. In a form letter to friends and colleagues dated February 7, 1985, Thea acknowledged,

> Admittedly last year was a hard one for me. Both my parents were ill most of the year. I had cancer surgery in March. Because the cancer had spread from breast to lymph nodes, I have been on chemo since April 1984. I finished the chemo yesterday, February 6, and this letter is my way of celebrating.
>
> I'm feeling well. (In retrospect I realize that the unaccustomed fatigue which I attempted to ignore for months and months before

the surgery was symptomatic.) I'll be having tests in April to confirm that I am as well as I feel. I'm scheduled to teach at Xavier University in New Orleans again this summer. I hope to work for the Diocese of Jackson again this year. I'm even hoping for an August business/educational/re-rooting/re-creational trip to Kenya for the Eucharistic Congress. Otherwise life goes on for me as usual, or at least as characteristic.[2]

On June 3, she packed up her belongings and moved from her family home at 136 Hill Street: "the house that has been home to me all my life," she wrote in a letter to friends. "I will carry with me many treasured memories of Mama, Daddy, family and all of you who have called or visited here throughout the years.... My daddy left seven guest books recording friends who came from January 1921 through December 1984. From time to time we all reminisced over those books. I miss my parents and those dear relatives and friends who have gone home, but I'm trying to journey on."[3]

Thea again took up residence at Holy Child Jesus Convent among the other Franciscan Sisters of Perpetual Adoration, who ministered at Holy Child Jesus School and parish. She recovered well from a second breast cancer surgery followed by seven weeks of radiation, joking to friends about her "certified radiant woman status."[4] Gradually she adjusted to a prescribed megavitamin therapy coupled with a nutrition regimen designed to deprive any stray cancer cells of nourishment. Her previous favorite foods were a thing of the past. Her friend Sister Antona Ebo said she never heard Thea, an enthusiastic gourmand, complain about her restricted diet.[5] She now enjoyed better physical health. People commented that she looked more like her beautiful, healthy self.

Before long her schedule filled up again. There were June trips to Wisconsin to spend time with Sister Dorothy Ann and the Kundinger family in Marshfield and a FSPA meeting in La Crosse. She accepted an invitation to speak at a CYO youth conference in Chicago, a Renew/RCIA program in San Diego, a workshop for women religious in Baltimore. She looked forward to teaching from June 23 to July 12 at the Institute for Black Catholic Studies at Xavier University in New Orleans, to workshops in Oxford, Mississippi, and in Dallas and Fort Worth. From July 28 to August 2, she was booked to give a workshop in New York City at the joint conference of black clergy, sisters, and seminarians.

Then came Africa. Almost two hundred friends, colleagues, and students responded to the Davis/Burns letter and contributed funds for the trip. Thea would have time to visit Sister Laurette Sprosty, FSPA, a former classmate, in Harare, Zimbabwe. Laurette and Thea had worked together from time to time over the years. From Zimbabwe Thea would fly to Kenya to spend ten days attending the Forty-Third International Eucharistic Congress. When that was completed, she would head to Nigeria to spend over a week with friends there.

On Saturday evening, August 3, Thea began a series of flights that landed her in Harare the following Monday, late afternoon, via Europe. Thea was thrilled to be actually on the "Mother Continent."

In a flash it was Saturday, and Thea was off to Nairobi. The trip was uneventful, and Thea headed from the airport to the Hilton International Nairobi in the heart of the capital city. She unpacked and prepped to comprehend the vast scale of the Forty-Third International Eucharistic Congress experience. One can easily imagine her dancing and singing, "Thank you, Jesus!" about her good fortune.

Fifty thousand clergy, religious, and laity from all over the world — including Pope John Paul II — were in Nairobi for the congress. With her congress host, seminarian Joseph M. Davis, SM, at her side, she immediately engaged Kenya's hospitable and happy people and congress participants.

Thea kept a card, which she later brought home, containing the words of the daily prayer of the participants: "God, Our Father, you are so good in giving us the Eucharist and the Christian Family. Grant us your Spirit to help us realize that this sacrament of your Son's death and resurrection is the source of love and life in the Family. Amen."[6]

Cardinal Joseph Cordeiro, archbishop of Karachi, Pakistan, gave the opening address. He said, "The uniqueness of this congress is that it is for the first time held in missionary Africa. This is something that should thrill the heart of every Christian, who with any sense of Church history will see, as it were, that the Church's life has come full circle. From the Africa that, in the early Church, staged Ecumenical Councils and Congresses, that produced Cyprian of Carthage and Augustine of Hippo, we are now celebrating the first International Eucharistic Congress in Nairobi in Kenya."[7]

It was a huge event for Nairobi and awesome for all who attended. Kenya's President Daniel Moi and other religious, civic, and business dignitaries were on hand to welcome the delegates. There were liturgies (including one led by the pope), workshops, and keynote speeches by Catholic leaders from all around the world.

Throughout the event, host Joseph Davis and Thea shared their intense interest in the African basis for African American culture. They relished the free experience of the church in Africa: participants spoke of the African soul in their music, dancing and laughter, a joyful and unified atmosphere.

At the end of the congress, Thea stayed two days for sightseeing before flying to Lagos, Nigeria, on Wednesday, August 21. Arriving in Lagos in early evening, she was greeted by Nigerian friends she had known in the United States, Sister Oresa Selo-Ojeme (a sister of the Sacred Heart). Thea stayed with her parents, Sir and Lady D. O. Selo-Ojeme in Benin City. Ten days later, on August 31, she reluctantly left her Mother Continent. She arrived back in Mississippi on September 1. The FSPAs were delighted to have her back home.

The local newspapers carried the travel news about the well-known Franciscan sister from Canton, Mississippi. Thea's desire to "be in touch with my roots" resonated well among the African American community. "I am interested in black culture," she told *Mississippi Today*. "If we as blacks are going to answer to the call to be truly Christian Catholics, we have to be truly ourselves." The paper also reported on some of the surprises that Africa held for Thea: "the large number of black cardinals, bishops, deacons, priests, nuns and the large number of dedicated religious lay people." This was different from the Catholic Church not only in Mississippi but throughout the United States. The spirituality of the people impressed her, reported the paper, along with the large number of Mass attendees, not only on Sunday but throughout the week: "It is a marvelous experience to go to an evening Mass on a weekday and find a church the size of St. Peter's Cathedral in Jackson filled with worshippers of different ages," she said.

But there was something deeper: "One of the most moving things for me is the realization that my sisters, mothers, and fathers in Africa recognize black Americans as belonging to Africa. These people received me warmly and went out of their way to help me experience their culture in its various forms. I am grateful to them for making me realize in a new way that I am an African American," Sister Bowman said. "I feel a responsibility to share in every way I can the insight, beauty, wholeness, and spirituality I saw in the African people with my American brothers and sisters of all colors."[8]

In her Christmas letter for 1985 Thea wrote, "Everywhere I went in Africa I was welcomed as a relative and made to feel truly at home. I met people who looked and thought and moved like me. Since I left one of my Nigerian brothers and his wife named their little girl "Thea." I feel most honored and happy for that newest evidence of my kinship with the continent of my ancestors. I hope to return to Africa someday."[9] Her hopes would be realized, but in ways she might not have expected.

Chapter 22

LEAD ME, GUIDE ME

Thea's Christmas letter of 1985 not only looked to the past; it also pointed to some big projects of the future. She planned a series of consultations, from coast to coast, as well as her usual work in Jackson and at the Institute for Black Catholic Studies in New Orleans. By 1987, she looked back on a series of major accomplishments: trips across the country, including Hawaii, and in what would make her a celebrity, completion of taping a segment for NBC's *60 Minutes* filmed in Washington, D.C.; Canton, Jackson, and Raymond, Mississippi; and New Orleans. It was aired on May 3, 1987.

Her cancer was at bay: "My health continues even better than expected," she reported in a letter in 1986. "Dr. Sanders removed two suspicious tumors in September 1986, both benign. I feel fine. Somehow God is not through with me yet."[1] In fact, there was much ahead for her. Clearly the phone call from *60 Minutes,* preliminary interviews with host Mike Wallace and his producers, filming, and televising were extraordinary for this Mississippian. The Thea segment was inspiring, dramatic, and well produced. Paul and Holly Fine filmed the segment for CBS; Mike Wallace conducted the interview.

In a letter dated May 20, 1987, to Sister Thea, Paul and Holly Fine wrote, on CBS News letterhead:

> You sure did sound great every time I spoke with you the week after the piece aired on *60 Minutes*. For us it is a real high to know that the subject of our efforts is so pleased.
>
> You deserved every accolade to every close-up you received in every minute of our air time. It's not often that we find such a genuine subject who cares so much about people. You're quite a lady, to quote a viewer, *exquisite.*[2]

Thea was ecstatic and shared stories of the taping of the show with her friends:

60 Minutes was filmed over a two-year period. They filmed me in Washington, D.C., at the National Shrine with Archbishop (James) Hickey; at Hinds Junior College in Raymond, Mississippi, with the children from Holy Child involved in a program; in New Orleans, at St. Monica, my favorite church in New Orleans with Veronica Downs, one of my best friends and accompanists; at Holy Child in Canton's convent, outdoors in front of what used to be Sister Enrico's (Pudenz) store and is now the music room; at my house on Hill Street and around there, in the Canton cemetery and down and around the town; in New Orleans at the Institute at Xavier U. where I teach. They also filmed me at the doctor's office and the diocesan office, and Arista Otto's house and Beatrice Smith's house, but they chose not to use those pieces.[3]

Mike Wallace himself, who is anything but fawning, was genuinely impressed by Thea, and they enjoyed a relationship from that time forward. In the Foreword to the book *Sister Thea Bowman: Shooting Star,* Wallace wrote:

I don't remember when I've been more moved, more enchanted by a person whom I've profiled, than by Sister Thea Bowman. I confess I was a little skeptical when she was first suggested to me, but just one session with this remarkable individual convinced me; her openness, her compassion, her intelligence, her optimism, her humor captured me.

[S]he told me, "Many of our priests in their training and preaching didn't do much body work, so techniques of relaxation, techniques of rhythm, techniques of communication and expression that come from us in the black community, that is what they have to learn to be more comfortable with." And her priestly acolytes did, on camera, for us.

Halfway into our filming, I learned that Sister Thea was already fighting cancer, but I couldn't believe it, for she was so confident, so optimistic, so determined.

"But there aren't enough Sister Theas around," I told her. "One's enough," she promptly answered. "You ask my friends. They'll tell you that's plenty."

She was wrong. For I was one of her friends, and we need so many more like Thea.[4]

Her appearance to millions on *60 Minutes* became the context for talking about her from that point on, and other media became increasingly interested. The week the Thea segment was televised on CBS, Thea spoke in Cincinnati at St. Peter in the Chains Cathedral on May 5 and then backed up two hesitant young singers with her soaring presence in their duet of a song, "Lord Lift Us Where We Belong." The service, in a stately Greek-revival cathedral, was more in the style of Gospel revival that night.[5] She went from there speak at the archdiocesan seminary.

Wrote Marianne Cianciolo in Cincinnati's *Catholic Telegraph*, "She's not embarrassed to kick off her shoes in front of an audience and walk around in her stocking feet, to sing at the top of her voice or to boast about her hundred-year-old Uncle Harvey, who earned his high school diploma at age ninety-four. She did all these things at the LeBlond Lecture. 'I love people. I get a charge out of people,' is her explanation for her unreserved behavior. 'I really feel there is a spirit and an energy in a group. We can learn to tap that energy. Energy is power.' "[6]

Not long after, a headline from Paterson, New Jersey, told a similar story: "Mississippi Roots Create a Special Sister." Bill Sanderson's story was effusive: "She sings. She dances and claps her hands. She tells jokes. Yesterday, parishioners at the Our Lady of Victory Church in Paterson saw why Sister Thea Bowman's way of teaching the Gospels is a hit at Catholic churches across the country." Noting the *60 Minutes* appearance, he observed, "Several people asked her for autographs and to pose for pictures." The gist of the story was that Thea was bringing the vitality of the churches of her youth to the Catholic Church.[7]

Sister Thea's appearance on *60 Minutes* brought new people into her world. Letters of joy, congratulations, and gratitude flooded Canton, the Franciscan Sisters of Perpetual Adoration, and CBS. Most were laudatory, although some were not. Some examples:

Dear Thea, Greetings from Las Vegas! A few weeks ago our choir director was watching *60 Minutes,* and when he saw the preview with you in it, he called as many folks as he could. I am so glad I was home to get the call and see you. The show was wonderful. I should say you were wonderful. I liked it for several reasons — one was that you were so much like you — the Thea I remember from New Orleans.

I wish you peace and love, Thea, dearest, I am so proud of you! We [black folks] all are! Truly you are Gift to this country, this church, this race of people, this past, present, future, etc....

I watched you, literally drank you in on *60 Minutes* Sunday evening. I called up the folks everywhere to let them know that "our Sister Thea Bowman" was going to be featured on national television. You represented yourself and us gorgeously, as only you could, Thea....

Dear *60 Minutes* staff: We have shared the joy of Sister Thea Bowman in action while vacationing in Fredrikstad, St. Croix. It was at an early morning Mass for school children of St. Patrick's parish — out where the camera never reaches.

   She was just as convincing and uninhibited there as she is on national television....

Sirs: How did you happen to find Sister Thea? We found her interesting, inspiring and refreshing. Every time that I've thought of that segment of your program, I feel a lift. She is beautiful....

Dear Mr. Wallace: Being a long-time viewer of *60 Minutes* and a native Mississippian, I am often aware of the faults of my state. Some of my fellow Mississippians (a majority, actually) claim "bad press" when your show and other TV news magazines show us images of ourselves.

   Happily, I watched your segment of Sister Thea Bowman's Christian ministry. I have been in her audience (congregation?) on several occasions, and on each occasion, Sister Thea has lifted my soul, as well as my consciousness. Since I participated in the civil rights movement in my state in the '60s and '70s, I have cried with the memories that Sister Thea's allusions to those disturbed, turbulent times have made me face. But I have also rejoiced with her during her "sermons." (Yes, she preaches — but never in the manner of orthodox preachers; few ordained ministers in any denomination could successfully imitate the style of her emotionally and intellectually satisfying sermons.) She shows us the beauty and love and goodness and intelligence in herself and in ourselves. Without making me feel ashamed or uncomfortable about what my race has done to her race, Sister Thea makes me feel at one with her in what she calls our common goal: knowing and loving and accepting one another.

Thank you so much for showing me a mirror of my state that I can feel proud of.[8]

Jackson's television critic Jeff Edwards later reported, after a Mike Wallace retrospective was aired, "Susan Fox, assistant producer for *Mike Wallace, Then and Now,* said the Bowman interview is cited by Wallace as one of the most memorable and pleasurable of his career."[9]

Shortly after the May 1987 airing Sister Thea wrote to her friends, making a point of how competent and professional the production crew was. "More than anything I was grateful to be able to say to roughly sixty million people on five continents that we believe in God, ourselves, the future, and the possibility of working together to make this troubled world a better and more joyful place for all of us."[10]

To her classmate, Sister Marla Lang, FSPA, she added a postscript: "At present, I seem to be winning the cancer battle. I feel I'm living on borrowed time — grace time — and that has a freedom and excitement all its own."[11]

The TV show had made Thea a star of sorts. Father Clarence Williams (first mentioned in chapter 12) recalls something that happened not long after the airing. In Cleveland, at the time of a meeting of black Catholic religious leaders, he set about to film a videotape to encourage black Catholic vocations. The series he was taping was like a newsmagazine, he recounts. "You would have a song, then a segment then we would have a little drama, then a song and sign off." There was one problem, though: the pickup choir he had planned on did not materialize. "So I was just really disgruntled. Sister Thea walked by and said, 'What is going on?'" Williams explained that the filming crew was there, being paid on the clock, yet there was no choir. "'Well, I can sing a couple of songs for you,'" she said. "I was taken aback," says Williams. "Here was this now really international person saying, 'Hey, I'll knock off a couple of songs.' And she did! Joe Davis played, she sang, and the production crew couldn't believe that this woman from *60 Minutes,* who they all knew, was doing this. They were so excited to say that they had worked with Sister Thea!" That's the kind of person she was, says Williams. "She was not taken by herself — she was who she was."[12]

Meanwhile, life kept happening in Mississippi. Later in the year there were intercultural programs sponsored by the Diocese of Jackson for its sesquicentennial anniversary, consisting of seminars in Oxford, Natchez, and Jackson. The emphasis was church ministry among women, blacks, minorities, and Native Americans, and discussion of the civil rights movement and the changing South. Thea was one of several presenters. She spoke also at another event, at the University of Mississippi, "Catholics and Blacks in Mississippi."

Then there was the National Congress on Black Catholics (not to be confused with the conferences for clergy, seminarians, and sisters, mentioned in chapter 12). It was an outgrowth of the same energy that produced the influential 1984 pastoral letter on evangelization from the ten black American bishops, *What We Have Seen and Heard.* The congress was a renaissance of five National Black Catholic Congresses held in the late 1800s. This historic 1987 congress, which has met every five years since, was held in Washington, D.C., May 21–24. Fifteen hundred delegates attended to formulate and approve a national black Catholic pastoral plan. From its inception, Thea was involved in planning this conference. She was a delegate and also coordinated the thirteen-member delegation from the Jackson diocese. The congress was a springboard for a number of initiatives to focus the work of the church on the needs of the black Catholic community.

One of those needs was to bring African American cultural traditions, in a more focused way, into Roman Catholic worship. Thea played a key role in the 1987 publication of the seminal *Lead Me, Guide Me: The African American Catholic Hymnal.* The Most Reverend James P. Lyke, OFM, PhD, auxiliary bishop of Cleveland at that time, coordinated the hymnal project. In the preface to the book, Bishop Lyke wrote that *Lead Me, Guide Me* was born of the needs and aspirations of Black Catholics:

> For a long time, but particularly within the last two decades, Black Catholics and the pastoral staffs who minister to our people have increasingly seen the need for liturgical and devotional settings and hymnody that lend themselves to the unique and varied styles of song and expression that are characteristics of our people.
>
> Similarly, Black Catholics, who embody various religious and cultural traditions, wish to share our gifts with the wider ecclesial community and draw from the great musical corpus of our own Roman Catholic tradition and that of our Sister Churches. Thus, *Lead Me, Guide Me* is both universal and particular as well as ecumenical in composition. While the various national Black Catholic organizations and leaders have voiced these concerns, and

while in the past specific individuals have initiated proposals for this hymnal, the fact is that its origin comes from Black Catholics themselves.[13]

Thea wrote one of the book's introductions and was actively involved in helping to make the choices that resulted in the hymnal. In that introduction, "The Gift of African American Sacred Song," one can read much of what made Thea tick. The academic side of her succinctly explained the history of sacred song:

From the African Mother Continent, African men and women, through the Middle Passage, throughout the Diaspora, to the Americas, carried the African gift and treasure of sacred song. To the Americas, African men and women brought sacred songs and chants that reminded them of their homelands and that sustained them in separation and in captivity, songs to respond to all life situations, and the ability to create new songs to answer new needs.

As the introduction continued, she traced African American song from the earliest times (timelines included), through the development of the African Methodist Episcopal Hymnal (1801), the Fisk Jubilee Singers of the late nineteenth century, through Thomas Dorsey's and others' Gospel music of the early twentieth century. She brings in the groundbreaking work of Father Clarence Joseph Rivers, who opened the door for black sacred song in Roman Catholic worship during the liturgical reforms of the 1960s.

She put words to what most people gather through experience:

Black sacred song is soulful song — holistic: challenging the full engagement of mind, imagination, memory, feeling, emotion, voice, and body; participatory: inviting the worshipping community to join in contemplation, in celebration and in prayer; real: celebrating the immediate concrete reality of the worshipping community — grief or separation, struggle or oppression, determination or joy — bringing that reality to prayer within the community of believers; spirit-filled: energetic, engrossing, intense; life-giving: refreshing, encouraging, consoling, invigorating, sustaining.

In a truly autobiographical statement, she speaks of the Gospel singer as one "chosen from the people by the people to suit their immediate need:

Sometimes *I* feel like a motherless child

I just came from the fountain

I love the Lord

My Heavenly Father watches over *me*.

The first person pronoun, the 'I' reference is communal. The individual sings the soul of the community. In heart and voice and gesture the church, the community responds."

The singer lifts the church, the people, to a higher level of understanding, feeling, motivation, and participation. "Song," she writes, "is not an object to be admired so much as an instrument to teach, comfort, inspire, persuade, convince, and motivate."[14]

To the delight of Thea and all involved, *Lead Me, Guide Me* received wide acclaim. A hundred thousand copies were sold during the first four years after publication. It still is used extensively in churches throughout the English-speaking world.

In mid-November Thea flew to St. Thomas Island in the Caribbean, conducting joyous revivals from Monday through Thursday evenings to overflow crowds. Her themes included the family, youth, celebrating who we are. Thea explained that mission revivals are a "coming together in Jesus' name," to revive the spirits and "bring new joy into peoples' lives."[15] Additional high points of the year 1987 included an October guest appearance on the *700 Club*, a widely viewed Protestant evangelical television show.[16] With the Holy Child Jesus children and parishioners from the church of St. Benedict the Black in Grambling, Louisiana, Thea also appeared on the *Ebony/Jet Showcase*,[17] a network TV show. She was becoming well known.

Her plans for the New Year 1988 were full. She was already booked for short courses, seminars, workshops, conferences, retreats, and/or revivals in sixty sites, plus return trips to St. Croix and Africa. She confirmed two weeks with the Maryknoll sisters in Tanzania (to be discussed in chapter 24.) As the year drew to a close, Thea wrote in her holiday letter for the beginning of the new year: "1987 was a busy and happy year for me.... I suffered no major health crises, and I made a new commitment to choose health and life. One of my retreat resolutions was to take better care of me. That's been fun, too."

She then went on to chronicle her many commitments of the preceding year, literally from one end of the continent to the other: "I had an opportunity to talk and work with the wealthy and the destitute, children and the elders, people from many ethnic, cultural, and national backgrounds. I loved it." She commented on her new typewriter and her concerted effort to learn typing: "Dort [her housemate] says it's my new toy."[18] She mentioned, almost in passing, her *60 Minutes* appearance and then spoke of something that came out of the *60 Minutes* show. Legendary actor Harry Belafonte began exploring the idea of producing a film documentary of Thea's life, with Whoopi Goldberg in the role of Thea. Belafonte, of course, is the hit musician, movie star, civil rights activist, and supporter of anti-poverty programs, especially in Africa. Known as the "King of Calypso," he popularized music from his Caribbean heritage with his record-breaking hits of the 1950s (including "Day-O").

He had seen Thea on *60 Minutes* and was captivated by her vision. He decided her life should be filmed as a major Hollywood movie. News accounts reported that Whoopi Goldberg had agreed to play Thea. In the late summer of 1987 Belafonte's agents had invited Thea to California to discuss this potential film, depicting her life and ministry. She visited his home and family and had talks with Belafonte, his agents, and Whoopi Goldberg. While she was in Beverly Hills, in a letter to Sister Patricia Ann Alden, FSPA, then-president of the community, Sister Thea wrote her latest news on five sheets of hotel telephone pad paper. (Sister Patricia Ann, her good friend, had been principal at Blessed Sacrament School in La Crosse during the last year of Sister Thea's time there.)

> Fri–Sat
> Dear S. Pat,
> Right now I am in a $250 a night room at the exclusive Four Seasons Hotel in Beverly Hills — note $2.00 grapefruit juice — small. I've been here since Sunday as guest of Harry Belafonte and Whoopi Goldberg.
> I told you recently that several companies are interested in rights to my life — TV, movies, book. You said okay. So we're on the way.
> Harry Belafonte is impressed by my message. I am teaching values that he wants to further — positive self-image for Blacks, cooperation/collaboration, hope for national and international peace and justice based on knowing one another, loving, and working together. (Right now he's producing Winnie Mandela's story.) He wants to do a movie about Thea.

Friends in media will/are assist/assisting me in selecting an agent and a lawyer specializing in media industry. Before any contracts are signed industry lawyer will contact and negotiate with community lawyer, treasurer and/or whoever else needs to be contacted in FSPA.

Industry researchers will talk with my friends, students, relatives, sisters, co-workers, colleagues, opposers, etc., to round out a biography. Belafonte wants to purchase premier rights — which means nobody can do movies or TV before Belafonte or without Belafonte's approval. Books and articles and interviews are always okay. Lawyers (FSPA and industry) will negotiate terms. Agent will represent my interests.

I'll get paid for rights, for royalties, etc. I'd like to negotiate with FSPA to designate % to FSPA-St. Rose, Inc., % to educational opportunity and/or job training for the poor — both in terms of my wishes and preferences, in terms of FSPA/Catholic public image and the possibility of drawing public attention to the needs of the poor and concrete possibilities for helping to break the cycle of poverty. At this moment, by God's strange design, I am a name, a celebrity, a public figure. I know this too will pass quickly away. In the meantime I will try to use it for the Kingdom. Remember Tammy and Jimmie Bakker. Pray for me.

Whether I live or die, if the movie is done, it becomes a teaching tool that for a while will endure. Belafonte projects a message to 60 to 80 million in this country and more abroad. Pray for me, please.

Thanks for all you've been in my life.

Love,

Thea[19]

Thea's friend Oldenburg Franciscan Sister Francesca Thompson, herself from a family of professional actors, remembers, "After Whoopi had met her, you know I think they just fell in love with her and were just amazed at the kind of person she was." She recalls that Thea's visit had been during the same week that Thomspon had been the keynote speaker at the National Black Congress, in Washington, D.C., and that Thompson's photo, giving a speech to the gathering, had been on the front page of the *New York Times,* with quotes from her speech in which she sarcastically described herself as, the "Ku Klux Klanner's dream girl." She speculates that Harry and Whoopi must have thought, " 'Where did you crazy Black nuns come from? Who is this fool that they've got on the front page of the *New York Times* who made that statement?"

Thea would have said, conjectures Thompson, " 'Oh, she's one of my dearest friends! Would you autograph a picture for her?' " In her self-less style, says Thompson, Thea had indeed asked Whoopi to send a celebrity photo, autographed for Francesca Thompson — not for Thea Bowman. Whoopi agreed, but sent along extras for Thea and friends. The inscription on Thompson's? "To Sister Francesca Thompson: a 'Ku Klux Klanners' dream girl' from Whoopi Goldberg, the 'African Premier's Nightmare.' "[20] Thea thanked and updated the Belafontes and Goldberg in September 1987:

September 25, 1987
Dear Harry and Whoopi,

It has been embarrassingly long since you have heard from me — how much I enjoyed my brief stay with you, how much I appreciated your interest, concern, kindness; how much joy I brought to students and friends with the autographed Whoopi pictures and the Belafonte-Goldberg stories. Thank you for one of the most exciting weekends of my almost fifty years.

Thank you, too, Harry, for the contract, which I realize is still under negotiation. I want you to know that after the Belafonte-Goldberg offer I did not seriously consider any other — not even, as was suggested to me, as leverage for bargaining power. I know and respect the Belafonte name and reputation, remember my father's admiration for the name and dignity, have enjoyed the Belafontes' arts and culture since childhood, remember the Belafonte stance for Black folks, for poor folks and for justice, how you stood for the people (poor, disadvantaged, fearful) when professionally and personally it would have been easier and safer to remain uninvolved. So I can truly say to my folks that I have loved and respected the Belafontes for a long, long time. And in short time I learned to love Whoopi — the depth, the insight, the humanity and humility, the ability to see humor, dignity, and goodness in the discouraged, outcast, neglected, and unlikely; the acting genius, as well as the strength that enabled you to turn your life around. I have so many happy memories of my time with you and with Mrs. Belafonte.

Harry, you mentioned that if you decided to do a film you would be seeking to establish a base of support. There are a number of

people who know that you are considering the project and who
have expressed an interest in talking with you and possibly in collaboration. I do not pretend to know how your business works or
theirs, but I will list some names of people that would be interested
in speaking with you in connection with your intention to do a film
about my life.[21]

A list of names and phone numbers followed. Various film makers
and the *Ebony/Jet Showcase* all wanted in on the act. Thea was fast
becoming everybody's sister.

Now using a wheelchair, Thea came to the White House Rose Garden to receive a presidential courage award given to cancer survivors. (1988)

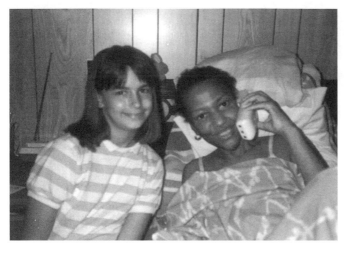

Thea spent much of her last two years in bed, on the road, or in Canton. People from everywhere came to visit, including 10-year-old Ann Sherberger, who asked, "Are you a saint?" (1988)

Miming "hear no evil, speak no evil, see no evil" (with Dorothy Ann Kundinger [l] and Carita Loving) reveals Thea's sense of humor during the Bouldin portrait unveiling. (1988)

Thea, with advanced cancer, gained healing when surrounded by friends, including Daniel Johnson and an unidentified friend who came to Canton to see Thea, and Dort (center). (late 1980s)

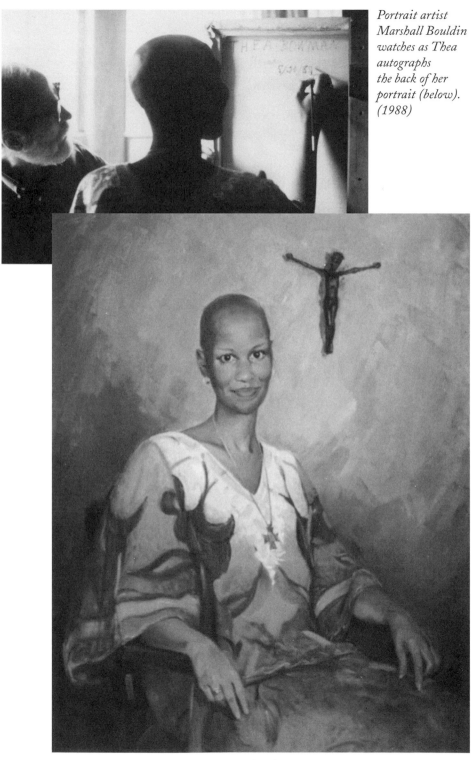

*Portrait artist
Marshall Bouldin
watches as Thea
autographs
the back of her
portrait (below).
(1988)*

*The portrait of Thea by renowned artist Marshall Bouldin today hangs in the
chancery office, Diocese of Jackson. Thea insisted on a portrait that showed the "true
truth": bald head, African garb, the suffering of Jesus.*

By then weak with cancer, Thea happily responds to an enthusiastic audience during her last appearance at Viterbo College, Humanities Symposium. (1989)
Photo by Patricia Tekippe, FSPA

*Fr. Roy Lee, presider, anchors the procession after FSPA memorial liturgy for Thea in
Mary of the Angels Chapel at the FSPA mother house in La Crosse, Wis. (1990)
Photo by Mary Beth Ripp*

St. Mary's Church in Jackson, Miss., was the site of Thea's funeral liturgy. (1990)

Thea is buried beside her parents in historic Elmwood Cemetery, Memphis, Tenn. The epitaph by Thea's name on the left: "She tried."

Sister Dorothy Ann Kundinger, FSPA, at the University of Notre Dame commencement, accepts the prestigious Laetare Medal, posthumously, for Thea, weeks after Thea's death.

At Holy Child Jesus parish, early in the school day on All Saints Day,
Thea coaxes a group of sleepy children to sing. (1984)
Photo © John Feister

With all kinds of love.
God bless you and yours. Thea

Chapter 23

WE SHALL OVERCOME—TODAY

April 4, 1988, marked the twentieth anniversary of Dr. Martin Luther King Jr.'s assassination. Five years earlier, the date had been designated a national holiday, driving the growth and energy of local community observances. The Milwaukee, Wisconsin, community invited Thea to be the keynote speaker for their 1988 event.

The Milwaukee celebration was a singular triumph for Thea. Free and open to the public, the program, "Martin Luther King: Seize the Vision," took place in Uihlein Hall at the Performing Arts Center in downtown Milwaukee. Widespread advance publicity ensured a large crowd.

In one of the advance stories, an organizer talked about Thea, the "first religious leader in the celebration's five-year history": "When Sister Bowman came to rehearse with the choir, you saw this little woman and you wondered how much of an impact she could have," said Rosa Givens, who organized the event, one of the largest in the United States. "But when she gets on stage she takes on this commanding presence. I was just astonished."[1] The article describes the two-hundred-voice choir combined from six choral groups that backed up Thea, as well as drummer groups from Native American and African American drummers, multicultural dancers, and high school students dramatizing the March to Montgomery. Previous years' events had filled the auditorium's twenty-three hundred seats; this event was expected to also be broadcast on local cable.

Other articles followed in the Sunday paper. Lyn L. Hartman wrote for the *Milwaukee Journal Sunday Magazine,* capturing the spirit and music of Thea. She wrote, "One of Sister Thea Bowman's missions is letting kids know that they are beautiful. That's part of how she pursues the dreams of Martin Luther King Jr." In the interview that followed, Thea spoke of Dr. King: "People keep saying, 'Where's the next Martin Luther King?' We're all called, I think. We're called by our citizenship, by our membership in the human race. We're all called to free ourselves and to free one another. I want our singing to be able to convey that, not just to ourselves, but to our children and to our elders."

In between all of the biographical information, Thea talks of her philosophy of music: "In African tradition, music was a tool for teaching. Song was used to give a lesson or a warning. It was used to praise, to censure or admonish, or to bring a kind of solemnity and celebration to reality and to make reality more memorable. Music is a way to deal with oppression, to come to peace with it, a way to center the soul, to calm yourself so you can make decisions."

Hartman also reported on Thea's comments to the choirs during rehearsal, urging the singers to find their truest voices: "There are two things I'm asking from you. I'm asking for your fine musicianship. But I'm also asking you for something that comes before that. Folks call it a primitive strength and energy. It has to come from the bottom of your feet, from the pit of your stomach, from your heart as well as your head. It has to come from all the times when somebody beat you down. Is there anybody here who doesn't know that kind of experience? Did you ever go to an old-time, back-in-the-woods, under-the-trees type of church? The elders would draw the spirit into the church. There was something about the old folks. They would start all kinds of synapses snapping. It's a kind of strength and power, that singing, that witnessing. It grips people at a level of heart and feeling and emotion. It's complete improvisation. People who know how to do it know.... That's what I want from you."

In the interview, Thea explained to Hartman, "I want to remind all of us that to celebrate Martin Luther King without being real about the dream is sacrilege." She listed the Beatitudes, feeding the hungry, clothing the naked, as King's dream. "By living the dream, I bring joy to my life. And by living the dream, I share that joy. It's contagious. I really believe that."[2]

Thea's actual speech was a triumph! A fresh, vital, radiant Thea was dressed in a two-piece figured blue African *bou bou* (top) and *lapa* (skirt). She wore her signature gold medium-sized hoop earrings. She plaited her luxuriant hair in braids wound on the sides and back of her head. Observant attendees noticed her FSPA gold ring was on the left hand middle finger instead of her ring finger because she had lost considerable weight. She was trim and beautiful.

A counter stool was placed next to the podium; Thea did not use it, even though, it would soon become clear, this was the last time she was able to stand during a talk. Her words, songs, gestures that afternoon in Milwaukee were powered by sheer soul-force. A photograph showing a side view of King in a pensive moment, arms folded across his chest, was dramatically projected on a larger-than-life-size screen when Thea first mentioned his name and remained on screen throughout much of the talk. Often the pianist played softly under her speaking, leading to her singing a spiritual. With dramatic intensity, she gracefully commanded the stage, moving from the podium when she sang. Like a Toscanini, she helped "conduct" the choirs' spirited Gospel songs, her own voice often soaring high above the massed chorus. Caught by her joy the audience frequently broke into sustained applause. The event was a tour de force, which was made all the stronger by her actual talk.

In it she remembered Dr. King, the true spirit of his life and of his selfless death: Martin was a man, not perfect, flawed as we are flawed, determined, dedicated. Martin was an ambassador for justice . . . an activist, an agitator. Call him what you will, he was willing to speak out, to march, to be jailed, to be cursed, to be spat upon, to be beaten and abused. He was willing to lay down his life for what he believed in. The grandson of a slave, he was able to talk with statesmen and politicians, the rich and the poor, the erudite and the illiterate, old people and little children, garbage collectors and farmers, presidents and princes. He was preoccupied with that struggle for freedom, strengthened by his belief that God would lead the oppressed to freedom.

Her talk was as much about King's dream as about King himself, "a dream of freedom, a dream deeply rooted in the American dream. A dream so vital that it has drawn people of all lands to these shores. A dream that dares to say, 'Give me your tired, your poor, your huddled masses yearning to be free.' " Interspersed through her talk, the choir broke into song; after this talk of Martin's dream, it broke into "America the Beautiful."

She brought her talk to a very pointed discussion about race relations in Milwaukee. "I read in one of your papers that Milwaukee is one of the most segregated metropolitan areas in the country. You have come together today to be about peace, to be about justice, to be about freedom, and to be about unity. And the celebration that we share is a mockery if the beauty we have shared we do not take back into our homes and our neighborhoods." She challenged the audience beyond complacency in serving the poor, in reaching out to help each other. "Think about the people who have brought you this far," she reminded them. It all ended with a quote from Dr. King: "I still believe that one day mankind will bow before the altar of God and be crowned triumphant over war and bloodshed, and nonviolent redemptive goodwill will be proclaimed the rule of the land. I still believe that we shall overcome." After the choirs and assembly sang the civil rights movement hymn "We Shall Overcome," the audience gave Thea and the assembled choirs a standing ovation. Event organizers presented red roses to Thea, which she distributed to dancers and singers who joined her on stage reprising "We Shall Overcome." Thea directed the large crowd to sing today in place of *someday,* "we shall overcome *today!*"[3]

Her rousing appearance was followed by an interview with MPTV personality Joe Smith for his *Smith and Company* program, televised Monday, January 18. Smith fired his questions about race relations to Thea, who in turn answered succinctly, though gently. Charmingly, relentlessly she articulated her points logically, explaining improvements in civil rights yet cataloging examples of continuing injustice and discrimination toward blacks twenty years after the King assassination. What follows is a substantial excerpt:

Smith: Your impression of yesterday's Martin Luther King Jr. celebration: Where are we now?

Thea: Some people would say that the dream has become a nightmare. We have definitely moved forward in terms of following the dream, of celebrating the dream. The legal machinery is in order. The nation is an institutional and constitutional reality. The validity of what King called the check has been written not only for black people but for all people who have come here to claim the heritage and to claim the dream.

Smith: But is there enough in the checking account?

Thea: There's enough in the checking account, . . . but not everybody has access. When I say that I mean King was demonstrating for the rights of the poor. He was demonstrating for housing, fair housing and decent housing. He was demonstrating for opportunity for adequate education, and not just adequate education opportunities, but adequate education for all the children, for all the young men and women. He was demonstrating for a land where we could love one another and where we could regard one another as brothers and sisters, and where we could work together toward the solutions of our common problems.

Smith: Okay, those are all the negatives. So what are the positives? How do we get ourselves out of that situation? You are a teacher by trade who's...

Thea: That's when we get ourselves out of that situation — by demanding of ourselves, demanding of the body politic, demanding of the public sector that we put top priority — high priority — on the education of our children and of our youth. And when I say education, I mean academic education. I mean physical education, vocational education, parenting education, moral and value education, cultural education. We need a total educational package and we need to make it available to everybody. And it's your responsibility; it's my responsibility. How can we impact the country in such a way that we get a clear message to our elected leadership that it is this what must be? I think to me the other priority is important. How do we say to this nation... and you hear all this conversation about people who are on welfare and who want to be on welfare? We have brilliant minds within this nation. How can we use the talent that we have to figure out a system that helps people who need help, that gives jobs to people who need jobs, that provides job training for people who need that training so that they can take advantage of a job that is in proportion to their talents? The IRS will track you down if you don't pay your taxes. Now why can't we use some of that kind of acumen — the kind of acumen that could get people into space? Why can't we use that talent and those brains to figure out a welfare system that is real and that works?

Smith: And you raise some excellent questions in trying to find the answers....

Thea: And what I want to say is that every one of us has a responsibility. We need to teach the children, the little five-year-olds, the little four-year-olds, that they can change things. They can make life better for themselves and for their families and for their country. And that even though they can't vote at this time they can be politically active. They can be involved in participating as citizens. I think that is the teaching at all levels. How do we teach the poor that they can change their lives? How do we raise up the young men and young women with the kind of confidence in themselves that says, 'I'm somebody! I am somebody special — even if I'm slow, even if I have a drug problem, even if my parents are gone, even if I don't have money — I'm somebody! — and that there are resources available in my community and that I have to reach out and grab those resources? And I say that if the child is five years old, how do we teach the children? And then there's something else I learned because there were people outside of my family — inside my family and outside of my family — who were willing to help me, to give me a chance, to give me an opportunity. And I know poor people who would use their money to put shoes on somebody else's child's feet, who would feed anybody who would come into the — you know. I think we have to return to some of the old value systems that says: If you know somebody, feed somebody; if you know how to read, teach somebody. If you know how to fix a car, teach somebody; if you know how to clean a room, teach somebody. If you know how to run a computer, if you're a radiologist, let somebody see. Let somebody hear what you do and try to inspire somebody — not only to take your place — but to surpass you in serving humanity. I think we could get some of these teachings.

Smith: Did you hear [Dr. King's] message when you heard him on the radio? What did you get from it?

Thea: Hope! Hope! Hope! I grew up in Mississippi. I grew up in Canton, Mississippi. I grew up under an institutionalized and legalized system of segregation and institutional racism. And for many of us it was a way of life that was unquestioned. We didn't like it. I didn't like drinking water out of the colored fountain when the bowl was broken and the white bowl had, you know, cold water. I didn't enjoy traveling and going for miles and miles without being able to use the restrooms because the restrooms were for white people. I didn't enjoy going into the store and waiting. I came in first, and I would have to wait until sixteen white people had been waited on before I had been waited on. I didn't enjoy hearing a seventeen-year-old, Miss Smith, call my mother, who was in her fifties, Mary, because she was black and Miss Smith happened to be white. But we never thought that we could change that. We never thought that we had any power to effect any change. And what King did for us was to help us to realize that the Constitution was on our side, that the American Dream was on our side, that there were good people, caring people, within this nation who did not know what was going on in some of these situations; that well-meaning people were doing racist things because they too were in this system that they did not question. And he (King) began to raise the questions, and he began to help us raise the questions, and he worked with the local leadership and taught us.

Smith: What was it in listening to him [King], or even going through your childhood of having to drink out of the bowl for colored people, what was it that didn't make you bitter through all of this?

Thea: I'm from Mississippi and the people who did not learn to contain their angers and their frustrations did not live long. [Pause] You do know what I mean — you learn very early on to wear the mask. So that if I had to work with you and I felt — not that I knew but I felt — that you were racist in your heart, I learned to guard my manner, to guard my feet, even to guard my thoughts, to guard my feelings and passions and emotions. I did that not because I hated you, but because I had to survive, because I had to have a job, because my children had to walk in safety.

Smith: Do you still have to use that mask today?

Thea: Sometimes.

Smith: Sad fact, isn't it?

Thea: Yes, it's a sad fact. . . . See, I walk in a number of different communities just as my Native American brothers and sisters [do], my Hispanic brothers and sisters, and my Asian brothers and sisters. We have to walk in more than one world. When I come into the world of academia, when I come into the world of business, or when I come into the world of politics or statesmanship, or into the world of international commerce or international conversation, I have to be bilingual, bicultural. I have to be able to talk your talk and to be able to talk it better than you can if I am going to be accepted and respected by many people in your society. And so what we say to our children is: you have to be bicultural, you have to be multicultural, you have to learn many ways, many styles — you have to be adaptable, if you want to survive. You have to adapt your speech; you have to adapt your dress; you have to adapt your manner; you have to adapt your ways of thinking and to give us flexibility.

Smith: If you had not become a nun, what do you think you would be doing?

Thea: I don't know.

Smith: What would you like to do?

Thea: I'd probably be teaching. I love teaching.

Smith: What is it about teaching? Is it the molding — the shaping of the mind?

Thea: . . . Well, I like children. I think they're much more fun than adults.

Smith: Okay! So you're not having a good time here?

Thea: Oh, yeah! But, you know, a lot of adults won't play with you, but the children will. And, in a remarkable kind of way, children will believe you if you tell them your truth. Not that you have a corner on the truth, but if you tell them your truth there's that intuitive grab — the children believe you. If you love them, they will let you love them. I am attracted to the freshness and the beauty of young people. I think it is so important that they learn to value themselves before the world has a chance to beat them down. I have worked in Wisconsin, for example, with children of affluence, and I have found the same kinds of insecurity and fear among some of these young people — of grade-school age, of college age — as I find among the poor. They're waiting for somebody else to tell them what to think and they live in fear of what others will think of them. And they don't realize their power: their power to reach out; their power to effect change; their power to grasp happiness and freedom. . . . See my dad was one of those people who felt that if you could read, you could do anything.[4]

After such a high-powered, successful event in Milwaukee, what came next was shocking. The following day, back home in Mississippi, Thea was running a high fever, and her back pain was undeniable. Her pulse was racing, too. After a day at home, the next day she went to her doctor, who hospitalized her for recuperation and tests. That night, January 18, x-rays showed, undeniably, that her cancer had returned. She went into the seclusion of treatment.

Several months later the rumor mill was buzzing among Thea's friends. In March, she put pen to paper, in another of her form letters to her broad network: "So many friends have recently asked where and how I am, what I'm doing and what I expect that I have decided to tell all," she wrote. It was a candid letter from a person who, though she loved the stage, preferred privacy when it came to health and personal matters.

"Frankly, I lost a month," she began. She chronicled her treatments for infection, the CAT scans that confirmed cancer's return, and the course of fifteen radiation treatments that followed. "All my late January, February, and early March engagements were cancelled, much to my regret," she explained. But, of course she had no choice. "For a month I ate and slept and did little else. I felt like a huge caterpillar: eat, sleep, eat, sleep, chomp, chomp, roll around in a wheelchair, drive poor old Dort crazy."

Sister Dorothy Ann Kundinger, her housemate and traveling companion, was again her caretaker. "Dort," wrote Thea with resignation, "passed pills, pushed food when the appetite was gone, carted me to radiation, etc., etc., etc. You know."

But, at letter's end, typical of Thea, she sounded a note of hope. She expressed the return of her strength, her doctors' satisfaction, and, referring to her previously mentioned caterpillar behavior, proclaimed, "I'm almost ready to do my butterfly act." She predicted to her reading audience her own return to the speaking circuit, although, she admitted, it would be a modified schedule, with time built in for "rest and recovery." I have to learn that the body is no longer eighteen years old and needs antique maintenance. But that's all right, too. We know that God has been good to me."[5]

Sure enough, in March she was in the Virgin Islands, at St. Patrick's Catholic Church, in Fredrikstad, on the west shore of St. Croix. Thea was happy to be out of the hospital, happy to be out of doctors' offices, and out of her house, she was even happy to be out of Mississippi, back on the missionary road. And the Virgin Islands weather was, of course, a joy.

A *Catholic Islander* article about the event, with an accompanying photo showing Thea in a wheelchair, was picked up and printed in several stateside Catholic papers. That news, of Thea using a wheelchair, being back in business, circulated rapidly among Catholics throughout the United States. And the comments of one parishioner, included after a vivid description of Thea's typical revival program of preaching, teaching, and singing, told a typical story: "Regular church is boring, but if every Sunday Mass was like this, I'd go every week."[6]

Even before her cancer's return, Thea's brave and exemplary role as a cancer survivor had been noticed. The American Cancer Society's Mississippi branch named Thea its choice to receive a national Courage Award, along with representatives from the other forty-nine states, at the White House at the end of March. The citation noted her battle with cancer since 1984 and credited her bravery and dedication in continuing her ministry in spite of the cancer. She and the other awardees received a citation signed by President Ronald Reagan: "The American Cancer Society salutes Sister Thea for her personal courage in her battle against cancer and for the hope and inspiration she gives all Americans in the fight for life and health."[7]

In early April, Sister Thea had two bookings in Madison, Wisconsin: at Mount Zion Baptist Church and at St. Benedict Retreat Center for a Lenten seminar, "Living Spirit/Woman Spirit." At the retreat center she crowed that she had choirs in lots of places and now she had one in Madison. The Mount Zion Inspirational Choir members joined her for the seminar at St. Benedict's. It was Thea's now well-tested style of coming into an area, locating local choirs, and putting them into a new setting where separated cultures could come together. People were thrilled.[8]

It would be easy enough to drop back into the whirlwind of Thea's schedule without noting what had become radically different. Up until this time, Thea, the unlikely Catholic sister, used her profound gifts in an unusual moment of growing awareness in America's cultural history. All of that, yes, but add to it the image of Thea, the wheelchair user, continuing her presentations. Now she brings the witness of suffering to her message of Gospel freedom and dignity. Much like Pope John Paul II would impress the world a decade later with his refusal to let Parkinson's disease stop him, much as he would make his disease a part of his message about the God-given dignity of human life, Thea's presence, that of a cancer survivor fighting to the end, would perhaps become her most lasting image.

The local Catholic press reported, glowingly, "Standing ten feet tall in a wheelchair, black eyes rolling and flashing, she lit up the room with her profound thought, easy humor, tender prayers, and soul-searing songs.

A recent end to the remission of cancer has incapacitated her body but not her spirit."[9] Wisconsin Governor Tommy Thompson sent his representative, David Duax, to present a commendation for her ministry and her courage as a cancer survivor. That cancer survivor, now facing cancer's return, boiled her message down to its most fundamental theme: the power of love. She lived in an even more loving way. More and more she told people that she loved them. She coaxed people coming for her speaking and singing to be kind, to be loving, to tell their children, their spouses, their families, their friends and colleagues, how much they appreciated and loved them. For commencement addresses Thea talked about the amazing power of love to graduating classes. Her words, backed by the witness of her suffering, her joyful endurance, her soul force, were potent and memorable.

Because her doctors so prescribed, Thea did take time to recuperate, to rest between appearances. Yet, at the end of April she enplaned again, this time flying to Baltimore for the Second Black Catholic Revival at the city's Basilica of the Assumption. On Monday evening, April 25, about a thousand Catholics and others packed the expansive cathedral church to hear Thea speak at the opening of the three-day revival. Bishop John Ricard, demonstrably proud of his friend, solicitously wheeled her through the crowds at the sessions.

The choirs of St. Bernardine and St. Edward parishes sang with Thea. "Inspiring" and "energetic" were the descriptors attendees gave to her talk-from-her-wheelchair.[10] Denise Walker's photo of Thea clad in blue African attire, head tilted far right because of her weakened neck bones, went out on the Catholic News wire and was published in the Catholic press throughout the United States.

Numerous articles gleaned from telephone interviews Thea gave to reporters during these months filled Catholic diocesan weeklies and other newspapers and magazines. The news of Thea's brilliant, exuberant presentations, her daunting travel schedule, the Cancer Courage award, her "keepin' on" spirit though cancer had spread to her spine and bones, captivated readers and Thea's legion of friends. Thea, the *60 Minutes* celebrity, gained fans constantly. She was continuously in the news across scores of cities in the eastern half of the United States and in national church publications. The few times when she was at home in Canton, visitors streamed to the convent door.

Sister Dorothy Ann (Dort) handled the increasing caregiving on the home front plus the activity Thea's engagements generated with constant good cheer and calm. Dort assumed more and more responsibility, acting as Thea's virtual secretary, trip planner, chauffeur, all-around personal assistant, nurse, and care-giver. Dort would later say that she considered serving and companioning Thea a privilege. She was there for Thea in every aspect of her demanding schedule. Thea remained independent to the end, but she was extremely grateful for Dort's help.

Thea rarely, if ever, complained about pain, or unpleasant medical treatments, or restricted diet, or difficult movement, or uncomfortable travel conditions. She put into serious practice the counsel she had gleaned from her elders about how to handle suffering. She moaned, she sang, she prayed, she swayed and rocked back and forth. She asked her friends to pray for her.

The Baltimore revival at the end of April was spirit-filled, a great event, if taxing, in the long line of others. When Thea returned to Mississippi, doctors once again admitted her to St. Dominic/Jackson Medical Center. The debilitating pain in her spine was, in her words, "like hitting your crazy bone again and again."[11]

Once statuesque Thea now could neither stand tall nor even hold her body erect for long periods. Tumors spread deeper into her bones. Her doctors, whom she trusted and whose advice she followed, prescribed another round of chemotherapy, with intense side effects. She remained an active and curious patient throughout her experience with illness. "I will be about the business of living for as long as I can," was her mantra. Characteristically she soon shared her adventure with cancer in a June 1988 letter to her friends and colleagues.

Along the way, commitments called, and Sister Thea answered. First, she gave a commencement address at Regis College in Weston, Massachusetts. Thea gracefully endured her hair starting to fall out, a side-effect of her recent chemotherapy, even standing before the assembly at Regis, where she was awarded an honorary doctor of laws degree on Saturday, May 21, 1988.

Hair loss aside, the commencement was a high point for Thea: it was her first honorary doctorate (though she had already earned an academic doctorate). The academic community at Regis's fifty-eighth annual commencement gave her a rousing reception as she was wheeled on stage. A photo was wired to media in New England of exultant Thea in academic attire, bald head covered with mortar board.[12]

Addressing the graduates who had come from all points across America and beyond, Thea told them they had come to a wonderland, "a

Regis wonderland of dogwood and pine, mansions and towers, tradition and ceremony, dance and internship, service, rivalry, affection, laughter and tears, pain, struggle, challenge, accomplishment, love, memory — no men!" As most commencement speakers do, Thea congratulated the nearly two hundred graduates for completing their courses and acquiring insights, skills, analysis, and judgment that would equip them for a lifetime of learning and growth. Now was their time for commitment, beginning and commencement. She talked about the role of women, drawing on her own insights from the black community: "Women's role is to give life. I challenge you to use your power; your personal power, your moral, intellectual, professional, economic, diplomatic, political power to give life, to nourish, protect, defend, and restore life.

"You are renaissance women, which means you must be reborn each day. Reborn in yourselves by helping growth in others and effecting life-giving change. As you rise, reach back and help somebody who needs your help. How will you serve humanity? How will you make a difference? Wherever you find yourself, share life, give life." Thea concluded her talk singing movingly, "My Living Will Not Be in Vain." The Regis College community gave her a standing ovation.[13] After the ceremonies a celebration dinner was attended by the honorary degree recipients, and friends including Boston's Cardinal Bernard Law (a one-time Mississippian) and Father John Ford, a member of the Missionary Servants of the most Holy Trinity order, which sponsored Holy Child Jesus Mission in Canton.

Returning to Canton, Sister Thea joined Sister Dorothy Ann in the major process of moving out of Holy Child Jesus Convent, which was closing, back to her childhood home on Hill Street. Friends helped to clean and shine the house. Dort coordinated tasks and pitched in with the physical labor.

Almost immediately after the official move back to the Hill Street house, Thea traveled to Indiana to give the keynote speech for the International Providence Symposium at St. Mary-of-the-Woods for the Sisters of Providence. Again singing, praying, and speaking from her wheelchair, she urged symposium participants to be special signs of God's Providence. Thea inveigled her audience of mostly women religious not only to talk about but also to provide opportunities to make multicultural experiences happen. These various sisters' congregations, all sharing a common charism of depending upon Divine Providence, have members serving in missions in Indonesia, Mexico, England, Taiwan, Puerto Rico,

Brazil, Germany, Canada, and Chile. "Engage your cognitive faculties,
your memory, your imagination, your body.... The voice your community needs to hear is your voice," Thea told the women.[14] Before
taking off to St. Augustine's Retreat Center in Bay St. Louis, Mississippi,
for her annual retreat, Thea wrote to myriad inquiring, concerned sisters and friends — all "Friends of Thea" — another general letter dated
June 5, 1988: Her physician's daughter upbringing shows in a clinical
description of her physical condition and medical therapies.

Greetings and love from springtime in Mississippi.

Thank you for your cards, letters, calls, and visits. I apologize
for the form letter, but I'm disastrously behind in correspondence,
and this is the best way I know to express my appreciation and to
bring you up-to-date on me.

In March, after nine weeks of R & R, radiation and recovery, I
learned how to travel in a wheelchair for revivals, retreat days, or
conferences in St. Croix, Chicago, New Orleans, Madison, Beloit,
San Antonio, Pittsburgh, Springfield, Washington, and New York.
May 2, I landed in the hospital again — chest and back pain. The
cancer had spread further in the bone.

May 6, I started a new course of chemotherapy, vincristine and
adriamycin administered intravenously for 48 hours, eight treatments altogether at nineteen-day intervals. If my blood chemistry
is cooperative, I should be finished by October, but I couldn't get
the treatment scheduled for May 27 because my white blood count
was too low. The drugs I'm taking can have serious side effects,
but I'm trying to pray and psych my body into positive response.
Please pray for me.

As a result of chemotherapy, I lost all my hair. Much of it fell
out when I was in Boston, where I gave the graduation address and
received an honorary degree at Regis College. Rev. Clarence Rivers
says, "Bald is beautiful." Grooming is surely easier, one swipe with
a damp washcloth and a touch of oil for sheen. Sometimes I wear
a short wig or my usual African head tie. Sometimes I wear my
bald head.

As of June 15, Sister Dorothy Ann Kundinger and I will be moving back to my old homestead. We're looking forward to returning
to the old neighborhood. Sister Agnes Wernimont will be moving to
Houston to minister in a child-care facility. The convent where we

lived used to house fourteen sisters. It was made of reclaimed army barracks and has seen more than forty years of Holy Child Jesus ministry, dedication, and history. It will be sold, moved, salvaged, and/or destroyed. My new address is 136 Hill Street, Canton, MS 39046. My phone number remains the same....

I plan to continue working for the Diocese of Jackson and also sharing the Good News wherever I can. This year I'm hoping to make retreat at St. Augustine Retreat Center, Bay St. Louis; summer school at Xavier University, New Orleans; workshops or conferences in Chicago, Terre Haute, New Orleans, Denver, Indianapolis, Oxford (Mississippi), Seattle, New York, Washington, Dubuque, St. Louis, Boston, Tanzania, San Diego, Toledo, Brooklyn, Tulsa, Pittsburgh, and Memphis. I hope I may be able to see you somewhere along the way.

May God be with you until we meet again.

Love,

Sister Thea Bowman[15]

Chapter 24

"LET ME LIVE UNTIL I DIE"

After her week-long annual retreat on the Gulf Coast, Thea's energy level rose. She was delighted to take up residence in New Orleans to teach at the annual Institute for Black Catholic Studies (IBCS). It is an understatement to say that the 1988 IBCS three-week-session was unforgettable. As it turned out, the summer session in 1988 was the last time Thea would teach at the institute. The next year she was unable to be away from medical treatments and home for an extended time.

Thea became aware that by now many people considered her a celebrity. Now that she was receiving the attention of Harry Belafonte and Whoopi Goldberg, who could deny it? Ever the Franciscan and the professional artist, she kept her wits — and her humility — about her.

Belafonte had arranged to be in New Orleans and expected to have unobtrusive interviews with Thea at Xavier. However, the institute and the university alerted media and gleefully celebrated his visit with a reception for both. The event was a watermelon party, a southern tradition, star-studded with influential blacks from New Orleans and beyond. It must have been quite a party; people lucky to have been there talked about the occasion with affection for years. And of course, in society style, it was fodder for New Orleans's *Midtown Picayune*.

Mary Donnelly knew Thea when they were both growing up in Canton. She went to the event and wrote it up, for the August 14, 1988, Midtown editions. Calling Thea a "spokeswoman for black Catholics" — which is saying something in New Orleans, with its sizable black Catholic population — the article went on to describe Thea's work and the fun of the party. Belafonte, the article said, "found himself dancing in a second line led by a black nun in a wheelchair."

Donnelly waxed on about Thea's stately presence, describing her as a "legend" to black Catholics and comparing her to "a museum sculpture of Egyptian Queen Nefertiti." Then she got into the heart of Thea's message: " 'For years the white Catholic Church imposed its Caucasian methodology on black Catholics,' she said. 'You see, we don't want to change the theology of the church. We just want to express that theology within the roots of our black spiritual culture.' The essence of Sister Thea's message is: 'Take the poor into your homes if you want to minister to them. Show them by example what it means to be Christian. Teach them, by example what it means to be a family.' "

Donnelly recounted various aspects of Thea's philosophy, landing on the way Thea has handled celebrity, " 'I guess the only difference between me and other people is I'm content to do my little bit. I don't do big things. People think you have to do big things to make a difference,' she said. 'But if each person would light his and her own candle, however small, we'd have a mighty bright world.' "[1]

In her thank you to Belafonte, Thea wrote, "Thanks for being with us as family. You brought much joy." She told Belafonte about another upcoming interview/research opportunity, at the upcoming National Conference of Black Sisters, Clergy and Seminarians.[2]

Belafonte had told Thea, according to Sister Francesca Thompson, how much he loved his time at the institute, saying, "It's been so long since anyone did anything for me without asking for something in return."[3]

In what had become an expected ritual, Thea, in July, updated her friends via a form letter.

> Greetings from Mississippi.
>
> For me summer has been reinvigorating and revitalizing — a retreat at Bay St. Louis; summer school at Xavier University; soulful liturgies; enthusiastic students; being surrounded by so many loving friends who worked, prayed, played, laughed, and cried together and shared much powerful faith and energy.
>
> Harry Belafonte came to Xavier to do preliminary work on the movie he and Whoopi are doing on my life. Folks at the Institute loved having him. We treated him like family. We had a reception with watermelon and Belafonte, song, dance, picture-taking, and fun.

She went on to describe her health as "improved," and gave clinical details of blood counts and so on. And she reported that she and Dort, with the help of friends, had moved back to Hill Street, her family home. Then she listed a stack of upcoming commitments, including her trip to Tanzania with Maryknoll.

"Thanks for your love, calls, visits, cards, letters, prayers. Thanks for keeping in touch." In a postscript to one of the letters sent back to La Crosse, Dort had added, "We're almost moved in here at Hill. No ramp for wheel chair access yet — but shortly it will be here. Hot here; humid, too."[4]

As was her annual habit since returning to Mississippi, in August Thea again was a featured speaker at the annual Faulkner and Yoknapatawpha Conference at the University of Mississippi in Oxford. (Yoknapatawpha is the fictional Mississippi county that serves as the setting for Faulkner's stories.) The list of her lectures from 1980 through 1989 at Ole Miss, in addition to showing a depth of scholarship, shows the breadth of what she had shared with this international gathering:

1980	Black Music and Culture in the Works of William Faulkner's Mississippi
1981	Faulkner's Understanding of Blacks
1982–83	Black Music and Culture in the World of William Faulkner
1984	Black Culture and Humor in the Writings of William Faulkner
1985	Black Women in the Works of William Faulkner
1986	Faulkner and His Humor
1987	Artistry and the Art of Black America
1988	Mr. Faulkner, Blacks, and Popular Culture Found in Requiem for a Nun
1989	Faulkner and the Ole Time Religion

Her intellectual acumen coupled with incorporation of African American song in her lectures when appropriate put her easily on the same level as other renowned Faulkner speakers who gave presentations at the annual conferences. In fact, over the years, she became one of the most attended presenters at the annual conference. At the 1983 conference she was soloist for "The *Sound and Fury* Symphony." Then, besides delivering a scholarly presentation on the black cook, Dilsey, in *The Sound and the Fury,* Sister Thea keynoted the opening session of the conference (Sunday, August 14) at the Lafayette County Courthouse on the famous Oxford town square. Her topic was "Black Music and Culture in the World of William Faulkner." The courthouse was filled to capacity that warm August evening, singing along with her and clapping when she broke into song.

As a Faulkner scholar, she hobnobbed with the likes of writers Toni Morrison, William Styron, Willie Morris; scholars Giles Gunn, Richard H. King, Karl F. Zender; critic Alfred Kazin; and numerous other Faulkner luminaries. In 1987 she wrote and directed a musical based on his work at the annual Faulkner event at Ole Miss.

Thea's music, talks, storytelling, and dramatic presentations were a highlight of the conferences for many, according to videotaped interviews with its planners.[5] True to her custom elsewhere, she recruited a local choir from the Oxford area to sing at the conference, naming it the "Christian Unity and Community Choir." As she had at performances of her local choirs all over, she would sing along, strongly, with lead singers, then back out and allow them to take the soloist spots. Her presence was that of an empowering teacher. She would tell the singers, "You can't be cute to sing. You've got to be ugly!"

Faulkner called his world a "postage stamp," and he was content delving deeply into the layers of relationships there. It was a mythical place, as Thea often said, one for which she had a fondness. In Faulkner's fictional world, the dynamics of racial and economic relations could be dissected and analyzed.

Shortly after the Faulkner event in 1988 Thea sat for a portrait — commissioned by anonymous donors — with Mississippi's famed portrait artist Marshall Bouldin. This artist, whose work hangs in the National Portrait Gallery, in Washington, D.C., said, at the time that his portrait of Sister Thea Bowman is among his finest, if not the finest.[6] September saw a rebroadcast of the Thea segment on *60 Minutes*. Thea found she was in constant demand.

In talks she sometimes described how Jesus of Nazareth frequently went away to pray, seeking respite from the crowds he encountered, as she said, "going to get me some R & R." Thea's friends encouraged her to get some R & R, yet she seemed led by a pressing need to be about her business. Though her body was fragile, her spirit enabled, perhaps compelled, her to fulfill invitations to speak and teach.

Around the time of her presentation to an assembly of Catholic sisters in Washington, D.C., she was interviewed by Arthur Jones of the weekly *National Catholic Reporter*. He talks of Thea, before the interview started, carefully easing "out of her wheelchair to lie down on her bed and pull the blankets up to her chin. The pain from the cancer that has spread from breast cancer to her bones is particularly vicious in her spine." He goes on, in his twelve-hundred-word profile, to explain the big themes in Thea's life at age fifty, fighting against cancer.

She tells Jones of her mid-1980s visit to a small Nigerian village, where she shared the platform with rising star Cardinal Francis Arinze, and mentioned that "if God gives me strength," she's going back. She tells Jones that she, at least in her heart, is certain of Nigerian heritage. Then he and she tell a story together:

> "It was a day I shall never forget. Everyone so kind and hospitable. I didn't know what to sing," she said. Her voice was tiring and had become softer. "What song would they know? I sang. And when I sang, that response — that *ululu* trill I had never heard before — it was music I'd heard in the old church in my childhood.
>
> "My grandfather was a slave. The people who told us the stories and sang to us were former slaves, Momma Tolliver, Momma Garrett, Poppa Lemmon, Momma and Poppa Wood.
>
> "When I sang, those village people acted like..." Sister Thea Bowman sank into the two pillows, bronze on white. She paused. Then she continued, "I sang 'Amazing Grace,' but did you ever hear a black woman do it?" From somewhere this moments-earlier fragile woman now filled herself with an incredible energy. From deep within, she started low. Then her magnificent voice soared with concert force. "Aaaaahaaaamayyyzinginging... grayayyyce. Hoo! Howowow...swee-eee-eee-eet the sound...." She stopped. "It moved me so," she said simply, and was quiet.
>
> After a while she said, "What moved me was the realization that these are my people, and I was home. In Africa I would go into homes. I went into the home of an old mother. She knew no English. I had perhaps ten words of Ibo. She hugged me just like my own mother."

He goes on with his biographical sketch of Thea and then closes with a reflection on Africa:

> Since her African visit, she said she has "tried to teach what I pray, to say to my people we must reclaim the vales and virtues that are our inheritance. To realize the whole African value of family and kinship: the African value of extended family, the African value of hospitality, what it means to African people just to recognize

another human being, to recognize the profound respect I owe you by the simple fact that you are a member of humanity," she said. "That was the Canton, the old church, of my childhood. How do we reclaim it?" she asked. Her voice was soft again now. Her head deep into the two white pillows.[7]

By now Thea's speaking presence had become closely intertwined with her witness as a cancer survivor. People who either knew her or had heard of her drove many miles to see her. People marveled that a wheelchair-bound person ill with cancer could speak and sing powerfully.

Headlines in the Clarke College newspaper in Dubuque proclaimed, "500 Cram Music Hall"; the local Catholic paper declared, "S. Thea Bowman Overwhelms Clarke Audience." The dailies in La Crosse were a bit more restrained, for example, "Nun Going Strong Despite Bout with Cancer" (*La Crosse Tribune*).

Dubuque's Catholic paper, the *Witness*, called her visit "a foot-stomping, old-fashioned revival" and described the audience as "eager." It told the story of an energetic, loud, and well-received presentation: "Reluctance turned to eagerness and quiet to shouts in her skilled hands. At times smiling, at times weeping, at all times praising the Lord, Sister Thea brought her unique message to Dubuque and left the gift of her inspiration with her listeners."[8] The student newspaper, the *Clarke College Courier,* quoted a freshman student, Roxanne Kobliska, saying, "It practically made me cry. She has so much energy and movement that it touched everyone."[9]

At the end of the evening, reported the paper, the audience stood and joined hands while stage members joined Thea in singing the civil rights ballad "We Shall Overcome." The religion writer for the *La Crosse Tribune* soon wrote a profile to update Thea's La Crosse fans:

Cancer has not dimmed Sister Thea Bowman's vision of a better life for all God's people. And the fifty-year-old Franciscan Sister of Perpetual Adoration still is doing all she can to make the vision happen. "I try, I try very hard," she says, explaining how she keeps up with a demanding speaking and performing schedule despite "constant discomfort" from cancer.

She has learned to live with the pain and to function in spite of it, she said last week. The ability to keep on with her life was one of the things she asked God for when she first became aware of the cancer, she says. "I didn't know what to pray for. I wasn't comfortable praying for healing. I wasn't comfortable praying for death. I was comfortable praying, 'Lord, let me live until I die. I just want to live fully,' she adds. 'By choosing life, I'm able to share my life fully with other people.' "[10]

Other reports talked of her need to spend time recuperating after performances. Finally, Mark Nepper, in the *Dubuque Telegraph Herald*, quoted Thea the teacher: "If there's anything in my life that I'm proud of, it's my students. To see my students comfortable, confident, and effective, and to realize I've had some small part in that is really the joy of my life," she said, tears sliding down her cheeks.[11]

At the National Religious Vocation Conference in St. Louis she appeared with a white blanket draped over African garb. Thea often got the chills because she expended every ounce of energy her fragile body had. Weakness aside, though, she delivered a powerful message: "So many white middle-class United States religious give the rest of us the impression that you think your way is the only way.... You won't try anything else; you won't get serious about anything else. In the United States, religious communities — nearly 90 to 95 percent Caucasian and middle class — need to listen to and learn from other cultures and recruit people from those cultures to go back and share with their people."

Her statements were boldly critical, but fundamentally inviting: "Some of you all are scared to get some of us coming around. We talk too much; we talk too loud. We play our music. We don't eat your food ... and you are worried about how to incorporate us into you and some of us don't really want to incorporate us into you. [But] we would like to walk, work, pray, and play with you." She worried aloud that people would think her cold for saying these things, but she pleaded the urgency of the case of a woman without much time. Then she hit the nail on the head, the nail of all of the well-intentioned white religious who discriminate in spite of themselves, who say, in her words, " 'We want to walk in solidarity, but we don't know how.' The answer is so simple. I challenge us to find those answers."[12]

Finally, the time to fly to Africa was at hand. It was September. The Maryknoll sisters in Kenya had invited Thea to come and conduct some workshops for their sisters and to invite along a teaching partner. Thea chose another African American religious sister, Eva Marie Lumas, SSS (Sister of Social Service), one of her former students from Xavier's Institute for Black Catholic Studies, to come along. With some trepidation

("What if Thea became too sick to conduct the workshops? What if she died in Africa?")[13] Eva Marie found funding to expand the party to include a backup presenter (Holy Name Sister Marie de Porres Taylor) and Dort, to help Thea if she weakened. The topic Thea and Eva Marie had chosen over the summer was "Racism in Ministry." When the medical doctors gave their approval to Thea, all systems were go.

Thea and Dort met Eva Marie and Marie de Porres in Amsterdam; then the foursome completed the journey to Nairobi, Kenya, together. It was a twenty-four-hour trip for Thea, and she was visibly uncomfortable. While the others slept, reported Lumas, Thea brushed up on her French with a person seated next to her. At 10:30 p.m. they arrived, but Thea's wheelchair was lost in the luggage, probably still in Holland.

The Maryknoll sisters met them. Lumas remembers: "We were each given a *khanga*" (an African cloth to be used as a skirt, shawl, or scarf). Norma's face registered her alarm at Thea's physical condition. Norma had not seen Thea in three years. At that time, Thea's cancer had been in arrest. She had been forty pounds heavier, moving around with her strong, determined walk, had a full head of braided hair, and generally looked as if she could move a train by the power of her will alone. Now she was slumped in a chair, her bald head covered with a scarf, her eyes were red with fatigue, her face was swollen, and any attempt to move was timid and obviously painful."

Africa brought new life to Thea, though. "Everyone, except Thea, was somewhat afraid," recalls Lumas. The next morning was a different story. The travelers awoke to the sound of Thea up and about, joyously singing, making breakfast. There were a few days in Nairobi before the group would head the 150 miles or so cross-country to the workshop assembly in Arusha, Tanzania.

During the stay in Nairobi there was time for preparations, for visiting, and for meeting some of the local people with whom the Maryknoll sisters worked. One of those meetings became a tearful event, recalls Lumas: "One afternoon, Sister Pearl brought the women she worked with to visit. They sang and danced for us. Thea sang and the rest of us danced with them. It was Thea who first began to cry. She expressed her gratitude for their sharing. She expressed her pain that she had returned to the home of her ancestors, but she could not speak their language. She expressed her sorrow that her physical condition did not allow her to accept the invitation to visit their homes."

Eva tells of Dort trying to shoo the other sisters away from Thea so that Thea could rest — only to have Thea invite them back in when the coast was clear. "Thea seemed to draw her strength from all of the activity." Along the way, Eva Marie decided to trust the moment, she says. "I knew that if she didn't think you could do something, she wouldn't ask you to do it. Beyond that, I'd learned Thea could call forth gifts from people that they never knew they had, myself included." Thea's confidence made her self-confident, she says, and "her care made you know that a failure is only a temporary obstacle that could and would be overcome."[14]

Sister Norma Angel was one of the Maryknoll sisters in residence in Nairobi. Thea was clearly in a very weakened state, but, says Norma, "It is amazing what she did. I mean different groups came to talk to her. She was very observant." She observed the personal dynamics among the black and white sisters and challenged what she saw as somewhat colonial behavior: "You know she really called all of us," says Angel. "One of the things that she said to us as a group was, 'How much effort do you spend helping people to speak for themselves?' You know that we as missionaries tend to speak for the people. She said, 'You know it's time to create opportunities for the people to speak for themselves. What their life is, what their experience is, what their hopes and dreams and fears are.' " The sisters took Thea's advice to heart, says Angel.[15]

On the way to Arusha, the sisters traveled through some of Africa's most popular tourist country. They stopped to photograph exotic wildlife — wildebeests, leopards, and more — and in Masai villages to pick up souvenirs. Thea was a curiosity among the Masai because of her Masai-like baldness. After probing to see what clan she had come from and then finally accepting her as an American who wasn't sure of her African lineage, they gifted her with jewelry from various clans.

Sister Norma recalls an episode when Thea encountered a pregnant Masai woman who wanted to abort, for fear she simply could not afford to care for another child. Upon Thea's return to the United States, Thea arranged for a man strongly opposed to abortion to support the child: "I have something you might be interested in," Thea the bridge-builder said to the man. The child was born, and the man, who has since died, arranged for financial help for the family even beyond his own death. The Masai boy, now grown, is named Thea.[16]

When the sisters got to the Danish Volunteer Center, the travelers had to carry Thea upstairs to her room. Thea was embarrassed for all of the attention, but the sisters made light of it all: "We told her to think of herself as the Queen of Sheba being carried to see Solomon. She laughed, straightened her khanga, changed her posture and said, 'O, Honey, lead on!' "[17]

The days in Arusha were filled with difficult encounters between white missioners and African locals, not unlike some of the difficult gatherings Thea had spoken to in the American South. The Maryknoll sisters faced themselves with painful honesty, remembered Lumas. Then the Africans and the transplant missioners asked each other for forgiveness and assistance from each other for dealing with racism in the future, she recalled.

In her article for the *Thea News*, a newsletter published by FSPA from 2002 through 2008, Lumas remembered Thea saying that it was only while singing that she forgot the pain of her cancer. Then, reflected Lumas, "I wonder if she knew that her song had removed the pain, healed the sickness and broken the pain of many?"[18]

Chapter 25

SONGS OF MY PEOPLE

Thea was on a high after the magnificent Africa trip. She was keynote speaker for San Jose's Liturgical Festival, which took place in the Santa Clara Convention Center. Loretta Pehanich, writing for the *San José Valley Catholic,* attended the early October meeting. She saw the standing ovation for Thea; she witnessed the lines of people pressing forward to greet Thea and to present small gifts.

Pehanich interviewed Thea after her presentation. As in so many of these latter-day interviews, Thea would reflect on the deeper meaning of pain and suffering, which is not "in vain," according to Thea. " 'All of us have a reserve of energy,' she whispered after the presentation, spent for God and lying in bed. 'A part of what I teach and preach is the ability to and the necessity of drawing on that energy to give life to one another.' For the children, added Thea, regardless of 'when we are tired and discouraged.' She spoke of the work for justice, pleading that everyone could do something every day, no matter how small. 'Justice is not a nice thing we do sometimes. It is not an option,' she pleaded. And it's not about something happening within the four walls of a church: 'What you've been doing all week is what you bring to church on Sunday.'

"Reflecting on her own condition, she admitted, 'I think the Lord has ways of slowing me down.' But she also asserted her own attitude: 'I don't know what I can do until I try. Like today, I didn't know if I was going to make it.' " Speaking of her cancer, she longed for her dancing: " 'It's one of the things I miss most,' " not fully appreciated by Thea until it was gone. She recalled being in Africa the first time, in 1985, depending upon dance to communicate.

"The body says, 'I like you, I love you, I want to be in solidarity with you.' " It is the body at prayer. She spoke, too, of the difficulties of finding a place for black leadership within the church, of the personal frustrations of black Catholics, frustration in coming into a black spirituality and problems being accepted as leaders. The church needs to be

236

a nurturing place, pleaded Thea: " 'We need to find strength for living when we come to church,' she said. 'We need to feel the energy of the spirit among us.' "[1]

Not long after that, she paid a visit to Boston, where the *Boston Globe* documented her appearance at a workshop conducted at Cardinal Cushing High School. Thea proclaimed to the area teachers, amid applause, "Black is beautiful! White is beautiful! Brown is beautiful! Red is beautiful! Yellow is beautiful! All the colors and hues in between that God made us are beautiful. Straight hair is beautiful! Kinky hair is beautiful! Bald is beautiful!" Then she pulled off her headpiece to illustrate the point![2]

In her talk to the teachers, she touched on the many social problems that some of the students struggle against and encouraged tolerance and love. "Sometimes, children receive more love at school than they do at home." Thea's basic plea to the teachers was one of her constant themes: help the children to claim their inner beauty. "If they come to school feeling ugly, they are going to act ugly," she said.[3]

Interviewing people who attended the rousing presentation, accented by the performance of a local Gospel choir that "almost took the roof off the gym walls!" teacher after teacher expressed emotion: "She's given us a lot of hope," expressed one.[4]

Thea recalled to the *Globe* journalist what by now was her keen awareness of the breadth of racial challenges everywhere: "When I was a child in Mississippi, it was thought that everyone in Boston was rich, well-educated and talked 'proper,' that if you were a black in Boston, you could be a policeman and sit in the front of the bus. . . . Boston is the only city I know where school doors are locked during the day to keep troublemakers out."[5]

This is the picture of Sister Thea during the latter part of 1988: Using a wheelchair, storing her energy up to be able to give public speaking appearances, then collapsing, exhausted, into a bed for recuperation time, she, nonetheless, maintained a busy schedule. She went literally from coast to coast, and from north to south, speaking to all manner of groups. The speaking enlivened her, and she was able to pace herself for a schedule that would have challenged the most healthy of speakers.

While in California, she also spoke to the Young Presidents' Organization convention, by then a five-thousand-strong, still growing, international group of business leaders. Essentially, the group serves to foster corporate leadership through encouragement and practical training. A program note on the event said about Thea: "Be prepared to look within yourself and at others in a new light. Sister Thea's unique ability to inspire and to sensitize is sure to have a lasting impact on you."[6]

She spoke at a revival in Chicago and then to a national Family Life Ministries convention, held in western Ohio. The *Catholic Chronicle* noted the difference between her previous presentation style and her presentations with advanced cancer: "When [Thea] spoke in Toledo in April 1987 at a parish life conference, she moved constantly about the room, singing, preaching, going into the audience. This time she was joined by an ecumenical group of singers from Toledo and Detroit who did the moving for her...." Thea acted the cheerleader nonetheless, enticing the audience to chant along with her, "I'm somebody special; I'm God's child. You're somebody special. You're God's child." She also used one of her teaching devices, the word *salt* as an acronym: *S* for spirituality, *A* for attitude, *L* for love, *T* for time — with each letter, of course, serving as entrée for talk about a particular theme.[7]

She went on to Detroit to receive the G. Mennen Williams Award for Excellence, from a foundation that promotes dignity for people with disabilities. Thea's award was for inspiration. Within weeks she was in Boston again, this time at the prestigious Jesuit-run College of the Holy Cross. On November 12, Thea gave a scholarly presentation at the University of Tulsa, "Black and Catholic: Sharing our Giftedness." It is one of the relatively few times that she spoke from a prepared text, as Doctor Sister Thea Bowman, the scholar, easily could do. As usual, though, Thea was accompanied on stage by a local choir. A lively question-and-answer session followed.

Two days later she gave a major presentation in Niagara, New York, at the Forum on the Black Family. The program began with a glowing introduction and the presentation of several awards including the "Franciscan Woman of the Year" award from *Mustard Seed* presented to Thea by Kathleen Rimar, OSF, of the Stella Niagara Franciscans. Among many other things, she told the upstate New Yorkers, that, newspaper claims aside, "you all aren't in paradise yet. I've been talking with my friends here, and they tell me there is de facto segregation in Erie and Niagara counties!" This part of her presentation homed in on the growing social problems in the area, especially for blacks. She closed with her practice of having the audience, hands joined, sing together "We Shall Overcome."[8]

After the talk, the "fragile nun" as news accounts had begun to describe her, had a day to rest before she and Dort traveled to Newark,

New Jersey, to speak at the centennial of St. Rose of Lima parish in Roseville. She gave those gathered for the event what would become one of her signature exhortations during the time she had yet to live: "We need to tell one another in our homes, in our church and even in our world, I really, really love you."[9]

In the middle of all that travel, during an October stop in Canton, she and Dort had hosted an open house at 136 Hill Street. It was there that portrait artist Marshall Bouldin unveiled his Thea portrait. A Mississippi Educational Television crew was there, doing a profile of Bouldin, the only American whose work was included in both the 1988 and 1989 annual exhibitions of the Royal Society of Portrait Painters in London.[10] The portrait, by all accounts, is stunning. In a 2001 interview with one of this book's authors, Charlene, Bouldin said that it was Thea who persuaded him to paint her image without hair.[11] The painting, now housed permanently in the Diocese of Jackson chancery, has been reproduced many times and is now ubiquitous in places where Thea spoke, talked, or visited, and in convents, seminaries, parishes, schools, and centers named after her.

Two Mississippi natives with childhood Canton connections, including memories of young Bertha Bowman, had commissioned the painting anonymously.

Though exhilarated by the receptions she had received in Oklahoma, New York, and New Jersey, Thea and Dort were grateful to wend their way back to Mississippi for the Thanksgiving season. Thea took time while she was home to remember her friends all over the country. In her Thanksgiving message, one of five form letters, written with Dort's assistance, that she had mailed to her list of friends in 1988, Thea updated everyone on her Africa trip. She recalled her personal renewal, her wonderful visits, and tourist/pilgrim experiences, recounting that she had personally enjoyed being mistaken for a Masai. Thea also mentioned, "Because of the weakness, nausea, dizziness, mouth infection, and pain associated with chemotherapy, Dort has traveled with me everywhere since Africa. It's been fun, and it's surely made my life and work easier. We've been to Boston, Worchester, Chicago, San Jose, San Diego, Laguna Niguel, Toledo, Detroit, Brooklyn, Washington, Tulsa, Buffalo, and Newark."[12]

At the times when she was home in Mississippi, her Black Catholic Studies student and now friend Chicagoan Karen Horace came to be with her, and to provide some respite for Dort. Karen had taken to spending a few weeks after each institute session, which she had started attending in 1986. By now, the visits became needed assistance: "When Dort would have to go back home, I would stay and take care of [Thea] when she was ill, just seeing to her needs." Those times became treasures of Karen's memory: "I did it with pleasure," she says. In the years that followed Thea's death, she drew on those experiences: "When I looked for inspiration, I'd look to Thea. I'd think of the things she did, the things she said, her compassion," her willingness to face "the challenges of life."[13]

Krystal Records, a ministry of the media-savvy Daughters of St. Paul, in Boston, arranged to make a recording of Thea's Gospel music. The first audiocassette was called *Sister Thea: Songs of My People*. Producer Sister Christine Salvatore wrote the story of the production for Christian Koontz's collection of writings, *Thea Bowman: Handing on Her Legacy.* Christine tells of Thea's eagerness to do the project, "something she had always wanted to do." She writes of Thea characteristically taking charge of the project, choosing singers and instrumentalists who would be appropriate for the production, taking Christine where she was (wanting to create entertainment) and moving her to a deeper understanding of the deeply liberating role of African American spiritual music.

Salvatore recalls how sick Thea was when she finally came to Boston to record, in 1988, a year after the initial conversations had taken place: "The first time she came, she had sores in her mouth and could eat little but baby food and drink only soy milk. She did the recording sessions in the morning and by noon collapsed in a heap of pain. She desperately wanted to leave those songs behind as a legacy, and her determination and love kept her going."

People in the studio were "almost in tears," wrote Salvatore, "because of what the effort was costing her." She called Thea's endurance to sing, in spite of pain, "miraculous."

In her essay, Salvatore also reflected on Thea's philosophy of life, noting that, in her circles at least, some thought of Thea as "a bit on the radical side." She saw Thea, though, not as some kind of subversive, but rather as "a daughter of the Church in its truest form. Once she said something that I will always remember, that she believed we should preach a naked Gospel... that the Gospel should be preached as it was, without so many interpretations."

The two sisters had plenty of conversations between the recording sessions, and Salvatore, with her own self-doubts about being in the media spotlight, probed Thea's motivation. How does one know that she is not just self-promoting, asked Salvatore of Thea. "Thea gave me the best answer I have heard to that question: there is no answer, nor will there ever be one. 'How are you going to know?' she said. 'Why are you trying to find out? Just go ahead and act and leave it up to the Lord.' The old folks... had a prayer, she said: 'Use me, Lord, use me....' They believed that if you didn't ask the Lord to use you, He might put you aside and stop using you. So never worry about whether you are doing something for Jesus or for praise of others. Just do what you are doing for Jesus and tell him to use you.' "[14]

Five musician-friends, including Leon Roberts, the musical director at St. Augustine's Church in Washington, D.C., had joined her for the sessions. Even Boston's archbishop, Cardinal Bernard Law, had stopped by for a visit, near the beginning of the production days. Writing his regular column in the *Boston Pilot,* Law had commented on her travel schedule and wrote, "What makes this remarkable is that Sister Thea is suffering from cancer which has invaded the spine. I know that her pain is at times excruciating. Yet the transparency of her love of God and of all whom she meets, and her desire to share God's love with others, gives her an incredible energy which allows her to keep going after many would have justifiably given themselves only to rest."[15]

Franciscan Father Fernand Cheri, himself a choir leader, heard stories immediately from some of his close friends who were at the recording session. It was Thea's witness of personal sacrifice and her demand for excellence, even under tough conditions, that made the recording happen. "She modeled for them the patience they needed to make the recording come alive," he recalls, calling for retake after retake. It made quite an impression on the other musicians. "She wasn't going to settle for second-best," says Cheri.[16]

After Boston, while at home in Mississippi, Sisters Thea and Dorothy Ann attended the Jackson Festival of Thanksgiving, where Thea was honored, along with several other recognized Mississippi community leaders. Before the year was out, she was back to California one more time to speak in San Diego, at the National Conference on Catholic Youth Ministry, to more than fifteen hundred youth ministers and other diocesan and parish personnel from around the country, as well as from Canada and Guam.

After a brief respite in California, it was time to head back to Canton to begin a new type of adventure. During the previous summer

the New York publishing house Harper and Row announced plans
to produce a book about the life of Thea. In early December those
plans began to materialize. Thea became intensely involved in the book
project. The Harper and Row editors had a writer in mind, but Thea
preferred that a black writer tell her story: she recommended the award-
winning Mississippi poet and novelist Margaret Walker. Harper and
Row acquiesced.

Walker is best known for her landmark Civil War novel, *Jubilee,* and
her collection of poems *For My People.* She won the Houghton Mifflin Literary Fellowship when *Jubilee* was published in 1966. The novel,
called by some a black counterpart to *Gone with the Wind,* is a slave
narrative, inspired by stories of young Margaret Walker's grandmother.
Like Thea, Margaret was an accomplished academic professor. She spent
most of her teaching career at Jackson State University, Jackson, Mississippi, where a center she founded for the study of black people is now
called the Margaret Walker Alexander National Research Center.

Margaret Walker Alexander was aging and had health problems, but
she allowed Thea to persuade her to take on the writing project. "How
could I say no to Sister Thea?" she later recalled.[17] She drafted a manuscript, but it never made it beyond an initial draft. Thea had dictated
much of the book to Alexander during the last year or so of Thea's life:
Harper had wanted it to be in Thea's voice. The women considered it a
joint effort (they shared copyright), but it was a project Thea could not
see to the end. The manuscript languished after Alexander produced it,
and eventually it landed, unpublished, in Alexander's archives at Jackson State, after Alexander died in 1998. A copy is in the Thea Bowman
Collection in the FSPA Archives, La Crosse, Wisconsin, as well, and has
been quoted and referenced for some parts of this book.

In the manuscript's afterword, Alexander describes the joint efforts of
the two authors. She recalls that she had known Thea since the 1970s,
when Thea would bring students from Viterbo to Mississippi to expose
them to southern culture. "She particularly wanted me to read poetry
from my book *For My People* to her class. As scheduled, she appeared
with her students one morning about eleven o'clock. I remember she was
wearing the traditional nun's habit, her lovely face vibrant and wreathed
in smiles and her eyes afire with love."[18] Alexander learned much later
that Thea also visited another famous black author and photographer
in the area, Eudora Welty.

Alexander had been with Thea over the years at the Faulkner conferences (it was Margaret Walker who narrated the conference's videotape tribute to Thea)[19] and had even contributed an essay to Thea's book *Families: Black and Catholic, Catholic and Black.*.

After agreeing to write the book with Thea, Margaret set up a time in December to start, and Joseph Dyer, a priest who was a friend of both women, offered Margaret a ride. "I was filled with trepidation and felt I must steel myself for an ordeal I was not prepared to face. But Sister Dorothy Ann Kundinger welcomed us smiling and with arms outstretched, and I went into Sister Thea's bedroom where she was in bed. She looked as beautiful as ever, and my only shock was seeing her bald head."

The two agreed on the outlines of a biography and spent, according to Walker, about eight hours in various sessions recording autobiographical interviews for the book. "One day when I was there I voiced what many other people had said to me, 'I think Sister Thea is a modern-day saint.' " But, Margaret said, Thea and Dort talked it down, Dort adding that a lot of people flat-out wouldn't agree with her. "Then, Sister Thea asked me, 'What do you think a saint is like?' " Walker told her she had heard a saint is radiant, and certainly Thea was that. Clever Thea made a joke of it, much to the threesome's amusement, crediting the radiation treatments for her radiance!

Once Margaret asked about Thea's attraction to the Franciscans and was told their ministry was in the world, serving the poor. Walker, who actually knew quite a bit about St. Francis already, wrote, "Sister Thea was a true Franciscan, preaching, speaking, teaching, singing, and living the Gospel of Jesus to the poor, the children, and everyone with whom she came in contact. Love and joy were her constant themes and always it was fun to be around her."

In one of the 1988 interviews, Walker asked Thea about how she was coping with her cancer. Thea told Margaret that she had been advised to cut back on her schedule, which she had done, although, she said, "I have a lot of things scheduled way down the road and I'm trying to honor those commitments. Part of my approach to my illness," said Thea, "has been to say I want to choose life, I want to keep going, I want to live fully until I die. If my doctors say I can't do something, I don't do it. Otherwise, I try."

Thea told her, "I don't know what my future holds." But in the meantime, she said, "I am making a conscious effort to learn to live with discomfort, and, at the same time, to go about my work." It is the business of life that energizes her, she said. "A kind of strength and energy" came to her when she worked with people, particularly children.[20]

Thea took time from the Alexander interviews to keep up with some of her travel commitments, as promised, in Mobile, Alabama. Then an extraordinary invitation arrived, near the end of the year. The West Coast group of the Knights of Malta, a centuries-old Roman Catholic organization with ties to wealthy donors, invited Thea on a pilgrimage to Lourdes, France, May 3 to May 10, 1989, all expenses paid. Lourdes has been world-renowned as place of healing among Catholics ever since the reports that the Virgin Mary (Our Lady of Lourdes) appeared miraculously to young Bernadette Soubirous there in the 1850s. (The story is the basis of the 1943 classic film *Song of Bernadette*.) Health issues, though, compelled Thea to write regrets:

> I was delighted to receive your letter and so very pleased to be invited as one of the Knights of Malta "Malades" to visit Lourdes on pilgrimage. Having heard from childhood of the wonder and the faith at Lourdes, having heard of the Knights and your work for the Church as well as your concern for the sick, I was excited about visiting Lourdes as well as spending time getting to know some of the Knights and hearing more about your work.
>
> However, your letter explains that your guests must be able to "climb a few steps, such as getting on and off buses." At this time I am confined to a wheel chair. I have metastatic cancer in the spine, hips, legs, arms, ribs, shoulder blades, skull. At this point I am not able to climb/walk a few steps. I have prayed about it and done some experimenting, also talked with the people who work with and assist me. I would not be able to climb on and off buses in Lourdes.
>
> So I express my deep gratitude to the Knights for your offer of the pilgrimage....[21]

Thea celebrated her fifty-first birthday on December 29, a day when one of the authors of this book, John, visited Thea at her home, conducting an interview for *Extension* magazine. This was a far different visit from the interview visit of All Saints' Day, 1984, which had caught the whirlwind Thea, not so well-known beyond her circles, actively promoting black cultural identity in Madison County and beyond. Now she was in bed, with visitors coming and going and screenwriter Emma Pullen at her bedside taking notes for the Belafonte project.

That day, as planned, sitting up in bed Thea talked about reconciliation and how she was living with her cancer. These were the insights of a dying woman. "I believe that reconciliation means that I can accept my limitations, that I need to know other people," she said. "I can't do everything, but if I work with other people who can make up or supply what I lack, they have a gift that I don't have. True reconciliation means I can ask for help."

Her insights didn't stop at the personal, however. Here we see the social insight that was a major, though perhaps lesser known, dynamic in Thea's work as she matured. "I know you might say this sounds idealistic and it sounds like a dreamworld, but you and I know that there cannot be true reconciliation so long as you have people who don't have food to eat, who don't have decent housing, or money to meet their basic needs—how are you going to reconcile that?"

She went on, speaking of political power, "social power! Diplomatic power, persuasive power, you know, Mama power, Daddy power!" How can we unlock this "power of personal witness" and "get the word out," she implored.

Asked to reflect back to an interview four years earlier, where she said evangelization, "sharing the good news," was her most basic goal, she agreed that was still true. "I think a sense of humor and a whole lot of fun can help," she said, "insofar as we are reconciled and can enjoy each other's presence." That, she said, is loving one another.

Looking back, she said, "My basic approach was to try to promote activities that help different groups get to know one another. As we learn to know one another, we learn to appreciate one another, then we grow to love one another." Her favorite approach, she said, was to "bring people into situations where they can share your treasures, your art, your food, your prayers, your history, your traditions, the coping mechanisms that enabled you to survive." That opened the way for mutual understanding, for "points of convergence," that would lead to working together for the common good.

She said that her approach in Mississippi was to go where she was invited, and not to push too hard with programs and the like. "But I have attempted to speak wherever I was given a forum and to bring people together."

Reflecting on the church, she argued, as she had in public so many times, that the church is universal, a concept that was mistaken for so many years as uniform. "The beauty of universality is that the church is able to speak to people in whatever language they understand best — and we're not just talking about verbal language," she added. She mentioned ritual, gesture, story as examples of other "languages."

Encouraged to take a break and eat the lunch that Sister Dorothy Ann had brought to her bed, she cracked, "No, go ahead. I'm missin' *All My Children* anyway, so you might as well get through."

She continued to reflect on her life: "I wish I had danced more, I wish I had run around more, I wish I had used my body more joyfully and more creatively." She mentioned a pair of moccasins shown to her by a friend, made by his mother-in-law, a Winnebago woman who had, years ago, adopted Thea as her own. The moccasins were beaded on the soles, which meant that they were to be worn in eternity. "Every bead that was sewn into that moccasin was an act of love, and in presenting those moccasins to him she let him know that she realized he was dying. And in showing them to me, he was saying to me, 'It's all right, I'm ready.' That moment is always with me." He wore the moccasins at his death. "I guess what I'm saying," said Thea, "is I have been blessed to understand it's okay to die."

Had she reconciled with cancer? She recoiled at the question. "I don't want to reconcile with cancer, I don't want to reconcile with injustice... racism...sexism...classism. I don't want to reconcile with anything in my life or in my world that is destructive," she insisted, adding that that type of reconciliation should not be taught to children, either.

Finally, asked to revisit a theme from her 1984 interview, she talked about the spirit of joyfulness that allowed her to move forward. "I'm black," she reminded the interviewer, from a community that "has a long tradition of joy in the face of death." She spoke of the various layers of symbolism in the Negro Spirituals, saying, "When the singer was talking about home, that singer was probably talking about the home that was where the heart is, the home where she was loved, nurtured, comforted. That person was singing about someplace and somebody right now. But that person was also talking about the heavenly city, Jerusalem." Her tradition, the songs of the "old ladies at church," she explained, gave her a place of peace around death. "You know, the old lady said, 'Soon we'll be done with the troubles of this world; I'm going home to live with my God; I'm going to see my mother.'"

Then she added, "It's always 'hidee, hidee, and never good-bye,' " referring to Cab Calloway's classic song. After all, she said, after cancer's return, she never expected to live to see her fifty-first birthday.

Before the interview ended, Thea graciously posed for photographs, holding her one-candle birthday cupcake. She asked the interviewer to pull a shoebox down from her closet. In it were her beautiful, black plaits that the chemotherapy had sacrificed. But below the box there was a stack of copies of that original 1984 article from *St. Anthony Messenger,* which had been reprinted in a short-lived black Methodist publication. "When Mike Wallace wanted to know what I did in Mississippi," Thea said, *"this* is what I showed him." It was the story, from before her time of fame, of teaching cultural awareness as a survival tool to the very poor students whom Thea touched near her own home of Canton.[22]

That weekend, her dear friend from the Archdiocese of Cincinnati, Father Clarence Rivers, renowned African American musician, dramatist, and liturgist, came to Canton to see his old friend. Journalist Fabvienen Taylor, reported in *Mississippi Today* that "almost like a scene from the upcoming movie or a chapter in the book, the sound of spirituals could be heard Saturday, December 31, emanating from 136 Hill Street as thirty-five people sang during a special liturgy for Sister Bowman." Rivers hadn't expected a crowd to gather, but they did.

Clarence Rivers, as did Thea, believed in and promoted soulful liturgy for Catholics. Reflecting on Thea for the newspaper, he essentially offered "that's showbiz" as an explanation for her seemingly insatiable energy: "People impressed with Thea do not understand that she is an artist (in the theater of the church), that she is able to make the true things in life alive by her ability to perform even while she is very, very sick. That is the artist in her. People ask over and over again, 'Where does she get all that energy being as ill as she is?' Well, she doesn't have all that energy; she is a professional. She is an artist."[23]

Chapter 26

A NEWFOUND FREEDOM

You can tell a lot about a person by what she chooses to do when she knows her days are numbered. The year 1989 was the last full year for Sister Thea. She no longer was mobile without great effort, and she knew the cancer was winning, that her life was coming to an end. Although she could have done any number of things, made any manner of changes, it's significant to observe that she stayed her lifelong course as a Catholic, a Franciscan Sister of Perpetual Adoration, a representative of African American culture to the world outside of her African American home.

She remained a public speaker, long after others would have retired to nurse their own illness, and prepare for imminent death. In short, Thea would continue to march on the course she had set many years earlier, repeating what became her mantra of fulfillment, "Let me live, until I die." So 1989, in many ways, and, rather amazingly, was a busy year for Thea. In light of her condition, her public appearances carried the gravity — and in Thea's case, the joyful certainty — of the last words of a dying person.

The fact that her *60 Minutes* appearance had been televised nationally three times, the fact that Harry Belafonte planned a full-length movie about her life and message, starring Whoopi Goldberg with Emma Pullen writing the screen play, the news that Thea with some of her musician friends recorded a cassette with fifteen Gospel songs, *Sister Thea: Songs of My People;* the fact that Harper and Row contracted award-winning Mississippi poet and novelist Margaret Walker to write about Thea's life, all of these newsworthy stories kept Thea on the national scene. Even in a wheelchair she was in constant demand to appear at major Catholic events. Of course, no one knew how long Thea would be active. She had proven an unpredictable character up to this point.

Media across the United States, especially in the communities where Thea had spent time in recent years, were quick to notice this unusual story. "Can't Keep a Good Nun Down" read the *Jackson (Miss.) Daily*

News.[1] Roseville, New Jersey's *New Community Clarion's* headline was "A Living Inspiration Shares the Good News."[2] Others in Texas and Iowa talked about her book and film projects. Catholic newspapers across the country followed her story closely. Thea knew why all this attention was coming her way; the performer in her knew the unusual opportunity before her.

At the Radisson Hotel in Denver in February, where Thea was invited to speak at the general session of the Twenty-First Mile Hi Congress on "The Threshold of Creative Ministry," she told a reporter, Christine Capra-Kramer:

> There is an urgency about my life. I know I have not got long. Because of the cancer I am deciding what is important and not important....I want to leave something behind. My role in life is to open people up to life, so that they might realize their own talents. So many people have gifts they haven't realized. God has given me a grace to see in people what they have.

Capra-Kramer wrote that Thea said the cancer has freed her so that she might say what's on her mind. But there are also fears.

> I'm afraid of pain, being helpless and incapacitated. Yet, I believe there's a plan, and I try to go with the program. All I ask of God is that I be able to live fully until I die. That takes away a lot of the anxiety and what happens doesn't matter. I want to love until I die. And, as I've always said, I want to have a good time![3]

She was having a good time, living a good life even as she was hurting.

Thea and Dort traveled to Jackson that January to celebrate Dr. King's birthday. The next day in Memphis, Jeff Bowman, eleven-year-old second cousin of Sister Thea Bowman, accepted, on her behalf, the 1989 Bishop Topel Ministries "Thea Bowman Justice Award."

Bishop Topel Ministries (BTM), named for Catholic Bishop Bernard J. Topel of Spokane, Washington, is a prayer-centered national network of Christians committed to prayer, service, hope, and support for the needy (materially, spiritually and emotionally) and the people who minister to the needy. Topel himself had led a simple, prayerful lifestyle of Christlike love for the poor, which inspired people across the nation to follow his example. The network reaches twenty-three states and the District of Columbia.

The announcement of the 1989 recipient was made in Portland, Oregon, by Mary Medved, director of Jesuit Volunteers, Northwest, and chairperson of the BTM national selection committee for the award. Medved said the national board elected to honor Sister Thea Bowman — including naming the award after her — in recognition of her lifelong daily example as a Christ-bearer who brings all of us Christ's joy, his music, his unity, his justice, his faith, his hope, his love, and his peace.

Thea had selected her young cousin intentionally to associate the dreams of the emerging generation to the dream of Dr. King: "My hope is that all of us today and every day will work and pray to create the climate so that his generation can realize the dream of freedom and opportunity and unity in love," she told the paper. Thea's Memphis relatives, of course, participated in the event.[4]

At the end of the month, Sisters Thea and Dorothy Ann flew to Los Angeles, making their way to Serra High School. Thea gave the keynote address at the second African American Youth Conference sponsored by the Catholic Archdiocese of Los Angeles. At that event, she sounded another of her keynote themes: "If anybody asks you who you are, tell them, 'I'm a child of God.' "[5]

In Texas, she gave a Mardi Gras Concert on February 5 at Corpus Christi Cathedral, where she was joined by members of various local Gospel groups, and told the press, "The songs of faith are my heritage."[6]

A week later, correspondent Rachelle Ramon wrote a further reflection on Thea's visit:

Sister Thea surely expended a lot of energy during her concert that Sunday night. . . . Wearing traditional African clothes that were gifts from her former students, Sister Thea began the concert by explaining that Mardi Gras, the traditional celebration before the penitential season of Lent, is "a time to celebrate life, to celebrate hope, to celebrate joy and celebrate resurrection." . . . By the end of the concert, Sister Thea had almost everyone on their feet, waving handkerchiefs (a Mardi Gras custom) in jubilation and holding their clasped hands high. Her message of concern for others and appreciation of all the races God has created touched those present.

Sister Thea, whose slim face, high cheekbones, and bright eyes belie her age, seems unfazed by all the attention. Her soft voice quickens when she speaks about issues that are important to her, including our responsibility to each other. "Some of us tend to forget *we* are the church," she explained. "Whatever the church needs to do — *we* need to do."[7]

Icy traveling conditions forced cancellation of a February 6 event, so Thea moved on to Houston for her next engagement, a three-day workshop, "Stepping to the Drum Beat." The meeting attracted more than five hundred participants and was welcomed by some commentators as one of the most important conferences dealing with the black family ever held in the Southwest. Just what is family in the African American context, with its history of forced destruction of families by slavetraders and then the continuing stressors of poverty and racial discrimination? This workshop set out to identify some common ground, affirming black family values and traditions, looking at the roles from immediate to extended to ancestral. Bonds to the ancestors and to God are affirmed through spirituals, songs, dance, drums, and biblical understanding.

Sister Thea and her friend and colleague Father Joseph A. Brown, SJ, were keynote speakers. Both emphasized that strong black families were the key to conversion. "We're the church," Thea told those gathered. "We, as family, need to assume our full role in the church." Sister Thea and Father Joseph captivated their listeners, young and old, with their dynamic messages, setting a challenging tone for the symposium.[8]

Soon Sister Thea journeyed to the University of Notre Dame for a Sunday evening ecumenical service on campus, featuring the "Voices of Faith" choir, a Gospel choir consisting of African American students, white students, and supporters from the surrounding churches in the black community. In a letter to Thea Holy Cross priest Don McNeill wrote, after the event,

> The Voices of Faith ensemble also challenged and assisted us in a moving way throughout the prayer service.... This unified form of prayer was unique in my experience at Notre Dame. Your gift of pulling people together by providing hospitality for members of the community in the chapel who were not black to learn about and receive the gift of black spirituality broke down many barriers.[9]

In March her travels continued, in Florida, Mississippi, then Pennsylvania. Later that month she was back in her former academic stomping grounds in La Crosse, at Viterbo, for a humanities symposium. After they arrived in La Crosse on a wintry Friday afternoon, Thea's hosts, classmate Sister Jean Kasparbauer and one of this book's authors, Sister

Charlene, ensconced her in a guest suite on first floor of St. Rose Convent. Immediately Thea eased her body onto the bed. There she remained horizontal until Sunday evening and a rehearsal at St. Rose with Viterbo College choir director Dan Johnson-Wilmot and his choir. Sister Dorothy Ann occupied an adjoining room during their stay and, as she did in all their travels, tended to Thea's needs. Friends joined them in the room, for meals were brought in.

Retired FSPAs living at St. Rose Convent as well as FSPAs living in La Crosse and nearby towns visited and were delighted to have their beloved sister in the Franciscan motherhouse. There was a steady stream of Viterbo faculty and administrators, former students, friends living in western Wisconsin, southeastern Minnesota, and northeastern Iowa who came to say hello to *their* Thea. Dort cautioned her to rest. Thea, however, preferred to see friends. Once again, her people energized her! Viterbo friends even brought pizza — at her request.

Weak as she looked, the symposium planners offered her the chance to cancel. In the days leading up to the performance, the offer was repeated, but Thea assured them she would do it. In the hours before the symposium, Thea rested in the Green Room until it was time for her to be introduced and wheeled onto her familiar stage, where she had often performed as a soloist and with her Hallelujah Singers. But the moment Thea came into view, a March morning in Wisconsin became electric!

The Viterbo crowd greeted *their* Thea with a sustained ovation. Thea took it from there, pitching higher the energy in the thousand-plus-seat main theater, with its standing-room-only crowd. From the orchestra past the first balcony, to the second balcony the audience's rapt attention was riveted on the formerly tall, strong, poised, beautiful Sister Thea and every word she spoke or sang. Though her spine burned in pain, though cancer made even simple movement difficult, though she was contained in her wheelchair, Thea smiled, teased, spoke with wisdom, sang, taught, gestured like the artist they had known her to be. Viterbo's concert choir sang with her spiritedly. A group of Gospel singers who had joined Thea a year ago at two appearances in Madison came for the Sunday rehearsal. They joined the student singers creating an authentic Gospel flavor. Then she spoke:

> I want to take you back to where you first believed. I want to take
> you back to where you were loved and nurtured and sheltered. I
> want you to remember the people who taught you faith and hope

and love and joy; people who taught you to love yourself and to believe in yourself. Who taught you to love your family, to love justice, to love sisterhood and brotherhood and fatherhood and motherhood and world harmony.

I want to take you back to those who gave you a transcendent vision of a God who is one, who is above us all. Some of us call him Creator; some of us call him Earthmaker. My folks say that he is a father to the fatherless and a mother to the motherless, a God of peace and a God of war. Rest in a weary land. I want to take you back to those who taught you the possibility of a world order built on mutual understanding and mutual appreciation and mutual respect, on giving and loving and caring. And so we get in touch and know what we are talking about.

At that point she named the many European, Latin American, African, and Asian nationalities present, asking each group, in turn, to stand up, and accept the applause of the entire audience. Then, she continued:

When all God's children get together, what a time, what a time, what a time....Did we miss anybody? If we come together, bringing our history, our experiences, our survival and coping mechanisms, our rituals of celebration, our unique ways of thinking and planning and relaxing and walking and talking and working and praying and playing and being, what a gift we can be to one another and to our churches and to our world....

Our world has reached a moment of unparalleled progress and opportunity. The winds of change are swirling around us. And we have within ourselves the capacity to free ourselves and to free one another.

My grandfather was a slave. And he used to talk about slavery, because he said if we understood about slavery we might be able to understand about freedom. My granddaddy said the worst kind of slavery is not the slavery that comes from outside with bonds and chains and forced labor. The worst slavery is slavery that comes in your own heart and your own mind and your own home and in your own church and in your own community.

Let's get in touch with the enslavement that keeps us from reaching out to one another and being to one another the cause of freedom and the cause of strength and the cause of life....

"Let my people go!" she proclaimed and then she listed some of the spots of oppression in the world of 1989: South Africa, China, Chile. Then she added a local touch: "Let my people go in Madison, Wisconsin, and in Milwaukee.... We're talking about sharing the world, folks."

She spoke of freedom, especially freedom from the fear to reach across the barriers that separate one group from another, the barriers that separate one person from another. "When your self-esteem goes down, then your hostility goes up. Your conflict goes up. Conversely, when your self-esteem is high, then hostilities go down. So if you feel a need to go beat up on somebody, look into your self. I'm somebody special. I'm God's child.... We must accept ourselves and one another and go about the business of building."

She gave a strong challenge to the all-white folks gathered to celebrate Thea's presence among them: "We sit here and we're real nice today. But on a regular basis we can do a job on one another. What do you all say about black folks? And if we admit them, they will lower our standards." It must have been awkward, if not shocking. "Some of you got an attitude for folks on welfare. That's because you've never been there. And you think of folks who have worked hard all their lives, worked harder than you've ever thought about working, and don't have money for food, don't have money for medical care, don't have money for decent housing."

She talked about prejudice against all minorities, not just blacks. Then she turned it around, to the prejudices of blacks against whites. "We do a job on one another." She implored her audience to think and talk differently, asking them to proclaim, together, "Black is beautiful. White is beautiful. Red is beautiful. Brown is beautiful. Yellow is beautiful...." The litany went on. "And then we come to the hardest part: to take your finger and point it to yourself and say *I* am beautiful.... When I can say I'm beautiful, I can look at my sister and look at my brother and I can see the beauty. I can find it and name it and affirm it."

Later she got to her basic point: "Insofar as we love one another, insofar as we come together to help one another, we prepare for change. ...We can help one another...to be co-creators of a new world in which we tolerate the boundaries of race and class and education and money." In then end, she announced, "Glory, glory, hallelujah! Let us sing a song of freedom. Let us sing a song of love. That's the answer. It's not that complicated."

At the very end of her talk, she told her most personal truth: "If I can help somebody as I pass along, then my living will not be in vain."[10]

The Viterbo community gave her a standing ovation. Her talk, nearly forty-five minutes long, had been a resounding success.

While Thea was in La Crosse, Patrick Kerrigan, of Viterbo Public Relations, interviewed her and drew forth some of Thea's Viterbo memories. She spoke in fond terms of her alma mater: "I remember Viterbo as a refuge. School was a place to go to enjoy life," she said. But she added that it was a "lonely experience for me culturally, because very little of what I studied pertained to my past, my experience, the contributions of my people." She then spoke of her career as teacher, how she tried to get into her students' heads and make them think, how she exposed them to live Shakespeare so they would understand what they were reading. "I was convinced" she said, "that literature is an incentive for most people."

In literature, she said, "you meet people who tell you things that your best friends, your closest friends, won't tell you. You have experiences of life through characters, and these prepare you to understand the reality that you attempt to live."

She spoke of her attraction to St. Francis, another of the deep strains in Thea's psyche. Speaking of Francis and his followers, she described minstrels and troubadours, "going about the countryside, teaching the good news, singing and praising. Somebody like me, a teacher of the English language and literature, was made to be a minstrel and troubadour."

She loved Francis the peacemaker, she said, and typically of many Franciscans, she recognized that "there's also a kind of craziness that is Franciscan.... People took time to laugh, time to play and it wasn't an isolated thing.... [At Viterbo] there was a closeness and kind of love that was Franciscan. Is it still like that?"[11]

On Tuesday morning, Jean drove Thea, Dort, and Charlene to Menomonie, Wisconsin, where Thea had an afternoon engagement for a group of Catholic women. Again Thea rose to the occasion. She was clearly exerting a heroic effort to follow through on her commitments. Later in March, Thea returned to the Midwest, to Fergus Falls, Minnesota, where she spoke at a Kiwanis luncheon. Far removed as this was from Thea's Mississippi roots, she was totally at home with the Minnesota business leaders. For their part, they were first caught a bit off-guard, but by the end of her talk they warmed to Thea. She told the Kiwanis Club she was preaching and teaching about a kind of religion that teaches faith in oneself, that has to do with a vision of a world that's bigger than ourselves, our successes and our business.

She said, "It has to do with reverence for yourself, for your employees, for your customers. . . . If you work for me or I work for you we need to be good news to each other! . . . Give me that old-time religion that believes in the power to change, in faith in humanity, in good business," she proclaimed. "What are you going to do to help somebody?"

Then she answered herself, singing her by now trademark: "This little light of mine, I'm going to let it shine, let it shine, let it shine."[12]

Another memorable event with Thea in the first quarter of 1989 took place at Mercy College in Detroit. At this "Remembering Rachel" conference on women's spirituality, with the Detroit archdiocesan choir, Thea illustrated with song, interspersed with her inimitable reflections, the unique spirituality of African American women.

In an interview before the event with Catherine Haven of the *Michigan Catholic* (April 7, 1989), Thea said she was always about the business of living and spreading the Good News.

> The mission is to worship, it's to teach, but it's also to feed the hungry, to clothe the naked, to shelter the homeless, and to teach the children, to heal the sick and to bury the dead. The Catholic Church all over this country has asked black people, you know, what can we do for black people? And the uniform answer from the black Catholic bishops down to the poor in the city and the poor in the rural areas has been *education*.[13]

Thea challenged the group to get past the obstacles to making education the priority and help black people move ahead.

Observer Brigid Johnson, liturgist and director of campus ministry at the time, remembered Thea as a "priest of God." In her article in Christian Koontz's book devoted to Thea's works, she told of the impression Thea had made. Thea was so weak when she arrived that organizers wondered if she would even be able to participate in the workshop. But she rested for two days, and mustered the strength to perform.

> At 7:00 p.m. Thea and the choir were in place on stage. Thea sat in her wheelchair, dressed in a white liturgical gown, most of her hair gone, a result of many sessions of chemotherapy. Draped over her shoulders was a colorful stole, embroidered with the names of Old Testament women.

Thea began to sing and speak, quickly engaging the choir on stage and the audience to join in singing with her. . . . Thea was radiant! She had at times an impish smile as she invited us "white folk" present to loosen up and put ourselves into the music. She spoke of church, of God, of Jesus, of people, of relationship, of respect, of culture. She would speak a little, sing a little, and speak some more.

She often smiled gently, and with her right elbow resting on the arm of her wheelchair, she waved her left arm in approval, her open hand toward the audience. . . . About forty-five minutes into her performance, I was struck with the powerful realization that Thea Bowman was being priest to God's people. That whole group of several hundred of us was being lifted up in prayer.

When we find ourselves in a situation where a holy person is standing before us, uniting us, proclaiming the Good News to us, and raising us up by lifting our minds and hearts, then indeed we can say, "Thanks Be to God!" This is what Thea Bowman did that evening at Mercy College. She truly was priest to us and to our church.

Early Christian writings speak of those who lived through martyrdom for their faith as being among those who presided at Eucharist. . . . Perhaps the sufferings Thea Bowman experienced in her years of illness constituted a similar kind of martyrdom. She became a stronger and more powerful witness even as her body was weakened by the cancer consuming her. She was truly an unusual woman, somehow able to get up out of her deathbed numerous times and travel across the country to speak to one group after another.[14]

May was a heady month for Thea. Editors of the Catholic monthly *U.S. Catholic* added her to its distinguished roster of *U.S. Catholic* Award recipients, which since 1978 has included luminaries such as Elisabeth Schüssler Fiorenza, Archbishop Raymond Hunthausen, Sister Theresa Kane, Sister Candida Lund, Kathleen and James McGinnis, Sister Mary Luke Tobin, Archbishop Rembert Weakland. The magazine's award is presented to persons furthering the cause of women in the church. Thea was cited for reminding the church of the role women have played in handing down a living faith from generation to generation through many difficult circumstances. The presenters proclaimed that Thea had sparked an awareness of the many gifts African American

Catholics bring to the life of the church.[15] The award was given by editor Mark Brummel, a Claretian priest, in the Chicago offices of *U.S. Catholic* on May 11. A delegation of friends from the Chicago area represented her. Though Thea could not be present, she took part via phone.

Wild horses, though, could not keep Thea away from Clarke College in Dubuque, where she was invited to give the commencement address and receive her second honorary degree. The graduating class, many of whom had been in the audience when Thea spoke at Clarke in 1988, voted her their number one choice for speaker. Before the event a friend asked her over the telephone what she planned to speak about to the graduates about. Thea responded, "Power!" Her friend said, "You, a humble Franciscan talking about power?" Thea moaned, "How long have I been with you and you do not yet understand. I will talk about the greatest power, love!"

Headlines from Dubuque newspapers testify that Thea achieved her objective. One hundred and fifty graduates listened spellbound during the energetic fifteen-minute address.

> Your education gives you a power nobody can take away from you. Use your power to make a better world. I want to challenge you not just to make a difference but to change the world. Use your power, your own unique power, your position, to help somebody who needs it.... Say to the world that I want to make this world a better place for all of us. That's how you celebrate what you've learned and achieved.... Be upwardly mobile. In a world where some people use their neighbors' hearts as stepping stones, resist destructive forces.... Be alive, be alert, and wherever you find yourself, share life.[16]

It was hard for the people gathered to believe this powerful woman was actually in a wheelchair. Her zesty spontaneity was contagious. The audience was wildly appreciative. Excerpts of her speech and a taped interview were featured on national television on CBS *Morning News* in a graduation feature the following Tuesday. She appeared along with four other commencement speakers, E. L. Doctorow, Lee Iacocca, educator Lauro Cavazos, and athlete Sid Thrift.

Immediately Sister Thea and Sister Dorothy Ann took off for Louisiana, where Thea gave the commencement address on Sunday, May 13, at Xavier University in New Orleans. Thea was the recipient of her third honorary degree, presented by university president Norman C. Francis.

Thea was also invited as speaker at the 113th Boston College commencement, but her worsening physical condition prevented her from flying East.

From her Canton home at 136 Hill Street, Thea wrote the first of her two 1989 general letters to her friends around the country. As usual, she catalogs where she's been and where she's going to be — pretty much coast to coast, every city listed not so much out of pride as out of a desire to see her friends: "perhaps we'll meet along the way." There's news of her advancing cancer, and her treatments, and the curtailing of her travel plans, by her doctors. She jokingly calls her letter an "organ recital," listing her many physical problems, being typed by "someone else" because of her sore right arm. She then goes on with a chatty letter, reminiscent of the letters she once had written from Wisconsin to her mother:

> Since my last form letter, Dort and I received two bird feeders and a stash of bird food. We enjoy watching cardinals and chickadees that frequent the feeders. About fifteen goldfinches used to come but they've left for the summer. We've entertained mockingbirds, blue jays, two kinds of woodpeckers, mourning doves, purple finches and two species we haven't identified. We've enjoyed the springtime.... Thank you for all your calls, cards, letters, visits, flowers, and prayers. Special thanks to Mrs. Cornelia Johnson, who addressed the envelopes for these letters. I love you. — Thea[17]

Chapter 27

UNFORGETTABLE THEA

In June 1989, Thea was invited to go before the semiannual assembly of the nation's Catholic bishops, held that summer at Seton Hall University in South Orange, New Jersey. It would be remembered as a historic public appearance.

One theme of the meeting was evangelization among Catholic minorities, and Thea's presentation was clearly the high point. At the beginning of her presentation, with a voice that unfurled like an airplane banner, Thea seized the attention of the bishops, singing, "Sometimes I feel like a motherless child." Their attention was riveted on her. Often during the talk, the bishops interrupted her with sustained applause, sometimes with laughter. At her conclusion, she sat before the room of two hundred or so men, overwhelmingly older, white men, a sea of black clerical suits, and, as was her practice with other groups from time to time, she directed these bishops to stand, cross arms, clasp hands, and join her in singing "We Shall Overcome." Thea had called Archbishop Eugene Marino of Atlanta, Bishop John Ricard of Baltimore, and Professor Albert Raboteau of Princeton to stand beside her wheelchair and clasp hands with her. Some of her brother bishops were seen with tears streaming down their cheeks. Even some of the reporters, sitting in the press area at the side of the hall, were so moved.[1]

Catholic News Service reporter Jerry Filteau, who made a career of covering church events, reported:

Sister Bowman . . . enthralled the bishops with her half-hour speech. She spoke to them about black sufferings and hopes, contributions and needs, history and future, and above all, faith, in the U.S. Catholic Church. . . .

Dressed in an elegant African American gown, her voice clear and resonant, eyes sparkling and hands animated, Sister Bowman's only betrayal of the advanced bone cancer ravaging her body was the wheelchair she sat in as she spoke.

Cardinal Bernard F. Law of Boston told the bishops afterward that in his many years of bishops' meetings it was the first time he "was moved to tears of gladness in this assembly."[2]

During her talk, Thea had taken the bishops down the course of black Catholic history, not only in the United States, but also in the church beyond. She spoke, of course, of slavery and how the exploitation of black Americans has been an ongoing crippler. "Proud, strong men and women, artists, teachers, healers, warriors and dream makers, inventors and builders, administrators like yourselves, politicians, priests. They came to these shores in the slave trade. Those who survived the indignity of the middle passage came to the American continents bringing treasures of African heritage, African spiritual and cultural gifts, wisdom, faith and faithfulness, art and drama.

"Here in an alien land, African people clung to African ways of think-ing, of perceiving, of understanding values, of celebrating life, or walking and talking and healing and learning and singing and praying," she said. "African people here became African Americans. Expressing faith in the God who loves and saves, they embodied and celebrated their own lives and their own values, their goals, their dreams, their relationships." She talked about what it means to be black and Catholic.

It was a door to education, she said, due to the work of generous reli-gious communities, but communities who, at the same time, historically would not admit blacks. "What does it mean to be black and Catholic?" she asked. "It means that I come to my church fully functioning. That doesn't frighten you, does it? I come to my church fully functioning. I bring myself, my black self, all that I am, all that I have, all that I hope to become, I bring my whole history, my traditions, my experience, my culture, my African American song and dance and gesture and move-ment and teaching and preaching and healing and responsibility as gift to the Church."

Thea tackled her topic from several angles, but the heart of her lecture was the rightness, the fullness of black spirituality, in all of its expres-sions, and how the Catholic Church needs to be open to that. She chided the bishops not to be distant with their local black Catholics. "If you get enough fully functioning black Catholics in your diocese, they are going to hold up the priest and they are going to hold up the bishop. We love our bishops, you-all."

She took a stand for black leadership within the church, and for black participation, from the grassroots, being integral to church decision-making and planning. "Black people who are still victims within the church of paternalism, of a patronizing attitude, black people who within the church have developed a mission mentality — they don't feel called, they don't feel responsible, they don't do anything," she lamented.

She made a strong plea for deeper commitment to education. At the end of her talk, preacher that she was, she broke into a rousing conclusion, and made her special appeal to the bishops gathered:

> Now, bishops, I'm going to ask you-all to do something. Cross your right hand over your left hand [clasping hands on either side –ed.]. You've got to move together to do that. All right now, walk with me. See, in the old days, you had to tighten up so that when the bullets would come, so that when the tear gas would come, so that when the dogs would come, so that when the horses would come, so that when the tanks would come brothers and sisters would not be separated from one another.
>
> And you remember what they did with the clergy and the bishops in those old days, where they'd put them? Right up in front, to lead the people in solidarity with our brothers and sisters in the church who suffer in South Africa, who suffer in Poland, who suffer in Ireland, who suffer in Nicaragua, in Guatemala, in Northern Ireland, all over this world.[3]

As she had with so many other assemblies, she implored them to sing with her "We Shall Overcome." Thea was glowing when she finished. She had delivered well, and she knew it. At the end of her presentation, she was presented a bouquet of red roses. No maternal elders were there in this room to whom to redirect the gift. Sweetly she said: "In the name of all the mothers and grandmothers and aunts and friends, all the women who have brought you to priesthood, who have nurtured you toward episcopacy, who have strengthened you in faith and hope and love so that you can be the Church of Jesus Christ, I accept these beautiful roses."[4]

"Her speech was, you know, so challenging, sharing what it meant to her to be a black Catholic," recalls attendee Bishop William Houck, of her own Jackson, Mississippi, diocese. "She was challenging the bishops to understand the different cultures and to be open to that in the church...."[5]

Archbishop Daniel E. Pilarczyk, who was president of the U.S. bishops' conference at the time and chair of the meeting, recalled years later, "I stood there thinking, this is surreal!" It was unprecedented to see this group of "grumpy old guys" standing there, arms crossed, clasping hands, he dryly observed.[6]

The event was widely reported and captured the imagination of many throughout the United States. Years later, Sister Marie Augusta Neal, a Sister of Notre Dame de Namur, would write, "When I reflect on Thea Bowman, her life and work, the first thought I have is that she made the bishops dance."[7]

In 1988, Thea had talked at length with Margaret Walker Alexander about prayer, which became increasingly important to her in 1989, as cancerous tumors continued to spread throughout her body. Thea prayed in the style she had learned from the "old folks," that same type of moaning that had eased Vyry, a protagonist in Walker's groundbreaking novel, *Jubilee:*

> That summer, after her son was born, Vyry was seventeen years old. She was now a woman and both her childhood and adolescent years were swept completely behind her. She lived from day to day with no hope. Even the days had lost their color. Life was the same as always, drab and hopeless, with always a slender undercurrent of a nameless fear. Whatever happened could not be good. Only evil could happen, and more evil, and it was this evil that peopled all her fear. Nevertheless she began to unburden herself as Aunt Sally had by lifting her voice in song. She was surprised to hear the dark rich voice of Aunt Sally come out of her throat. She was surprised to discover how much she enjoyed singing and what a relief she felt when she sang. The days always went faster singing.[8]

What follows are Thea's reflections on prayer, a lengthy excerpt from her previously unpublished interviews with Walker:

> Often, I find myself talking with God [in prayer] about my illness. I was reared in a community in which prayer was natural. Growing up, I was around old people whose prayer was not only consistent, but shared. Something good would happen and some

old woman would just break out in prayer. Very early, I learned traditional black modalities of prayer — words, symbols, phrases, songs, prayers. Older folks used to say God is my father and my mother and my sister and my brother, my pearl of great price, my lily of the valley, my rock, my sword, my shield. God's a god of peace. God's a god of war. God's water when you're thirsty, bread when you're hungry. God is my doctor, my lawyer, my captain in the battle of life, my friend, my king.

I find that the old prayers come back to me. For example, I recall an old man who would get up in church and say, "I thank you for another day of life because this very night many folks have been laid out on their cooling boards. I ask you for strength to bear the burdens of the day. I know that whatever comes to me is sanctioned by your holy hand." The old styles of prayer bring me comfort. When I'm tired, weak and in pain, I find myself turning to these prayers quicker than I used to. When I hurt I like to sing some of the old songs:

> Precious Lord, take my hand.
> Lead me on, let me stand.
> I'm tired, I'm weak, and I'm worn.
> Through the storm, through the night
> Lead me on to the light.
> Take my hand, Precious Lord, lead me on.

I find that prayer and song can take me beyond the pain.

Our old folks would go to church and pray, and they'd come home happy. Within the traditional prayer of the black community, there were ways of controlling the mind, the mood and even the body, and doing it in Jesus' name. I thank God for that gift of my people.

The approach to prayer of my folk has always been holistic. We seek a prayer of total engagement. We want to fully engage our mind so that we can say, "Were you there when they crucified my Lord?" I want to remember the Jesus of the Gospels, the Jesus who was promised in the Old Testament, the Jesus who was despised and rejected. I want to think of the Jesus who said, "Take up your cross and follow me." I want to think of the Jesus who said, "All you who are heavily burdened, come to me."

The mind is conscious not only of my need but of the needs of my brothers and sisters who are suffering all over, in South Africa, in Guatemala, in Poland, in Bangladesh, in the fields of California. Our prayer tradition attempts to go to God with feeling and passion, and emotion and intensity. I want to be a part of what Jesus felt as He hung on the Cross. I want to feel the anguish. I also want to feel the love that motivated Him to save us. He's the Almighty Word who leapt down from heaven. He's the son of the eternal Father who became human like us in all things save sin. Yet, he accepted the sufferings of a lifetime as a human being to give us life. I want to feel that love, that compassion.

Trying to understand my suffering helps me to understand the gift of my Savior and the love of my Savior. In order to do that, I need to engage my memory and imagination, not just my mind and feelings. The old songs help me do that. "Were you there when they *nailed* Him to the tree?" Stop and think about it, hear the hammer, see the crowd gathered. Try to realize what it must have meant for His mother to stand and watch.

In their holistic prayer, black people use the mind, memory, imagination, feelings, passion and emotion. The body also has a role. You'll see black people in prayer humming to themselves or rocking and swaying. Again, there's the effort to engage the totality of human energy in prayer, to engage ourselves as individuals and with our brothers and sisters in the community. Holistic prayer can make you feel better physically. It can move you beyond consciousness of the body and beyond consciousness of ordinary human surroundings. Abraham Maslow talks about peak experiences.

I think prayer for us can and should be a peak experience. We can achieve altered states of consciousness by the massive concentration of human energy — the mind, feelings, imagination, will, and body — in search of transcendence. Black folk never thought those states of altered consciousness were unusual. If the Church did not move together on a regular basis to praise the Lord in ways that were enhancing, entrancing, and revitalizing, my folk thought the prayer wasn't authentic.

Father Clarence Joseph Rivers expresses it in terms of "Roman Catholic liturgy that does not leave us revitalized and invigorated isn't authentic." In other words, traditionally black folk pray with the expectation that prayer will make a change in life. If you're in sorrow, you'll find comfort and consolation; if you're heavily burdened, you'll find relief; if you're lonely, you'll find friendship in Jesus and in the praying community; if you're joyful, your joy will be doubled because you shared. In prayer you will find the strength to keep on keepin' on.

An old lady I remember from my childhood said, "I come to church, I come to the meeting, I lay my burden down at the door. I ain't no fool, I know I got to pick it up again. But I come to God and I come to my church family to find some strength so I can go back and pick it up and carry it a little further." I remember old people sitting out on their porches and moaning on and on. I've found out that moaning is therapeutic.

What's ahead for me now is life for a while and then death. It's as simple as that. When I first found out I had cancer, I didn't know what to pray for. I didn't know if I should pray for healing or life or death. Then, I found peace in praying for what my folks call "God's perfect will." As it evolved, my prayer has become, "Lord, let me live until I die." By that I mean I want to live, love, and serve fully until death comes. If that prayer is answered, if I am able to live until I die, how long really doesn't matter. Whether it's just a few months or a few years is really immaterial.

I grew up with people who believed you could serve the Lord from a sickbed or a deathbed. The great commandment is to love the Lord your God with your whole heart, your whole soul, your whole mind, and all your strength. As long as I have any mental facility, I want to keep on loving. I want to keep on serving. That's what I hope to be about. My illness has helped me to realize how fragile our hold on life is. I always thought I was going to live to be an old woman, like my mother and my father and all the other old people I knew and was close to when I was a child. But I no longer think that. My time isn't long. Now, I just want to find ways to make the most of the time I have left.

I am using the traditional black prayer in facing the cancer. My people used to say — and they still say — sometimes you have to moan. I remember old people sitting out on their porches and moaning on and on in a kind of a deep, melodic hum. I've found out that moaning is therapeutic. It's a way of centering, the way you do in centering prayer.

You concentrate your internal energies and your powers in prayer or wordless outcry to God. Old people used to say the words from Scripture, "When we don't know how to pray the Spirit intercedes for us with inexpressible groaning." So sometimes you just moan.

Yes, I too, moan sometimes and I sing sometimes. When I'm sick and don't have the internal resources to pray as I would like, I sing or moan or hum. Because the songs are so familiar, it is an easy way to pray, to unite myself with God. When I have pain, I find it goes away when I hum or sing. When I concentrate on the song I forget the pain.

When I had a bone marrow biopsy, the doctor who was supposed to do it had a problem getting into my bone. Another doctor had to be called. A procedure that was supposed to take fifteen minutes took forty-five. As the pain increased, I hummed; after a while, I sang. Maybe they thought I was crazy, but it was my way of dealing with the stress and pain. I've found it works. It's a lesson I learned from my people and my heritage. Worshipping, hearing people praying, singing the songs — is helpful. I find myself carried by the prayer of the community. It gives me peace and support — and joy.[9]

After returning to Mississippi from speaking to the U.S. bishops in New Jersey, Thea needed rest. Her friends, saddened that the end might be nearer than anyone wanted, began to fete her. Holy Child Jesus Mission Church and School sponsored a tribute to Thea, under the name of an alumni event.

Much to her regret that summer, Thea had to cancel teaching at her beloved Institute for Black Catholic Studies at Xavier University in New Orleans. She was, however, in for a surprise. As Birnam Wood came to Macbeth, IBCS would come to Thea. On July 4, two busloads of Xavier students, faculty and friends rolled into Canton. It was a day of tributes, stories, singing, tears. Thea was overjoyed with the affection showered on her.

The group of faculty and students spontaneously decided to come to Canton to pay her a visit. In that group was C. Vanessa White, then a student, now a professor of spirituality at Chicago's Catholic Theological Union.

Two large buses left New Orleans, recalls White, one a "study" bus, to accommodate those students who needed study time; one more relaxed. When they got to Canton, they gathered at Holy Child Jesus Parish, in order to perform for the now fragile Thea Bowman. "I remember that you could sense that she was in pain, and we had been told that she was not able to speak because of her illness, but you could also sense that she needed to be there," White says. "For the next two hours — through song, preaching, dramatic expression, dance — we poured out our love for Sister Thea. It was the most profound, the most religious experience I have ever had, the sense of community coming together."

This was an expression of the Body of Christ, which Christians try to name and express in their gathering, says White. "It was multigenerational, it was lay, religious, older, younger, black, white, Latino." At the end of the two hours Thea herself motioned for the microphone and began singing the spiritual, "Done Made My Vow," White recalls. "I remember that those in attendance were crying," says White, as the words of the song came forth: "Done made my vow to the Lord, and I shall never go back. I will go, to see what the end would be."

Now a member of the IBCS faculty, Dr. White looks back on that as "the moment when the Institute was fully realized," she says: "You saw the power of black spirituality, the power of how the spirit of community can revive — and it did."[10]

During this time of rising black Catholic consciousness, important events were occurring outside of Mississippi as well. Father George A. Stallings, priest of the Archdiocese of Washington, D.C., formed a breakaway congregation for black Catholics, the "Imani Temple," and declared that his church would be separate from Rome and many of its mandates, including mandatory priestly celibacy, prohibition of abortion and birth control, and exclusion of women from the priesthood. Stallings said he had lost patience with slow change. As efforts were underway to resolve the rift (eventually, in February 1989, the Archdiocese of Washington formally expelled Stallings and his followers) there was a crisis in the black Catholic community. It was a rift that made national news, even in the secular media. "Which side are you on?" was the question of the day.

On the West Coast, at Sunday Mass on July 9, 1989, Franciscan Father Jim Goode, OFM, Pastor of St. Paul of the Shipwreck, San Francisco, referred to Thea's address to the bishops' conference when addressing the Stallings crisis. The problem was not George Stallings, preached Father Goode; it was racism. He preached about Thea: "Over the past year many Catholic organizations and institutions have awarded and honored the work of Sister Thea Bowman, who is also a friend of mine and a wonderful blessing to her people. But the question for me is, do we have to be in a wheelchair or facing death's door to be respected and fully validated by the Roman Catholic Church? What about the many black religious women and men who are daily struggling with and for their people? Why has the Church hesitated in recognizing their leadership and withheld support of their ministry in the black community?"[11]

News about Father Goode's statement reached Thea, but she made no comment.

Back in Mississippi, Harry Belafonte was beckoning. A photo of Belafonte sitting at Thea's bedside, taken July 28, 1989, flashed around the country. Belafonte brought his screenwriter Emma Pullen along to continue interviews with Mississippians who knew Thea. Pullen and Belafonte had interviewed Thea in Canton the previous December. Later, not long after Thea's passing, Pullen drafted the screen play for the movie about Thea. By then, however, Belafonte had become absorbed in the Haitian struggle.

At the same time, there was a desire on the part of the Franciscan sisters to have editorial input into the final product. With Thea's death and her intellectual property clearly in the hands of her Franciscan community, Belafonte's interest in the project waned. In 1994, Belafonte's option on Thea's story expired without a film ever being produced. Whoopi Goldberg, by then, had been cast in the unforgettable role of a singing black Catholic nun-impersonator in *Sister Act,* released in 1992, in some ways a tempting parallel, but with no evident connection to Thea's story.

A few days after Belafonte's July visit, Sisters Thea and Dorothy Ann packed the wheelchair in the van for a drive north to Oxford, for yet another Faulkner conference, this final year for her on a subject close to her heart: Faulkner and Religion (see chapter 24 for a description of the conference and her earlier participation). Thea loved meeting and greeting and conversing with Faulkner enthusiasts from all over the world.

The 1989 gathering was a gala event. At the opening reception the beautiful Bouldin portrait of Thea was exhibited in the Ole Miss art museum, where it remained on display for about a week. The exhibit was popular, and the portrait was greatly admired. The portrait, and the attention it created, made Thea smile, she said. She was keynote speaker for the opening session Sunday evening with a presentation entitled, "Ole Time Religion."

One can see her moving presentation to the conference in a video tribute, *Are You Walkin' with Me?* produced by Lisa N. Howorth of the Center for the Study of Southern Culture. The tribute, narrated by Margaret Walker, gives an overview of the programs Sister Thea Bowman presented at the annual Faulkner Conferences from 1980 to 1989, in which she used music and drama, as well as the spoken word, to reveal the importance of the African American voice and experience in Faulkner.

In her 1989 speech, Thea told those gathered that "Faulkner helped me to understand my state...to understand the glory and the shame of it" and to "understand the white folks — their ways of feeling and thinking." She asked the group, many of whom were white, "Are you with us? We can stop and explain this stuff, but I'm asking you, Are you with us?"

In a friendly way, she chided the white participants toward more active participation: "They think they're being erudite when they're being quiet."[12]

Sister Thea made her illness a tool of her teaching, and she refused to let advancing cancer stop her until she was near the point of death. So in the final months of 1989, Thea, in advanced, crippling cancer, was still making speaking appearances. She spoke to the National Office of Black Catholics and the National Black Lay Catholic Caucus at Emory University in Atlanta on August 5 and then conducted a three-day renewal in Aurora, Colorado, on August 24 and 25. Four days later, she spoke to a group at Sacred Heart Seminary in Detroit and then, within a week or so, to Gaston Hall at Georgetown University. On September 10 she was off to St. Stephen's Church in Minneapolis for a memorial concert and healing service with persons living with AIDS and related illnesses. Thea asked those gathered to pray for her, as well. On September 14 she flew to Charlotte, North Carolina, where she spoke from her wheelchair about "Walking toward the Promised Land."

At all these events Thea was accompanied by local singers, choirs, and musicians and, of course, by her faithful companion Dort, Sister Dorothy Ann.

While in Denver, she had been interviewed by religion writer Terry Mattingly, who was then writing for the *Rocky Mountain News*. He broached the topic of sainthood:

"You see, I'm black," she said, with a quiet laugh. "I guess the word 'saint' has a different meaning for me. I was raised in a community where everyone grew up believing they were supposed to try to be what we call a 'saint.' We were always saying things like, 'The saints would be coming in to church today' or 'The saints will really be dancing and singing this Sunday.' . . . I know people are looking for sources of hope and courage and strength. I know it's important to have special people to look up to. But, see, I think all of us in the church are supposed to be that kind of person to each other."

Then Mattingly quoted a local priest, Richard E. Breslin, who said, "I think people start talking about people being holy when they sense a special quality in that person. Sometimes you just have that sneaking suspicion. It's kind of neat to be able to meet a person and experience that, . . . to be able to put your finger on that special quality we can only call holiness."[13]

By now, a video about Thea, produced by Catholic media house Liguori, was being distributed. She had participated in the preliminary taping a year earlier. *Almost Home: Living with Suffering and Dying* focused on Thea's lessons on how to die with dignity and faith. Through song and story, she shared in the video something of her struggle with terminal illness and the confidence and courage with which she lived her life fully. Producer David Howard wrote:

[On the first day of taping] we walked into Thea's home, 136 Hill Street, and Dort said Thea was still in bed and was not feeling all that great. Our crew, Julie Yellen, the videographer, Dennis Finnegan, the grip, and I simply entered Thea's bedroom and in moments we began shooting.

Of course, one of the first things she did was sing. Out came "Deep River" in a magnificently emotional moment. Thea was so willing to let you in and let her gifts come out.

At the unveiling party, when Thea's portrait was presented to the public, I asked her what her favorite song was, and with a little encouragement from her friends seated around her, Thea broke into a very sultry, man-stealing version of "I'm a Big Fat Mama." It was pure Thea.

Early on, we were informed that at 12 noon most days Thea's and Dort's work came to a halt for one hour — "Holy Hour" — *All My Children* [the popular soap opera].[14]

Ultimately, the Liguori video received the Religion in Media Silver Angel Award, an Emmy, a Gabriel Award, and a Wilbur Award and has been used widely since that time as an educational tool.

Gayda Hollnagel wrote a review of the Liguori video for the *La Crosse Tribune* in August of 1989. In it she said, "The radiance and enthusiasm is inspiring. But, when she is at home and away from public view, she admits to sharing those moments of doubt common to terminally ill people...in a voice quaking with emotion and with a sad smile, she says, "Goodbye. It's been good to know you." And then she offered this parting advice: "And keep on keepin' on."[15]

There were several other media projects for this seemingly unstoppable woman. *Sister Thea: Ole Time Religion* was the theme of a series of religious-education videotapes produced by Gerard Pottebaum of Treehaus Communications from Loveland, Ohio. In the colorful videos — eight fifteen-minute programs for use from grade six through adult, recorded before the spring of 1989 and released that summer — Thea, singing spirituals along the way, inspires viewers to live ole time religious values: working, praying and playing together.

She also found the energy, somehow, to record a second audiocassette of spirituals, a set of Christmas songs, all Negro Spirituals, entitled, *'Round the Glory Manger*. St. Paul Books & Media also released with the set a booklet containing lyrics and score.

By now, in the last half of 1989, Thea was still "keepin' on." She and Dort went to New Orleans on September 22 and back to Canton for a September 25 "Thea Night in Canton." It was held by Holy Child Jesus parishioners, musicians, Holy Child School Choir, Sacred Heart Church and Community Choir, neighbors, townspeople, business leaders, Friends of Thea. The production was called "This Is Your Life, Sister Thea." It included sisters, priests, and bishops with blessings, reflections, gifts, and refreshments. She went on to Louisville, Kentucky, to Our Mother of Sorrows Church on September 29 to be the keynote speaker at the first general session in a three-part Consistent Life Ethic series sponsored by the archdiocese there.

The last few months of the year, after which she was unable to travel, marked the birth of the Thea Bowman Black Catholic Educational Foundation, started by then-Vermonters Dr. Leonard and Mary Lou Jennings. The Jenningses had been supporters of Catholic education for African Americans over the years, but they wanted to do more. They were sent to Sister Thea back in 1984, and the wheels started turning. Thea encouraged them to go national.

Sister Maria Friedman, FSPA, wrote up the story in the premiere issue of the aforementioned *Thea News:*

> Mary Lou made six trips to Canton, Mississippi, to work with Thea on a mission statement. With that, the Sister Thea Bowman Foundation was born. Thea was with Len and Mary Lou at St. Michael's College, in Winooski, Vermont, on October 19, 1989, when several Catholic university presidents and five bishops joined with them to officially launch the foundation.

Thea, according to Friedman, was set on the foundation targeting higher learning opportunities for black students and carefully refined the mission statement to reflect that. That statement is "another example of her logical, scholarly, historically astute writing," wrote Friedman. As Thea said, reported Friedman, " 'It takes more than one parent to raise a child, it takes more than two parents, to raise a child, it takes a whole church.' "[16]

The mission statement acknowledges the destructive force that racism has been, from slavery up until today. Yet it also acknowledges the great gifts of black people: the genius and creativity, the faith, richness of literature and arts, especially in song and in dance. The mission of the educational foundation is to forge a new beginning by providing each child with a quality, value-based education. The foundation will "establish the means by which to rekindle and enliven the hope and the opportunities which Catholic schools can offer to black children."[17]

For Thea, given her passion for education, the foundation's inauguration was a momentous occasion. In addition to the bishops who came, there were the presidents of Catholic University, the University of Notre Dame, and Boston College. This work was seen as significant in the broader educational community, in all of these places that somehow had shared in Thea's story. The *New York Times* said Sister Thea brought many people in the crowded chapel at St. Michael's to tears when she thanked those who worked on the foundation and those who had helped "the young people who are already claiming the victory because somebody, somewhere, somehow, has given them a chance."[18]

Thea was garbed in colorful African attire, seated in a wheelchair. Draped around her shoulders to protect against any autumn chill, a Kente cloth, purple, gold, orange, red, and green, a sign of African royalty and the power of the extended African family.

On Thanksgiving Day, November 26, 1989, Thea wrote a general letter to her friends, filled with recent activity, her state of health, and plans for the coming months. It was like her usual "report to the troops," chronicling, in detail, her still-full travel schedule, and the many events that have constituted this chapter. She reports that she's on chemotherapy again, that she fights ear infections, and now reports an electrically powered hospital bed. After describing the beautiful birds that frequent her windowsill, she returns to the maddening schedule of upcoming commitments: "In January I hope to be in Maryknoll, New York, Prescott, Arizona; in February, Notre Dame, Indiana, Canton, Mississippi, Shreveport, Louisiana; in March, Orlando, Washington, D.C., Indianapolis, Chicago, Los Angeles; in April, Madison, Wisconsin, Philadelphia, Notre Dame, Indiana; in May, Minneapolis and La Crosse. God willing, perhaps we'll meet along the way. Until then, thanks for your calls, cards, visits, flowers, gifts, love and prayers. My prayers are with you."[19]

Her traveling days would end before all that could happen. In fact, she was at the same time soberly preparing for her own end. Her fellow Franciscan, Celesta Day, a former FSPA vice president, recalled listening to a television interview aired at Christmastime, called "Heart of the Nation: A Christmas Special with Sister Thea Bowman," during Thea's last year. The interviewer, a priest, asked her if she ever got scared. She replied, "I get scared! I am afraid of pain. I am more afraid of disability. The time will come when I can't work at all. I don't like that, but I am preparing myself. The old folks say, so long as you're in your right mind you can help somebody. If you are paralyzed and can't move, you can still listen, you can praise God, you can help." Asked further questions about whether she believed in the afterlife, she replied by singing several of "the songs of my mothers and fathers, my people's songs," including:

> This world isn't my home.
> I'm just passing through.
> I'm gonna set at the welcome table,

I'm gonna drink from the golden fountain,
I'm gonna shout glory, alleluia,
I'm gonna see my sainted mother,
I'm gonna talk to my King Jesus.[20]

The December issue of *Ebony* magazine ran a story titled, "How Celebrities Will Celebrate Christmas" with pop singer Whitney Houston, the Reverend Jesse Jackson and family, U.S. Secretary of Health and Human Services, Louis Sullivan, M.D., velvet-voiced singer Luther Vandross, and now-celebrity Sister Thea Bowman. There was a photo of smiling, standing, braided-haired Thea in a gorgeous red African dress, with a caption detailing Christmas plans: "Sister Thea Bowman, Catholic nun, will have warm apple cider and plenty of cookies on hand.... The Kundinger family [Dort's] also will bring a holiday feast, which will include a variety of African and German-American specialties. 'We might have wedding dumplings, sauerkraut and some black-eyed peas so everyone will have something they like,' says the wheelchair-bound nun...."[21]

As it turned out, Thea was sick with nausea most of Christmas Day.

Dort wrote to one of Sister Thea's FSPA friends the next month, explaining that, by the end of 1989, Thea was not able to leave the house for Mass, even the holiday Masses. Bishop Brunini, now-retired, had offered always to help in any way he could, so Dort had called him and asked him to come to the house and say Mass. He gladly obliged. "My mother and sister were here, Thea and me," wrote Dort. "We had liturgy in Thea's bedroom. It was truly a grace-filled time."[22]

Thea, by now, was wracked in pain.

GOING HOME

Dort remembers when the end was truly at hand, the evening of December 8, 1989. She remembers, "it was one of the few times I saw Thea cry." The *Inside Edition* TV crew was taping a segment on Thea, and Holy Child Jesus children's choir at church, in Canton. Thea couldn't make the high notes. Amazingly, it was a first. "My heart sank, I can still see the look on Mr. Watson's face." (Harry Watson was Thea's accompanist at Holy Child Jesus.)

Later, after their night prayers, Thea talked about what had happened and started to cry. "I just held her." The loneliness of the big little girl with the difficult name of Bertha, who had suffered the taunts of her childhood friends, returned to her. She had written a poem about it, at a retreat in 1988, remembers Dort:

> Only child, lonely child
> Daddy's daughter
> Grandpa's child, Daddy's kid
> Mama's sweet little, poor little,
> Little black lamb. . . .
> Only child, lonely child
> Grandpa died Aunt Bertha died
> Charlotte [Bonneville] died Joe [Nearon] died
> Mama died Daddy died
> The Lord is my light and my salvation
> Thank God there's you.

By now, Thea required assistance in and out of bed, in and out of her wheelchair; she asked friends who came by to write letters she dictated and signed, recalls Dort.[1]

Now, not much more than a month after the mournful night, following her singing failure, Thea dictated the last of her now-famous "form

letters" to Dort. The letter is shorter than usual. It has no extensive cat-
alog of engagements — those cancellations were very difficult for Thea,
recalls Dort. Thea is weakening each day, yet characteristically she is
concerned about her friends. "Greetings from Mississippi," she writes.
"I apologize for being behind in my correspondence. Life has been a little
hectic here. . . . " She then goes on to explain why she's not been writing — as if people would have expected a dying woman to keep up on her
correspondence! "I had to cancel all my January commitments and what
February will bring God knows. I ask your prayers. I'm very weak but
my spirits are good and I'm trying to keep on keeping on." She concludes
with an apology for being "slow to respond to your generosity."[2]

Thea's strength ebbed. Elected leaders and other Franciscan Sisters of
Perpetual Adoration came to visit, to validate that Thea was receiving
the best possible medical care, and to say grateful and sad goodbyes to
their dear sister. Other friends and colleagues came from near and far to
visit and linger one last time. Thea absorbed their energy and was happy
to see them. Dort, constant, untiring caregiver, fielded calls, knocks at
the door, frequent visitors, streaming correspondence with gently sweet
care. Many people from the neighborhood and parish came by with
food, gifts, and offers to do whatever they could.

In the little white shotgun home on 136 Hill Street walls and shelves
were adorned with plaques, certificates, awards. The honorary degree
academic hoods were displayed in a bookcase, and the awards kept
coming, from the many areas of her life, from the many elements of her
identity. Perhaps one of the finest for her would have been the University
of Mississippi's award for Outstanding Mississippi Leader in Religion,
an award Thea received but didn't live to see. That year, 1990, her friend
Margaret Walker Alexander received the parallel award for the arts.

Early in February, Thea mustered all her strength and traveled to
Jackson, with Dort, of course, to the annual Black Catholic Congress
meeting. There nearly three hundred people met at St. Joseph High
School to launch a permanent diocesan office for ministry to black
Catholics. The new office was established to implement the National
Black Catholic Pastoral Plan, which promoted and supported evangelization and addressing long-term needs of the African American Catholic
community. Thea's steely determination throughout her years of ministry
had helped to lead black Catholics to positions of church and parish

leadership. Representatives from all parts of the diocese grouped themselves according to deaneries to elect representatives for the new board of directors. They also voted to hold a diocesan congress twice a year.

Speaking with a firm voice, Thea gave the welcoming address from notes she had dictated to Dort. "We have come together because there has got to be a new way," Thea said, speaking as Director of Intercultural Awareness for the Diocese of Jackson. "The formation of a permanent diocesan structure will enable us to do what we are supposed to do, that is, to be fully functioning black Catholics." She ended her talk with the 1960's song, "We've Come This Far by Faith" and asked to be taken back to Canton.[3]

Dort remembers that Thea had wanted to die in the same place her parents had wanted to die — at the Hill Street Bowman home.[4] Mrs. Bowman had died, though, in the hospital, in November 1984, and Dr. Bowman died, in his sleep at home before the year was out.

Her childhood friend, Flonzie Brown Wright, now of Ohio, would come to be with Thea whenever Flonzie came to town to visit her own aging parents. At one of those last visits, Flonzie recalls, "I remember her getting up from the bed and going into, I think, the bath area, and when she came back, of course, she was walking very very slow, and my heart was so torn up. I said to Thea, 'You know, if I could just take your pain for one day, I would do it.' And she stopped in her steps. She said, 'Flonzie, you don't want *no* part of this.' "[5]

Now, in March 1990, days and nights melded for Thea. Chemotherapy was no longer fending off the tumors. Thea was confined to her bed most of the time as her body grew more fragile. But she wasn't finished. For *Thea News,* Beth Erickson, editor, wrote of an event that happened in mid-March, when Daniel Johnson-Wilmot and the Viterbo Choir were on tour throughout the United States. They stopped in Canton, because he wanted his choir to meet her. Calling ahead, he heard from Dort that of course, Thea wanted to see them as well. The group crowded into Thea's small house and sang, "Roll, Jordan, Roll." Johnson-Wilmot remembers, and that after the line, "I want to get to Heaven," Thea "burst into tears and said how beautiful it was.... She had a need to sing and a need to express," he said. When the choir returned from their tour in New Orleans, on their way north, Thea requested that Dort drive her out to the McDonald's by the highway to see them. "She wanted to see the choir one more time," said Johnson-Wilmot. "How desperately she wanted to sing. Our choir was very special to her because she had trained us 'white folks' to do her music."[6]

Thea had been asked, some weeks back, by *Mississippi Today*, the newspaper of the Jackson diocese, to write a meditation for the week concluding in Easter, Holy Week. From her bed Thea dictated the piece. "Let Us Resolve to Make This Week a Holy One." It was the poignant testimony of a gifted, inspirational speaker at death's door. Upon Thea's death on March 30, two weeks before Easter, National Catholic News Service picked up the essay. Catholic newspapers across the United States and Canada printed it as a reflection piece during Holy Week, concluding in Easter, which was April 15 that year. In addition to the outstanding editorial quality of the submission, its publication was kind of a tribute to Thea on the part of Catholic newspaper editors across the continent. Over the phone, Thea had dictated,

> Let us resolve to make this week holy by claiming Christ's redemptive grace and by living holy lives. The Word became flesh and redeemed us by his holy life and holy death. This week especially, let us accept redemption by living grateful, faithful, prayerful, generous, just, and holy lives.
>
> Let us resolve to make this week holy by reading and meditating, holy Scripture. So often, we get caught us in the hurry of daily living.
>
> As individuals and as families, reserve prime time to be with Jesus to hear the cries of the children waving palm branches, to see the Son of Man riding on an ass's colt, to feel the press of the crowd, to be caught up in the "Hosannas," and to realize how the cries of acclamation will yield to the garden of suffering, to be there and watch as Jesus is sentenced by Pilate to Calvary, to see him rejected, mocked, spat upon, beaten, and forced to carry a heavy cross, to hear the echo of the hammer, to feel the agony of torn flesh and strained muscles, to know Mary's anguish as he hung three hours before he died.
>
> We recoil before the atrocities of war, gang crime, domestic violence, and catastrophic illness. Unless we personally and immediately are touched by suffering, it is easy to read scripture and to walk away without contacting the redemptive suffering that makes us holy. The reality of the Word falls on deaf ears.

Let us take time this week to be present to someone who suffers. . . .

Her essay goes on with more specific encouragement for people to participate fully in the liturgies of Holy Week, sharing our suffering with that of people worldwide, building peace in our homes and beyond, praying together, reaching out to the poor, "seeking to go all the way for love as Jesus went all the way for love."[7]

By the time people read Thea's message, she was a week or more gone, basking in the love of her sweet Jesus, her parents, her beloved ancestors.

Leadership members from Thea's Franciscan community joined Dort, parishioners, and friends at her side as she died, and, being the teachers that they are, documented in detail her final days. One visitor, Celesta Day, FSPA, a registered nurse, was surprised to see so many books, so much research material among Thea's possessions. She wrote, "I should have known. . . . She was an intelligent, reflective scholar and I saw the signs of it all about."

Celesta's notes indicate that Thea was relaxed and conversant in her final days, but, to Thea's own surprise, exhausted. By Tuesday of her final week, Celesta reports, "Thea began to let go. She seemed to have answered her own question about when the time was to be." It was at that time, after a final visit to the doctor, that Thea and Celesta had a conversation about the state of things.

Thea had used the ride back from Jackson, on that Tuesday, as a time to talk things over with Celesta. After comparing notes on what she had heard the doctor say, Thea told her, "I can't trust myself to do anything. If I can't do anything, I'm not interested in living. Do you understand?" then Thea added, "I feel guilty, there is more to do. But not my will, but Thine, be done. I really want what God chooses for me, no matter what that is." Thea made a cryptic admission to Celesta at that point, the meaning of which one can only speculate: "I never prayed for death but one time. I never will again."

At home, she was helped back into bed and now was ready for her final journey. On Wednesday, she fell in and out of a coma, a condition that lasted for a few days. At one point, she awoke and, with help, was able to walk to the bathroom. At another time, she partially awoke, acknowledged her friends, and asked, "Let me go, okay?" On Friday, March 30, at 5:00 a.m., Sister Celesta lit a candle.[8]

Dort recalls the end: "Before 5 a.m., I woke up because Sister Celesta was moving around the bedroom." (Dort was sleeping on the second bed in Thea's room.) "I asked what she was doing. She was lighting a candle; Sister Thea's breathing pattern had changed. I sat on Theas's bed; she was sitting almost straight up to help with breathing. I put her right hand in my lap and held her and asked Celesta if we could have a few minutes alone. I whispered, 'Thea, it's Dort.' She straightened her head, moved her shoulders, and tried to open her eyes. I repeated often, 'Thea, many friends have said "Good-bye." It's okay to die. Don't be afraid. Your Mama and your Daddy and Joe [Nearon] are waiting for you in heaven. You are not alone. Don't be afraid. I love you. Good-bye, Thea.' Her head turned to the side, shoulders dropped, she didn't try to open her eyes anymore."[9] Thea passed into eternity at about 5:20 a.m.

Sisters Celesta, Grace McDonald, FSPA former president and archivist, and Addie Lorraine Walker, SSND, came in. As loved ones would around anyone who has died, they stood around the bed and prayed. Wrote Celesta, "Addie spoke of the angels leading her into paradise. I spoke gratitude in my heart to God for the gift of her and for her merciful passing. After we prayed and watched quietly for a time, we put on a cassette tape of Thea's music. We sat around her bed listening to her songs of her people and sipped coffee. Father Charles Burns, SVD, came. After prayer, we again sat with Thea for a time."

Then Dort bathed the body, Addie clothed it with a fresh gown, and, Celesta continues, "We closed her eyes again and propped her chin. After each of us kissed her and thanked her, we let her go."

Father Bede Abram OFM, Cap., a friend of Thea, earlier had said at her bedside, "God is going to look at you and say, 'Well done, good and faithful daughter!'"[10]

Chapter 29

WINNING THE GAME—
FOR EVERYBODY

Thea's death was a national event within Catholic circles and beyond. CBS rebroadcast the 1987 *60 Minutes* segment, now for the fourth time. The *New York Times* published an obituary. Of course, local media in both Wisconsin and Mississippi reported as well, as did the national Catholic press. The *New York Times* obituary mentioned Thea's memorable presentation to the nation's bishops, but added, "The work of Sister Thea, a Canton native who was the granddaughter of a slave, was far more than symbolic." The obit listed her work for intercultural awareness in Jackson, her faculty position at Xavier's Institute for Black Catholic Studies, and the Thea Bowman Educational Foundation in Vermont as evidence of that.[1]

There was a memorial service at Holy Child Jesus Church in Canton, with the funeral in Jackson (moved to a larger location than planned due to large crowds), but her burial was in Memphis, where she was laid to rest next to her parents at historic Elmwood Cemetery. At the Canton memorial service, held Monday, April 2, Thea's body was dressed in colorful African garb. One long-stemmed red rose was by her beautiful head. It was "a genuine celebration," Beth Erickson remembered. "Daniel Johnson-Wilmot, Viterbo music professor and 'adopted brother of Thea,' reflected on his experience at the wake. '[I] was nervous about singing "There Is a Balm in Gilead."'" When his time arrived to sing toward the end of the wake, the pianist had gone outside. For a split second, he wondered what to do, and then he just began singing, "There is a balm in Gilead." After a short while, the pianist returned and began to accompany." Johnson-Wilmot told Erickson, "I was crying and suddenly the whole room started singing. She gave her gift back. It was like magic."[2]

Thea's FSPA sisters, back in La Crosse, held a memorial service on April 2, in the same Maria Angelorum Chapel where Thea had celebrated so many significant moments.

Thea's childhood friend Mary Queen Donnelly wrote for the April 28, 1990, issue of *America*, the influential Jesuit magazine read by academics and Catholic Church leaders from parishes to the Vatican. That issue featured a full-page sketch of Thea, the first time a black woman ever graced its cover. The pride and awe Donnelly felt about her friend is evident. "They streamed into Holy Child Jesus Church in Canton, Mississippi, and the following day into St. Mary's in West Jackson much like the shepherds and kings of old sought out the balm of Gilead in the cave at Bethlehem," she wrote. "...They came from the four corners of the United States — from the West Coast, from the East, from the Franciscan mother house in La Crosse, Wisconsin, to Sister Thea's hometown in Canton, where she received the roots and heart of her special evangelizing. They arrived in buses, cars and by train — Black, White, Catholic, Protestant, Jew — the hierarchy of the Catholic Church, the recognized and the unrecognized, men, women and children — especially the children. For they knew they were special in the eyes of Sister Thea."

Donnelly's memoriam touches on much of Thea's career, but perhaps one passage sums up the woman: "At a time of much division in the Church, Sister Thea possessed the charismatic gifts to heal, to bring joy to the Church.... 'Be woman. Be man. Be priest,' Sister Thea would say. 'Be Irish-American, be Italian-American, be Native-American, be African American, but be one in Christ....' This was her song, and no one sang it more eloquently than Sister Thea Bowman."[3]

Childhood friend Flonzie Brown-Wright, at Thea's request, sang a song, "Zion's Hill," one that they had listened to decades earlier, sung by Earnest Gannett, who owned the row of "little shotgun houses" where Flonzie had lived, near young Bertha Bowman. Thea had asked Flonzie to sing it and had hoped that Flonzie would earn a singing part in the ill-fated Belafonte movie, Flonzie recalls. She sang, with the emotion of a childhood friend who still marveled at the amazing woman that Thea had grown into, once the kid across the way who wanted to "play nun." "There waits for me a glad tomorrow / and beyond this veil of sorrow." Thea herself had sung that song at both Dr. and Mrs. Bowman's funerals.[4]

The NBC-affiliate television station in Jackson broadcast the funeral services from Jackson, which were rebroadcast nationally on the Catholic cable network, EWTN, several times.

The funeral itself was a glorious event, attended by a crowd that had started in Canton and reached its peak in Jackson. Thea's great friend, Father John Ford, Missionary Servant of the Most Holy Trinity, delivered the eulogy, encouraging all to be strong:

> Even in the face of human suffering and anguish and death we must, this day, not only renew our belief that God will come, but we must also find ways to imitate this irreplaceable woman. There is no other Thea. None other will come in our lifetime. We must recognize that, even as we come to celebrate her new life. We must need to find a way, somehow, to imitate Thea who took the psalmist's words literally. "Wait for the Lord with courage. Be stouthearted and wait for the Lord."[5]

Thea was buried on Wednesday, April 4, 1990, in Elmwood Cemetery, in the Rite of Committal, led by Bishop James Lyke of Cleveland, formerly of Memphis. Fittingly, Memphis's St. Augustine Church choir sang.

The epitaph she had requested was inscribed on her white tombstone: "She tried."

In La Crosse, on April 5, Rev. Roy Lee, then at St. Philip Neri parish, Milwaukee, presided at a spirited liturgy in Mary of the Angels chapel at the FSPA motherhouse. Daniel Johnson-Wilmot directed the Viterbo College Choir in rousing Gospel songs.

Tributes to Sister Thea came from friends far and wide. New York's Cardinal John J. O'Connor was among the many who saluted her in print. In his archdiocesan newspaper column, he wrote, "Friedrich Nietzsche said: 'The world no longer believes because believers no longer sing.' He didn't know Sister Thea Bowman, dark nightingale. I am grateful that I did." He called her a "quintessential woman," a "quintessential religious" a "quintessential black...never a whit self-conscious.... When Sister Thea talked 'soul,' I knew that most of what I had listened to before had been stereotype. For her, 'soul' was all the misery of the crucifixion and all the glory of the resurrection."

He said he suspected that no one had a "deeper understanding of the Mystical Body of Christ.... Sister Thea was quintessentially a Church-woman." That's why, he said, the "bishops of the United States listened to her so raptly. . . . There was a quiet in her suffering, a dignity, a nobility that never made light of pain, but never treated it as an impossible burden." That he compared to the crucifixion, which, he said, she accepted "as a gift beyond measure."[6]

Eventually, memorials sprang up in various parts of the nation. Nearly two decades after her passing, at the time of this writing, her friends still marvel at the contribution that Thea made. Longtime companion Sister Antona Ebo says what many would agree with: "Her greatest gift was communication." And if that communication rocked the boat, so be it: "She wanted people to come out and speak very candidly about what they were experiencing and what they had seen and heard," says Ebo. "Empowering woman" is a term that sums up Thea's presence for Antona: "She brought forth the best that was already there."[7]

Bishop William Houck, now retired from Jackson, Mississippi, recalls, "She was insightfully aware of her own dignity as a woman and as a Black woman. She combined that with great love of the Catholic faith," he adds, "deeply in love with God — and as a result, in love with people."[8]

Says Father Clarence Williams, who many times over the years shared a stage or speaking platform with Thea, hers was a "victory that she had in her whole life from that little small place of Mississippi, to the very cold north of Wisconsin, to her days in DC, to her going around the country, just inspiring people."

She stood alone among her community, says Williams, because "the capacity for leadership is not an equal opportunity employer. Some people, like St. Paul, can say, 'You take Jerusalem; I'll take the world.' Because the capacity for leadership is not democratic. Like the NFL," he continues, "some are virtuosos. Those are the ones who win the game for everybody."

That virtuosity played itself out in many arenas, he says, as she delivered substance in addition to her personal charisma. "She could not only sing a spiritual, but she could tell you what the spiritual meant. She was a cultural communicator; she was also an interracial communicator, a theological and arts educator. She had all these skills — they were just so powerful and all in one person." Comparing her "star power" to that of an athlete like basketball star Michael Jordan, he sums up: "She had spiritual intelligence, and she could communicate it."[9]

Flonzie Brown and Thea's childhood friends were simply awestruck by Thea, says Flonzie. "A lot of that stemmed from the fact that we watched her grow. We know her. She's ours. She's a native daughter. To see her, to see Thea Bowman, who once wore all of the [nun's] garb, now in Church, clapping and dancing, singing Gospel songs, teaching Gospel music,...it was just awesome." Flonzie knew Thea never to be a "worldly" woman, yet, "How did she know those moves?" she asks. "I mean, she could rock, and she could sway, and she could do her shoulders, and she could step back — ." To Flonzie she was a sister, in the African American sense of the term: "There's always an aura about these 'sisters,' in what they wear, and how they wear it."[10]

Thea's colleague Sister Jamie Phelps finds Thea's legacy in her selfless, nonjudgmental way of relating with others. "People like people who sense their needs and respond to them generously in support and love," observes Phelps. "She would focus on the aspects of their personalities, their gifts that were good, and encourage and nurture that. Don't we all want that kind of person?"[11]

Thea's close friend Sister Addie Walker, sums up Thea's gift: She was "a black woman of faith who lived it with great freedom and integrity, and not without cost." She was God's child, says Walker, and thus was free to follow a different path. "Many of us try to meet with other people's expectations, try to live what other people expect....She didn't live with that."

"In my words," says Walker "her teaching style was always to forsake the process and save the people." That legacy still lives, she says, because "people who were taught by her are still affected by her"; her teaching "still burns within them....I think her impact will be long-lived because she was an embodiment of love. She affirmed the very being of persons."[12]

"Thea is one of those people who remain loyal," says Father Fernand Cheri. And within that loyalty she got other loyal people to reexamine their charism, their basic gifts and commitments. "That's what she did to the Jesuits," he says, speaking of a challenging talk she gave to a national conference. "That's what she did to bishops," in her famous presentation. That loyalty, he says, is how she could remain both black and Catholic.[13]

But her commitment, her willingness to remain in an all-white community, wasn't such a jump for Jesuit theologian Father Joseph Brown. He would say that the character of her work, off on her own compared to many members of her community, and her loyalty to Catholicism, were to be expected: "There is no reason to break from a community when the work you are supposed to be doing actually reflects the mission and history of that community. They [the FSPA sisters] went into Mississippi to teach in unrepresented communities. Thea spent her entire life doing that and by trying to bring people together in an inclusive way." That, he says, "was an embodiment of their charism. I think they are beginning to recognize that now.

"One of the things that has made me very sad is that she wrote almost nothing," reflects Father Brown. Yes, there are collected speeches, and video recordings of Thea in action, but "her teaching and her entire way of preaching was a form of black theology that you don't often see in the Catholic Church," says Brown. "Most of the people who are considered black Catholic theologians have been trained in European methodologies and apply that to black theology."

It wasn't that her style was uneducated, he adds. "Her singing was part of her theology because performance is part of black theology. As an artist she understood the value of rhetoric, performance, communication." Using all of that, he says, "she could overwhelm some people because her personality was pure, as pure as possible, and unfiltered." That didn't mean it wasn't complicated, he explains: "She was playing about three or four notes at the same time."[14]

And, on those notes, we come to the end of this story. Some years after Thea's passing, her companion for many years, Sister Dort Kundinger, said that Thea, a bird-lover, known in her youth as "Birdie," considered the mockingbirds of the world as her own. "Calling to them, singing short phrases to them, they could imitate her."

As a young postulant, said Dort, Thea had reveled in the chickadees outside her window at the River Pines Sanatorium in Wisconsin, taming the birds first to come to her windowsill and eventually, to eat crumbs from her hand.[15] It was that patience, and a fundamental respect for others, that marked Thea's life. Her desire to engage people, to bring forth their song and blend it with both hers and others,' made Sister Thea Bowman unforgettable. That is Thea's song.

NOTES

Chapter 1 / In Thea's Own Words: Life in Canton

1. Thea Bowman, "Passing beneath the Southern Sun," *Touchstone* (Viterbo College, La Crosse, Wis.), Winter 1959: 5–11; written at age twenty-one.

Chapter 2 / Ancestral History of Hope

1. This may be oral history. The highest recorded temperature in the states Thea mentions is 115 degrees Fahrenheit.

2. Unpublished penciled notes written by Thea Bowman, 1980s, Thea Bowman Collection, FSPA Archives (La Crosse, Wis.), no. 16, no. 1.1.2.3. B. 1 F.1.

Chapter 3 / The Parents: Mary and Theon in Love

1. "Couples Share Their Togetherness" *Mississippi Today* (Jackson, Miss.), February 10, 1984.

2. Bowman family scrapbook, Thea Bowman Collection, FSPA Archives (La Crosse, Wis.).

3. Ibid.

Chapter 4 / Young Bertha

1. Charlene Smith, FSPA, in conversation with Bertha/Thea during formation years in La Crosse.

2. *Baby Book,* Thea Bowman Collection, FSPA Archives (La Crosse, Wis.).

3. Ibid.

4. Ibid. for all of the preceding.

5. "Readin' and Ma," essay written at St. Rose High School, Thea Bowman Collection, September 19, 1955.

6. *Baby Book.*

7. Margaret Walker and Thea Bowman, "God Touched My Life: The Inspiring Autobiography of the Nun Who Brought Song, Celebration, and Soul to the World," unpublished manuscript, Thea Bowman Collection, FSPA Archives (La Crosse, Wis.), and Margaret Walker Collection, Margaret Walker Alexander Research Center, Jackson State University (Jackson, Miss.), 1992.

8. Essay written at St. Rose High School, Thea Bowman Collection.

9. Frances White, "Motherhood" on a prayer card in the Thea Bowman Collection, FSPA Archives (La Crosse, Wis.).

10. Celestine Cepress, FSPA, *Sister Thea Bowman: Shooting Star* (Winona, Minn.: St. Mary's Press, 1993), 76.

11. *Sister Thea: Songs of My People* (Boston: St. Paul Books and Media, 1989), 7.

12. Thea Bowman, Autobiography, written as a novice in 1958, Thea Bowman Collection.

13. *The Non-Catholic in the Catholic School* (Washington, D.C.: National Catholic Educational Association, 1984), quoted in Cepress, *Sister Thea Bowman: Shooting Star,* 92.

Chapter 5 / School Days in Canton

1. Thea often referred to her "grandfather" as a slave, a statement many journalists, including one of this book's authors, John, repeated. In this quote, she identifies the grandfather as her "father's father," who was Edward Bowman. He was born in 1874, about a decade after the Emancipation Proclamation (1863) and the Thirteenth Amendment (1865). Edward was born to parents who were former slaves, Nathaniel and Katherine Bowman. Perhaps being from a family of former slaves, he referred to himself as a former slave. Alternatively, perhaps young Thea simply misunderstood and, having lost him to death while she was a teenager far from home, never had a chance to correct this with "Grandpa Ed" as an adult. There could be some other explanation: one can only speculate.

2. Celestine Cepress, FSPA, *Sister Thea Bowman: Shooting Star* (Winona, Minn.: St. Mary's Press, 1993), 24.

3. Charlene Smith, FSPA, conversations with Bertha/Thea during formation years. Similar account in Margaret Walker and Thea Bowman, "God Touched My Life: The Inspiring Autobiography of the Nun Who Brought Song, Celebration, and Soul to the World," unpublished manuscript, Thea Bowman Collection, FSPA Archives (La Crosse, Wis.), and Margaret Walker Collection, Margaret Walker Alexander Research Center, Jackson State University (Jackson, Miss.), 1992, 01.8.

4. Walker and Bowman, "God Touched My Life," 01.12.

5. Ibid., 01.13.

6. Ibid.

7. Ibid., 01.24.

8. Ibid., 01.11.

9. Cepress, *Sister Thea Bowman: Shooting Star,* 18.

10. Sister Mileta Ludwig, FSPA, *A Chapter of Franciscan History: The Sisters of the Third Order of Saint Francis of Perpetual Adoration 1849–1949* (New York: Bookman Associates, 1950), 254.

11. Ibid., 254–55.

12. Ibid., January 29, 1948, 255.

13. Ibid., 256.

14. John Feister, interview with Flonzie Brown-Wright at Miami University, Middletown, Ohio, August 16, 2007.

15. Ibid.

16. "She Inspires Thousands, but Who Inspires Her?" *CUA Magazine* (Winter 1990): 7–8. Quoted in Cepress, *Sister Thea Bowman: Shooting Star*, 18.

17. John Feister, interview with Flonzie Brown-Wright at Miami University, Middletown, Ohio, August 16, 2007.

18. Judy Ball, "A Woman Wrapped in Courage," *Mustard Seed* (January 6, 1989): 1–2.

19. *The Non-Catholic in the Catholic School* (Washington, D.C.: NCEA, 1984), 20–25, quoted in Cepress, *Sister Thea Bowman: Shooting Star*, 92–93.

20. Thea Bowman Collection, FSPA Archives (La Crosse, Wis.).

21. Ibid.

22. John Feister, interview with Flonzie Brown-Wright at Miami University, Middletown, Ohio, August 16, 2007.

23. Ball, "A Woman Wrapped in Courage," 1–2.

24. Thea Bowman, "Passing beneath the Southern Sun," *Touchstone* (Viterbo College, La Crosse, Wis.) (Winter 1959): 10.

25. Holy Child Jesus School fundraising letter, Thea Bowman Collection.

26. John Feister, interview with Flonzie Brown-Wright at Miami University, Middletown, Ohio, August 16, 2007.

27. Ibid.

28. Ibid.

29. Ball, "A Woman Wrapped in Courage," 1–2.

30. Prayer card, Thea Bowman Collection.

Chapter 6 / Following St. Francis — to Wisconsin

1. Charlene Smith, FSPA, conversations with Bertha/Thea during formation years.

2. Bowman family scrapbook, Thea Bowman Collection, FSPA Archives (La Crosse, Wis.).

3. Thea Bowman Collection.

4. John Feister, telephone interview with Dorothy Ann Kundinger, FSPA, June 8, 2008.

5. *La Crosse Catholic Register*, August 1953.

6. Bowman family scrapbook.

7. Ibid.

8. Ibid.

9. Ibid.

10. Ibid.

11. Ibid.

12. Ibid.

13. "Death Claims Bowman after Brief Illness," *Madison County (Miss.) Herald*, January 1954.

14. Bowman family scrapbook.

Chapter 7 / Stepping Up

1. John Feister, telephone interview with Jamie Phelps, OP, New Orleans, June 17, 2008.

2. John Feister, telephone interview with Norma Angel, MM, Maryknoll, New York, March 20, 2008.

3. John Feister, telephone interview with Dorothy Ann Kundinger, FSPA, June 8, 2008.

4. John Feister, telephone interview with Jamie Phelps, OP, New Orleans, June 17, 2008, for all of the preceding quotes.

5. John Feister, telephone interview with Francesca Thompson, OSF, Oldenburg, Indiana, June 18, 2008.

6. John Feister, telephone interview with Norma Angel, MM, Maryknoll, New York, March 20, 2008.

7. Bowman family scrapbook, Thea Bowman Collection, FSPA Archives (La Crosse, Wis.).

8. Ibid.

9. Ibid.

10. Charlene Smith, FSPA, in conversation with Thea during college years at Viterbo.

11. Bowman family scrapbook.

12. Ibid.

13. John Feister, telephone interview with Jamie Phelps, OP, New Orleans, June 17, 2008.

14. John Feister, telephone interview with Francesca Thompson, OSF, Oldenburg, Indiana, June 18, 2008.

15. John Feister, telephone interview with Fernand Cheri, OFM, St. Louis, June 25, 2008.

Chapter 8 / Laid Up

1. Bowman family scrapbook, Thea Bowman Collection, FSPA Archives (La Crosse, Wis.).

2. Ibid.

3. Ibid.

4. Charlene Smith, FSPA, in conversation with Thea during formation years. Also Margaret Walker and Thea Bowman, "God Touched My Life: The Inspiring Autobiography of the Nun Who Brought Song, Celebration, and Soul to the World," unpublished manuscript, Thea Bowman Collection,

FSPA Archives (La Crosse, Wis.), and Margaret Walker Collection, Margaret Walker Alexander Research Center, Jackson State University (Jackson, Miss.), 1992, 02.13.

5. Bowman family scrapbook.

6. Ibid.

7. Ibid.

8. Ibid.

9. Ibid.

10. Ibid.

11. Ibid.

12. Ibid.

13. Thea Bowman Collection, FSPA Archives (La Crosse, Wis.).

14. Celestine Cepress, FSPA, *Sister Thea Bowman: Shooting Star* (Winona, Minn.: St. Mary's Press, 1993), paraphrase from 22.

15. *St. Joseph's Journal,* Thea Bowman Collection.

16. Thea Bowman Collection.

17. Bowman family scrapbook.

18. Ibid.

19. Ibid.

20. Ibid.

21. Ibid.

Chapter 9 / Becoming Sister Thea

1. "First Negro," *La Crosse (Wis.) Tribune*, August 10, 1958.

2. Charlene Smith, FSPA, and Thea in Dramatic Production course Viterbo College Summer School, 1959.

3. Celestine Cepress, FSPA, *Sister Thea Bowman: Shooting Star* (Winona, Minn.: St. Mary's Press, 1993), 24.

4. Bowman family scrapbook, Thea Bowman Collection, FSPA Archives (La Crosse, Wis.).

5. Ibid.

6. Ibid.

Chapter 10 / Civil Rights from Afar

1. John Feister, interview with Flonzie Brown-Wright at Miami University, Middletown, Ohio, August 16, 2007.

2. Rev. J. F. McRee, quoted in Flonzie Brown-Wright, *Looking Back to Look Ahead* (Dayton, Ohio: FBW and Assoc., 1994), 48.

3. John Feister, interview with Flonzie Brown-Wright at Miami University, Middletown, Ohio, August 16, 2007.

4. Thea Bowman, *The Concept of Negro in American Literature*, Thea Bowman Collection, FSPA Archives (La Crosse, Wis.), 1961 box 15, folder 4. This is the source quoted for material to end of this chapter.

Chapter 11 / Home Again

1. Margaret Walker and Thea Bowman, "God Touched My Life: The Inspiring Autobiography of the Nun Who Brought Song, Celebration, and Soul to the World," unpublished manuscript, Thea Bowman Collection, FSPA Archives (La Crosse, Wis.), and Margaret Walker Collection, Margaret Walker Alexander Research Center, Jackson State University (Jackson, Miss.), 1992, 02.15–16.

2. "The Negro Needs Understanding," *La Crosse (Wis.) Tribune*, July 28, 1963.

3. Ibid.

4. Ibid.

5. "What the Negro Wants: Sister M. Thea, FSPA, of Canton, Mississippi, Delivered a Most Perceptive Address," *La Crosse (Wis.) Times Review*, August 7, 1963, 7.

6. *The Voice of Negro America*, LP record produced by Holy Child Jesus School (Canton, Miss., 1967).

7. Ibid.

8. Thea Bowman, "Literature and Art," July 18, 1964, Thea Bowman Collection, box 15, folder 4.

9. John Henry Newman, "Communication through Literature," in *Reading for Understanding*, rev. ed. (New York: Holt, Rinehart and Winston, 1960), 265.

10. Bowman, "Literature and Art."

11. Ibid., 63.

12. Lewis Carroll, *Through the Looking Glass* (Oxford: Oxford University Press, 2007), 185.

13. Charles D. Burns, SVD, "Deep in Their Hearts, Lord, They Do Believe," *Divine Word Messenger* (St. Augustine, Fla.) (March–April 1965): 40–42

Chapter 12 / Sister Thea Goes to Washington

1. Margaret Walker and Thea Bowman, "God Touched My Life: The Inspiring Autobiography of the Nun Who Brought Song, Celebration, and Soul to the World," unpublished manuscript, Thea Bowman Collection, FSPA Archives (La Crosse, Wis.), and Margaret Walker Collection, Margaret Walker Alexander Research Center, Jackson State University (Jackson, Miss.), 1992, 02.17.

2. Charlene Smith, FSPA, in conversations with Thea in the 1960s.

3. Walker and Bowman, "God Touched My Life," 1992, 18.

4. Ibid.

5. John Feister, interview with Dr. Joseph Sendry at Catholic University of America, English Department, Washington, D.C., November 6, 2007.

6. John Feister, interview with Glenmary Father Robert Dalton at Glenmary Home Missioners headquarters, Cincinnati, October 25, 2008.

7. See chapter 5, note 1. This story of the hog-calling slave is perhaps a reference to Katherine Bowman.

8. John Feister, interview with Rev. Clarence Williams, CPPS, at the Paulist residence, Washington, D.C., November 14, 2007.

9. Ibid.

10. Ibid.

11. John Feister, telephone interview with Antona Ebo, FSM, St. Louis, December 17, 2007.

12. Ibid.

13. Ibid.

14. John Feister, interview with Rev. Clarence Williams, CPPS, at the Paulist residence, Washington, D.C., November 14, 2007.

15. John Feister, telephone interview with Antona Ebo, FSM, St. Louis, December 17, 2007.

16. John Feister, telephone interview with Francesca Thompson, OSF, Oldenburg, Indiana, June 18, 2008.

17. Ibid. for all of the preceding quotes.

18. Thea Bowman, *The Negro in Education,* Thea Bowman Collection, FSPA Archives (La Crosse, Wis. 1968).

19. Abbé Germain, Marc'hadour, "Complete Explication and Critical Analysis of the 'Ruful Lamentacio of the Deth of Quene Elisabeth,'" *Moreana Review* (June 1970): 93.

20. Walker and Bowman, "God Touched My Life," 1992, 02.17.

21. Thea Bowman, Thea Bowman Collection.

22. Thea Bowman, "The Relationship of Pathos and Style in *A Dyalogue of Comforte Agaynste Tribulacyon*: A Rhetorical Study," Thea Bowman Collection.

23. Ibid.

Chapter 13 / An Emerging Awareness

1. *Lumen* (Viterbo College, La Crosse, Wis.), November 1971.

2. John Feister, interview with Rev. Clarence Williams, CPPS, at the Paulist residence, Washington, D.C., November 14, 2007.

3. Joan Chittister, OSB, *In Search of Belief* (Liguori, Mo.: Liguori Triumph Books, 1999), 69–70.

4. Charlene Smith, FSPA, in conversation with Thea during 1970s-1980s.

5. Ibid.

6. Margaret Walker and Thea Bowman, "God Touched My Life: The Inspiring Autobiography of the Nun Who Brought Song, Celebration, and Soul to the World," unpublished manuscript, Thea Bowman Collection, FSPA Archives (La Crosse, Wis.), and Margaret Walker Collection, Margaret Walker Alexander Research Center, Jackson State University (Jackson, Miss.), 1992, 03.9.

7. "Albertus Plans Program about Black Culture," *Milford (Conn.) Citizen*, March 28, 1971.

Chapter 14 / To Europe

1. Thea Bowman, Thea Bowman Collection, FSPA Archives (La Crosse, Wis.). Quotes from what follows and itinerary are drawn from this source, except as noted.

2. John Feister, interviews with Thea Bowman, Canton, Mississippi, and surrounding area, November 1, 2 and 3, 1984.

3. "Sister Bowman Returns from Study in England," *Madison County (Miss.) Herald*, August 17, 1972.

Chapter 15 / The Most Powerful Woman on Campas

1. "Symphony Marks 'Sweetheart Night,' " *La Crosse (Wis.) Tribune*, February 2, 1972.

2. Dr. Truman Hayes, "Soloist Zgodava Stirs Audience," *La Crosse (Wis.) Tribune*, February 14, 1972.

3. Most Reverend James P. Lyke, OFM, PhD, ed., *Lead Me, Guide Me, The African American Catholic Hymnal* (Chicago: G.I.A. Publications, 1987), no. 285.

4. Margaret Walker and Thea Bowman, "God Touched My Life: The Inspiring Autobiography of the Nun Who Brought Song, Celebration, and Soul to the World," unpublished manuscript, Thea Bowman Collection, FSPA Archives (La Crosse, Wis.), and Margaret Walker Collection, Margaret Walker Alexander Research Center, Jackson State University (Jackson, Miss.), 1992, 13.

5. Lesley Ann Stugelmeyer, "Musings on 24 Years at Viterbo–Tribute to FSPA," Thea Bowman Collection, FSPA, Archives (La Crosse, Wis.) 1999.

6. Tim Claussen, untitled, Thea Bowman Collection, 1990.

7. Ibid.

8. Janet Gottfresden, "Woman to Be First Black Instructor at Viterbo," *La Crosse (Wis.) Tribune*, August 24, 1971.

9. Barb Umberger, "Sister Thea Bowman on the Move," *Lumen* (Viterbo College, La Crosse, Wis.), October 30, 1975.

10. Thea Bowman Collection.

11. "Viterbo Will Repeat Black Culture Program," *La Crosse (Wis.) Tribune,* March 24, 1974.

12. Barb Umberger, *Lumen* (Viterbo College, La Crosse, Wis.), May 1974.

13. Thea Bowman Collection, FSPA Archives (La Crosse, Wis.), from notes for workshop by Thea Bowman entitled, "What Do You Say When You Don't Say What You Mean?" at Superior Diocese Teachers' Institute, Mount Senario College, Ladysmith, Wisconsin, October 9, 1974.

14. Thea Bowman, "Dream Is Fading but Isn't Dead," *La Crosse (Wis.) Times Review*, April 1978.

15. Pat Moore, "Indian Pair Teaching Indian Literature Class" *La Crosse (Wis.) Tribune,* February 9, 1975.

16. "A Member of the Wedding," *La Crosse (Wis.) Tribune*, April 4, 1978.

17. Ibid.

18. Unpublished notes, Thea Bowman Collection.

19. Debby Smith, "Thea's Regional Exchange: A Convert Returns," *La Crosse (Wis.) Times Review*, July 27, 1978.

Chapter 16 / Sister to the World

1. Margaret Walker and Thea Bowman, "God Touched My Life: The Inspiring Autobiography of the Nun Who Brought Song, Celebration, and Soul to the World," unpublished manuscript, Thea Bowman Collection, FSPA Archives (La Crosse, Wis.), and Margaret Walker Collection, Margaret Walker Alexander Research Center, Jackson State University (Jackson, Miss.), 1992, 15.

2. John Feister, telephone interview with Bishop William Houck, Chicago, November 19, 2007.

3. Ibid.

4. John Feister, telephone interview with Antona Ebo, FSM, St. Louis, December 17, 2007.

5. John Feister, telephone interview with Bishop William Houck, Chicago, November 19, 2007.

6. Thea Bowman Collection, FSPA Archives (La Crosse, Wis.), "Report of Progress on Inter-Racial and Inter-Cultural Awareness and Exchange" to Bishop Joseph B. Brunini, August 31, 1978, box 15, folder 10.

7. Ibid.

8. John Feister, telephone interview with Fernand Cheri, OFM, St. Louis, June 25, 2008.

9. John Feister, telephone interview with Jamie Phelps, OP, New Orleans, June 17, 2008.

10. John Feister, telephone interview with Antona Ebo, FSM, St. Louis, December 17, 2007.

11. Ibid.

12. Thea Bowman Collection, "Report of Progress on Inter-Racial and Inter-Cultural Awareness and Exchange."

13. Unpublished personal calendar and agendas from 1970s and following, Thea Bowman Collection.

14. Ibid.

15. Thea Bowman Collection, from notes by Thea Bowman.

16. John Feister, telephone interview with Antona Ebo, FSM, St. Louis, December 17, 2007.

17. Mary Thomas, untitled articles in the *Gramblinite* (Grambling, La.), November 3 and 17, 1978.

18. " 'Most Dioceses in the South Have Large Black Populations' — Sister Thea," *Mississippi Today* (Jackson, Miss.), November 19, 1978.

19. John Feister, telephone interview with Bishop William Houck, Chicago, November 19, 2007.

20. Ibid.

Chapter 17 / Beyond Mississippi

1. Thea Bowman, "Jackson Hosts National Black Convention," *Mississippi Today* (Jackson, Miss.), November 5, 1982.

2. Cullen Clark, "Black Catholics Convene in First Southern Meet," *Jackson (Miss.) Clarion Ledger*, August 6, 1983.

3. John Feister, telephone interview with Fernand Cheri, OFM, St. Louis, June 25, 2008.

4. Celestine Cepress, FSPA, *Sister Thea Bowman: Shooting Star* (Winona, Minn.: St. Mary's Press, 1993), 35. Similar quote in talk to U.S. Catholic bishops, June 17, 1989, Seton Hall University, South Orange, New Jersey. Also Charlene Smith, FSPA, in conversations with Thea during the 1970s and 1980s.

5. "If You're Black," *Louisville Record*, October 31, 1981, a news report of a talk Thea gave at Spalding College.

6. Unpublished personal calendar and agendas 1970s and following, Thea Bowman Collection, FSPA Archives (La Crosse, Wis.).

7. "Black Catholic Center Consideration at Xavier U.," *San Francisco Monitor*, July 31, 1980.

8. John Feister, telephone interview with Fernand Cheri, OFM, St. Louis, June 25, 2008.

9. Ibid.

10. Joseph A. Brown, *A Retreat with Thea Bowman and Bede Abram: Leaning on the Lord* (Cincinnati: St. Anthony Messenger Press, 1997), 8.

11. John Feister, telephone interview with Joseph Brown, SJ, at Southern Illinois University (Carbondale), June 19, 2008.

12. Ibid. for all of the preceding quotes.

13. John Feister, telephone interview with Norma Angel, MM, Maryknoll, New York, March 20, 2008.

14. John Feister, telephone interview with Francesca Thompson, OSF, Oldenburg, Indiana, June 18, 2008.

15. John Feister, telephone interview with Addie Lorraine Walker, SSND, Dallas, July 3, 2008.

Chapter 18 / Let Freedom Ring

1. John Feister, interview with Antona Ebo, FSM, in Dayton, Ohio, for *St. Anthony Messenger* magazine, March 2006.

2. Jean Martin, "Sister Thea Decries Apathy," *Selma Times Journal,* January 16, 1983.

3. Ibid.

4. John Feister, telephone interview with Antona Ebo, FSM, St. Louis, December 17, 2007.

5. Patrick Whelan, "Sister Thea Receives First Justice Award," *La Crosse (Wis.) Times Review*, February 10, 1983.

6. Margaret Walker and Thea Bowman, "God Touched My Life: The Inspiring Autobiography of the Nun Who Brought Song, Celebration, and Soul to the World," unpublished manuscript, Thea Bowman Collection, FSPA Archives (La Crosse, Wis.), and Margaret Walker Collection, Margaret Walker Alexander Research Center, Jackson State University (Jackson, Miss.), 1992, 04.8–10.

Chapter 19 / An Empowering Mission

1. John Feister, interviews with Thea Bowman, Canton, Mississippi, and surrounding area, November 1, 2 and 3, 1984.

2. See chapter 5, note 1, on page 290.

3. John Feister, conversation with Thea between interviews.

4. John Feister, telephone interview with Norma Angel, MM, Maryknoll, New York, March 20, 2008.

5. John Feister, telephone interview with Addie Lorraine Walker, SSND, Dallas, July 3, 2008.

6. John Feister, interviews with Thea Bowman, Canton, Mississippi, and surrounding area, November 1, 2 and 3, 1984.

7. Rev. Clarence Williams, CPPS, *Sr. Thea: Her Own Story, A Video Autobiography* (St. Louis: Oblate Media and Communication, 1991).

8. Margaret Walker and Thea Bowman, "God Touched My Life: The Inspiring Autobiography of the Nun Who Brought Song, Celebration, and Soul to the World," unpublished manuscript, Thea Bowman Collection, FSPA Archives (La Crosse, Wis.), and Margaret Walker Collection, Margaret Walker Alexander Research Center, Jackson State University (Jackson, Miss.), 1992, 03.23–24.

9. "I've Done My Work," words by George W. Caldwell, music by Carrie Jacobs-Bond, 1862–1946 (Boston: Bond and Sons Publisher), 70–73. Found on "Songs Everybody Sings" Web page.

10. Thea Bowman Collection, FSPA Archives (La Crosse, Wis.).

Chapter 20 / Families, Black and Catholic

1. Julie Horgan, "Different Cultures Have Gifts to Share, Nun Says," *La Crosse (Wis.) Times Review*, April 25, 1985.

2. Charlene Smith, FSPA, in conversation with Dan Rooney, Spring 2007.

3. John Feister, telephone interview with Fernand Cheri, OFM, St. Louis, June 25, 2008.

4. Thea Bowman, *Families: Black and Catholic, Catholic and Black* (Washington, D.C.: United States Catholic Conference, 1985), Introduction.

5. Peter Mara, "Sister Bowman Edits Book on Black Catholic Families," *Mississippi Today* (Jackson, Miss.), February 21, 1986.

6. John Feister, telephone interview with Addie Lorraine Walker, SSND, Dallas, July 3, 2008.

7. John Feister, telephone interview with Karen Horace, Chicago, June 18, 2008.

Chapter 21 / To Mother Africa

1. Thea Bowman Collection, FSPA Archives (La Crosse, Wis.).

2. Ibid.

3. Ibid.

4. Bowman letter to friends, Thea Bowman Collection.

5. Antona Ebo, FMS, video of presentation at Lent 2001 Thea event at Franciscan Sisters of Mary Center in St. Louis, Missouri.

6. Thea Bowman Collection.

7. "Papal Legate Opens Eucharistic Congress," *Congress Courier* (Nairobi), August 18, 1985, 17.

8. Beatrice Njemanze, "Sister Thea Bowman Touches Her African Roots," *Mississippi Today* (Jackson, Miss.), September 13, 1985.

9. Thea Bowman Collection.

Chapter 22 / Lead Me, Guide Me

1. Thea Bowman Collection, FSPA Archives (La Crosse, Wis.).

2. Ibid.

3. Ibid., 1987.

4. Celestine Cepress, FSPA, *Sister Thea Bowman: Shooting Star* (Winona, Minn.: St. Mary's Press, 1993), 9–10.

5. Firsthand observation by John Feister, who was in attendance.

6. Marianne Cianciolo, "Amen, Sister!" *Cincinnati Catholic Telegraph*, May 15, 1987.

7. Bill Sanderson, "Mississippi Roots Create a Special Sister," *Paterson (N.J.) Record*, 1987.

8. Letters from Thea Bowman Collection, FSPA Archives (La Crosse, Wis.).

9. Jeff Edwards, "Wallace Interviewed Bowman for *60 Minutes*," *Jackson (Miss.) Clarion Ledger*, Fall 1990.

10. Thea Bowman Collection.

11. Ibid.

12. John Feister, interview with Rev. Clarence Williams, CPPS, at the Paulist residence, Washington, D.C., November 14, 2007.

13. Bishop James Lyke, OFM, "Preface," *Lead Me, Guide Me: The African American Catholic Hymnal* (Chicago: GIA Publications, 1987).

14. Thea Bowman, "Introduction: The Gift of the African American Sacred Song," *Lead Me, Guide Me.*

15. "First Black Franciscan Order Nun Here on 'Mission of Love,' " *St. Thomas Island Daily News*, November 17, 1987.

16. Bowman letter to friends, Thea Bowman Collection.

17. Ibid.

18. Thea Bowman Collection.

19. Ibid.

20. John Feister, telephone interview with Francesca Thompson, OSF, Oldenburg, Indiana, June 18, 2008.

21. Thea Bowman Collection.

Chapter 23 / We Shall Overcome — Today

1. Tina Maples, "Nun Will Join King Tribute," *Milwaukee Journal,* January 15, 1988.

2. Lyn L. Hartmann, "The Message of Music," *Milwaukee Journal Sunday Magazine*, January 17, 1988.

3. Charlene Smith, FSPA, Video of King event in Milwaukee.

4. Joseph Smith, *Smith and Company* (Milwaukee: Milwaukee Public Television, January 18, 1988), Transcribed from video in Thea Bowman Collection, FSPA Archives (La Crosse, Wis.).

5. Thea Bowman Collection.

6. Creed S. Gillem, "Sister Thea Bowman Leads Spirited Mission at St. Patrick's," *Fredrikstad Catholic Islander*, March 16, 1988.

7. *Madison Catholic Herald*, March 31, 1988.

8. Veronica Deane,"Living Spirit/Woman Spirit," *Madison Catholic Herald*, April 9, 1988.

9. Ibid.

10. "Spirit of Revival," *Baltimore Catholic Review*, May 16, 1988.

11. Charlene Smith, FSPA, in conversation with Thea, 1988.

12. "Rejoicing at Regis," *The Pilot*, May 1988, 58th commencement photo.

13. Tim Monaghan, "Bowman Tells Graduates to Share Life," *Wayland-Weston (Mass.) Town Crier*, May 26, 1988.

14. Thea Bowman Collection, FSPA Archives (La Crosse, Wis.).

15. Ibid.

Chapter 24 / "Let Me Live until I Die"

1. Mary Donnelly, "Nun Brings Black Roots into Church," *New Orleans Midtown Picayune*, August 14, 1988.

2. Thea Bowman Collection, FSPA Archives (La Crosse, Wis.).

3. John Feister, telephone interview with Francesca Thompson, OSF, Oldenburg, Indiana, June 18, 2008.

4. Thea Bowman Collection.

5. *Are You Walking with Me? Sister Thea Bowman, William Faulkner and African American Culture* (Oxford: University of Mississippi Center for the Study of Southern Culture, 1990). Thanks to Sharon Sumpter, assistant archivist, Archives, University of Notre Dame, which contains the copy used for this research.

6. Charlene Smith, FSPA, telephone conversation with Marshall Bouldin, 2001.

7. Arthur Jones, "She Sings a Ululu Story That Begins in Africa," *National Catholic Reporter,* September 9, 1988.

8. "Evangelist, S. Thea Bowman Overwhelms Clarke Audience," *Dubuque Witness,* September 1988.

9. Greg Chesmore, "500 Cram Music Hall to Hear S. Bowman," *Clarke College Courier* (Dubuque), September 16, 1988.

10. Gayda Hollnagel, "Pursuing Her Dreams: Nun Going Strong despite Bout with Cancer," *La Crosse (Wis.) Tribune,* September 14, 1988.

11. Mark Nepper, "Sister Thea Moves Audience with Message," *Dubuque Telegraph Herald,* September 10, 1988.

12. Elizabeth Wimmer, "Bowman Keynote at National Vocation Conference," *St. Louis Review*, September 23, 1988.

13. Eva Marie Lumas, SSS, "Tatuonada, Ndade!" (Until We Meet Again, Sister!)" *Thea News* (La Crosse, Wis.) 2, no. 2 (September 2003): 4.

14. Ibid., 5.

15. John Feister, telephone interview with Norma Angel, MM, Maryknoll, New York, March 20, 2008.

16. Ibid.

17. Lumas, "Tatuonada, Ndade!" 7.

18. Ibid.

Chapter 25 / Songs of My People

1. Loretta Pehanich, "Sister Thea: 'My Mission Is Sharing the Good News...to Work for Justice,'" *San José Valley Catholic*, October 1988.

2. Gloria Negri, "Nun's Gospel of Love Lifts Educators' Spirits," *Boston Globe,* October 7, 1988.

3. Ibid.

4. Cardinal Cushing School Newsletter, Boston, Mass.

5. Negri, "Nun's Gospel of Love Lifts Educators' Spirits."

6. Thea Bowman Collection, FSPA Archives (La Crosse, Wis.)

7. Karen Katafiasz, "A Taste of Salt," *Catholic Chronicle* (Toledo, Ohio), October 28, 1988.

8. Renee Cowles, untitled *Niagara Index* (Niagara Falls, N.Y.: Niagara University, November 1988).

9. Burnell Williams, "A Living Inspiration Shares the Good News," *New Community Clarion* (Roseville, N.J.), December 10, 1988.

10. Amanda McCaughey, "Going beyond Features to Presence," *International Artist* (Scottsdale, Ariz), June–July 2004: 33–37.

11. Charlene Smith, FSPA, telephone conversation with Michael Bouldin, 2001.

12. Thea Bowman Collection.

13. John Feister, telephone interview with Karen Horace, Chicago, June 18, 2008.

14. Christine Salvatore, FSPA, "Sharing the Songs of Faith," in *Thea Bowman: Handing On Her Legacy,* ed. Christian Koontz (Lanham, Md.,: Rowman and Littlefield, 1991), 40–44. Sister Christine was director of Krystal Records when they produced the two audio recordings of Thea's songs: *Sister Thea: Songs of My People* (Boston: St. Paul Books and Media, 1989), a selection of traditional spirituals, and *'Round the Glory Manger* (1989), a collection of Christmas spirituals.

15. Cardinal Bernard Law, "God's Love Seen in Others," *Boston Pilot,* August 26, 1988. Cardinal Law, a longtime friend of Thea, would, decades later, resign his post and leave the United States under a cloud of trouble related to mishandling clergy sexual abuse.

16. John Feister, telephone interview with Fernand Cheri, OFM, St. Louis, June 25, 2008.

17. Margaret Walker and Thea Bowman, "God Touched My Life: The Inspiring Autobiography of the Nun Who Brought Song, Celebration, and Soul to the World," unpublished manuscript, Thea Bowman Collection, FSPA Archives (La Crosse, Wis.), and Margaret Walker Collection, Margaret Walker Alexander Research Center, Jackson State University (Jackson, Miss.), 1992, 07.3.

18. Ibid.

19. *Are You Walking with Me? Sister Thea Bowman, William Faulkner and African American Culture* (Oxford: University of Mississippi Center for the Study of Southern Culture, 1990).

20. Walker and Bowman, "God Touched My Life."

21. Thea Bowman Collection.

22. John Feister, interview with Thea Bowman, Canton, Mississippi, December 29, 1988.

23. Fabvienen Taylor, "Noted Author Writes Sister Bowman's Story," *Mississippi Today* (Jackson, Miss.), January 6, 1989.

Chapter 26 / A Newfound Freedom

1. Charlotte Graham, "Can't Keep a Good Nun Down," *Jackson (Miss.) Daily News,* December 31, 1988.

2. Burnell Williams, "A Living Inspiration Shares the Good News," *New Community Clarion* (Roseville, N.J.), December 10, 1988.

3. Christine Capra-Kramer, "There Is an Urgency about My Life," *Denver Catholic Register,* February 1989.

4. "National Award Honors Sister Thea Bowman," *Mississippi Today* (Jackson, Miss.), January 20, 1989.

5. "I Am Beautiful, You Are Beautiful," *Los Angeles Tidings*, January 27, 1989.

6. Rachelle Ramon, untitled, *South Texas Catholic* (Corpus Christi), February 10, 1989.

7. Rachelle Ramon, "Sister Thea Bowman's Life a Testament to Courage, Joy," *South Texas Catholic* (Corpus Christi), February 17, 1989.

8. Bob Giles, "Strong Black Families Called Key to Conversion by Visiting Speakers," *Texas Catholic Herald* (Houston), February 24, 1989.

9. Thea Bowman Collection, FSPA Archives (La Crosse, Wis.).

10. Ibid.

11. "A Final Farewell," *Strides* (La Crosse, Wis.: Viterbo University, 1990): 6–7.

12. Thomas Ebele, "Sister Thea Bowman: We Shall Overcome," *Fergus Falls (Minn.) Daily Journal,* April 4, 1989.

13. Catherine Haven, "Nun's Message: People Can Make a Difference," *Michigan Catholic* (Detroit), April 7, 1989.

14. Brigid Johnson, RSM, "Priest of God," in Christian Koontz, ed., *Thea Bowman: Handing on Her Legacy* (Lanham, Md.: Rowman and Littlefield, 1991), 51–53.

15. Charlene Smith, FSPA, in conversation with Mark Brummel, CMF, 2004.

16. Thea Bowman Collection.

17. Ibid.

Chapter 27 / Unforgettable Thea

1. John Feister, conversation with Jerry Filteau of Catholic News Service, Washington, D.C., May 31, 2007.

2. Jerry Filteau, "Weekly Roundup, June 19, 1989, Evangelization, Vietnam, Theologian Relations Occupy Bishops" (Washington, D.C., United States Conference of Catholic Bishops, Catholic News Service archives).

3. Thea Bowman Collection, FSPA Archives (La Crosse, Wis.).

4. Ibid.

5. John Feister, telephone interview with Bishop William Houck, Chicago, November 19, 2007.

6. John Feister, interview with Archbishop Daniel E. Pilarczyk, Cincinnati, March 15, 2008.

7. Marie Augusta Neal, SNDdeN, "She Made the Bishops Dance," in *Thea Bowman: Handing on Her Legacy,* ed. Christian Koontz (Lanham, Md.,: Rowman and Littlefield, 1991), 54–57.

8. Margaret Walker, *Jubilee* (New York: Houghton Mifflin, 1966), 150–51.

9. Margaret Walker and Thea Bowman, "God Touched My Life: The Inspiring Autobiography of the Nun Who Brought Song, Celebration, and Soul to the World," unpublished manuscript, Thea Bowman Collection, FSPA Archives (La Crosse, Wis.), and Margaret Walker Collection, Margaret Walker Alexander Research Center, Jackson State University (Jackson, Miss.), 1992, 04.4–8.

10. John Feister, interview with C. Vanessa White, Cincinnati, August 8, 2008.

11. Thea Bowman Collection, FSPA Archives (La Crosse, Wis.), also John Feister, interview with Jim Goode, OFM, September 12, 2009.

12. *Are You Walking with Me? Sister Thea Bowman, William Faulkner and African American Culture,* Lisa N. Haworth, producer (Oxford, Miss.: University of Mississippi Center for the Study of Southern Culture, 1990).

13. Terry Mattingly, "Charismatic Nun Shrugs Off Idea of Sainthood," *Denver Rocky Mountain News,* August 26, 1989.

14. David Howard, "Thea: One of a Kind," in *Thea Bowman: Handing on Her Legacy,* 38, 39.

15. Gayda Hollnagel, "Thea Video Offers Lesson in How to Die," *La Crosse (Wis.) Tribune,* August 7, 1989.

16. Maria Friedman, FSPA, "Thea Bowman Scholars Assured a Quality Education," *Thea News* (La Crosse, Wis.), March 2002, 1.

17. "Mission Statement," Thea Bowman Black Catholic Education Foundation, 1989.

18. "Nun Provides Young Blacks a 'Way Out of Helplessness,' " *New York Times,* October 20, 1989.

19. Thea Bowman Collection, FSPA Archives (La Crosse, Wis.).

20. Thea Bowman, "Heart of the Nation: A Christmas Special with Sister Thea Bowman," 1989, recalled by Celesta Day, FSPA, in written memories of Thea.

21. "How Celebrities Will Celebrate Christmas," *Ebony* (December 1989).

22. Thea Bowman Collection.

Chapter 28 / Going Home

1. Dorothy Ann Kundinger, FSPA, speech at "Theafest," held at Viterbo College, La Crosse, Wis., March 26, 2000.

2. Thea Bowman Collection, FSPA Archives (La Crosse, Wis.).

3. Ibid.

4. Kundinger, speech at "Theafest."

5. John Feister, interview with Flonzie Brown-Wright at Miami University, Middletown, Ohio, August 16, 2007.

6. Beth Erickson, "She Sang Because the Spirit Moved Her," *Thea News* (La Crosse, Wis.), March 2004, 5–6.

7. Thea Bowman, FSPA, "How to Celebrate Holy Week," *Mississippi Today* (Jackson, Miss.), April 6, 1990.

8. Celesta Day, "Trip from La Crosse to Canton the Last Week of March 1990," Thea Bowman Collection.

9. Kundinger, speech at "Theafest."

10. Day, "Trip from La Crosse to Canton the Last Week of March 1990."

Chapter 29 / Winning the Game — for Everybody

1. Dennis Hevesi, "Sister Thea Bowman, 52, Worker for Catholic Sharing with Blacks," *New York Times,* April 1, 1990, 30.

2. Beth Erickson, "She Sang Because the Spirit Moved Her," *Thea News* (La Crosse, Wis.), March 2004, 4–5, 7.

3. Mary Queen Donnelly, "In Memoriam," *America* (April 28, 1990), 420–21.

4. John Feister, interview with Flonzie Brown-Wright at Miami University, Middletown, Ohio, August 16, 2007.

5. John F. Ford, ST, "Waiting for the Lord with Courage," in *Thea Bowman: Handing On Her Legacy,* ed. Christian Koontz (Lanham, Md.: Rowman and Littlefield, 1991).

6. Cardinal John J. O'Connor, "A Quintessential Woman," *Catholic New York*, April 5, 1990.

7. John Feister, telephone interview with Antona Ebo, FSM, St. Louis, December 17, 2007.

8. John Feister, telephone interview with Bishop William Houck, Chicago, November 19, 2007.

9. John Feister, interview with Rev. Clarence Williams, CPPS, at the Paulist residence, Washington, D.C., November 14, 2007.

10. John Feister, interview with Flonzie Brown-Wright at Miami University, Middletown, Ohio, August 16, 2007.

11. John Feister, telephone interview with Jamie Phelps, OP, New Orleans, June 17, 2008.

12. John Feister, telephone interview with Addie Lorraine Walker, SSND, Dallas, July 3, 2008.

13. John Feister, interview with Fernand Cheri, OFM, St. Louis, June 25, 2008.

14. John Feister, telephone interview with Joseph Brown, SJ, at Southern Illinois University (Carbondale), June 19, 2008.

15. Dorothy Ann Kundinger, FSPA, speech at "Theafest," held at Viterbo College, La Crosse, Wis., March 26, 2000.

PERMISSIONS

FSPA: The authors gratefully acknowledge the unlimited access to and use of the extensive Sister Thea Bowman Collection in the FSPA Archives and Heritage Department, La Crosse, Wisconsin, including the Bowman Family Scrapbooks, Thea's writings (personal and professional, unpublished and published), appointment calendars, magazine and newspaper clippings, video and audio tapes of speeches and singing, photograph and slide collections, eulogies, and tributes.

Walker/Bowman: We are grateful for permission to quote from the Walker/Bowman unpublished manuscript *God Touched My Life: The Inspiring Autobiography of the Nun Who Brought Song, Celebration, and Soul to the World.* 1992 joint copyright held by Thea Bowman Collection, FSPA Archives, La Crosse, Wisconsin, and Margaret Walker Collection, Margaret Walker Alexander Research Center, Jackson State University, Jackson, Mississippi.

Viterbo College (now University): We also gratefully acknowledge the generous permission to quote newspaper and magazine articles from publications of Viterbo College (now University): *Lumen, Strides,* and *Touchstone.* Excerpts on pp. 6–11 are from the Winter 1959 issue of *Touchstone* article "Passing Beneath the Southern Sun," written when Sister Thea was twenty-one years old.

Milwaukee Public Television: We acknowledge with gratitude permission to quote extensively from the "Interview with Sister Thea Bowman" by Joseph Smith, *Smith and Company,* Milwaukee Public Television, MPTV, January 18, 1988. Transcribed by FSPA from video in Thea Bowman Collection, FSPA Archives.

INDEX